Academic Degree Structures: Innovative Approaches

PRINCIPLES OF REFORM IN
DEGREE STRUCTURES IN THE UNITED STATES

by *Stephen H. Spurr*

Dean, Horace N. Rackham School of Graduate Studies,
University of Michigan

A General Report Prepared for
The Carnegie Commission on Higher Education

MCGRAW-HILL BOOK COMPANY
New York   St. Louis   San Francisco   Dusseldorf
London   Sydney   Toronto   Mexico   Panama

*The Carnegie Commission on Higher Education,
1947 Center Street, Berkeley, California 94704,
has sponsored preparation of this report as a
part of a continuing effort to present significant
information and issues for public discussion.
The views expressed are those of the author.*

ACADEMIC DEGREE STRUCTURES:
INNOVATIVE APPROACHES

*Principles of Reform in Degree Structures in the
United States*

Library of Congress catalog card number 71-114293

23456789MAMM7987654321

10010

Foreword

Academic degrees are identified with both the ends and the means of higher education. For the American student, a college or university degree may be a prize for persistence, proof of ability, a letter of introduction into the company of "educated" men, or a ticket of admission to further study, a particular occupation, or a profession. For the colleges and universities, awarding degrees involves decisions that affect the pace of academic life; influence the breadth of the curriculum; prescribe the length of time an entering student will probably remain within the institution; affect the number of faculty members that must be hired and retained; determine the qualifications needed by members of the academic staff; and govern the relationships and prerogatives of students, teachers, and researchers. For all these reasons, degree policies inevitably become crucial considerations in college and university planning.

American degree structures have ancient origins, but they have been modified over the years as new degrees were created to recognize achievement in new subject disciplines or to certify practitioners in particular professions and occupations. Today, the once simple pattern of American college degrees is immensely complicated.

At the request of the Carnegie Commission on Higher Education, Dean Spurr has made an extensive investigation and analysis of these developments. His findings and recommendations are of great value.

Clark Kerr
Chairman
The Carnegie Commission
on Higher Education

February, 1970

v

Contents

Introduction

I accepted the invitation of Clark Kerr to study and write on alternative degree structures in American higher education with a mixture of enthusiasm and trepidation. The enthusiasm arose from my experience as a graduate dean in a complex university; from my consequent exposure to the very real inadequacies, inconsistencies, and failures of our present degree structures, particularly in the graduate schools; and from the realization gained through my involvement in the development of the *Candidate of Philosophy* concept that some academic reforms were indeed possible through changing degree structures. The trepidation came from several months' immersion in the literature of higher education dealing both with America and with western Europe, from the consequent realization that almost everything that could be said and proposed concerning degree structures has indeed been said and proposed, and from the consequent doubt that I could say anything new or half as well as it already has been said in the past. One cannot but be impressed with the iconoclastic perceptiveness of the critics of American higher education; with the occasional brilliance with which such writers as William James, Abraham Flexner, Robert Hutchins, Jacques Barzun, and David Riesman dissect our system; and with the enormous inertia of the system itself, which has evolved in its own ponderous way oblivious to the slings and arrows of outrageous educators. It is not surprising, then, that I, a botanist and forester, an erstwhile professional school dean, and a current holder of the one deanship in the university without a budget, without faculty, and even without space, should wonder why I ever got myself into this fix in the first place.

Be that as it may, the assignment was accepted and the report must be written. I have read a great deal. I have interviewed at length a selection of innovative and otherwise distinguished people in higher education both in this country and in western Europe. A list of these is to be found in the appendix. By the very nature of my assignment, few truly original ideas may be expected at this late date, and it is perfectly true that much of what I have to say has come from what I have read or from people to whom I have talked. The presentation and emphasis of the material and, it is to be hoped, some of the ideas and concepts, however, are mine.

The core of my presentation is to be found in Chapters 3 and 14, in which I propose first the basic principles and second my own synthesis of an idealized and generalized system of degree structures for American higher education. Chapters 4 through 12 deal with the several generalized degree levels and particularly with a few selected problems of current general interest. Foremost among these is the current concern about the development of degree programs for the training of college teachers, especially for the two-year colleges and the regional universities. Another topic of importance is the possibility of combining the last one or two years of secondary school and the first years of college into a unified collegiate program. Finally, in these chapters will be found attempts to generalize what is actually required in the curricula of our leading colleges and universities for the basic liberal arts associate's, bachelor's, master's, graduate intermediate, and doctor's degrees.

Relevant recent European experience with degree structures is dealt with in Chapter 13. Material here is derived from a good deal of reading, fortified by a month's travel in England, Germany, and France during which I interviewed a number of leaders in higher education in those countries. Differences between the total European and American educational systems are so great that there is little in European developments of direct relevance to American experience. At least, though, there are analogies to be drawn, lessons to be learned, and ideas worth exploring in their American context.

There are many omissions in this work. Perhaps most serious is the relative inattention given to the improvement of secondary education and the possibilities of better articulation of it with the undergraduate experience. Although proposals for combining advanced secondary school experience with the general collegiate experience have long been advocated in America and are briefly discussed in Chapter 4, limitations of time have prevented me from exploring fully the base of the pyramid of higher education and the possibility of improving the superstructure through modification of the substructure. Professional degrees, too, are given short shrift in this work—not because of lack of concern, but simply because of the exigencies of completion and the general feeling that professional degree structures are perhaps more generally satisfactory than those in the liberal arts. For these and other short-comings, I can only apologize.

Preliminary drafts summarizing my thinking have been constructively reviewed by Clark Kerr, David Riesman, Gustave O. Arlt, and F. Champion Ward. To the latter I am indebted for the most apropos quotation from *Troilus and Cressida* that initiates Chapter 3.

On this project, Miss Meredith A. Gonyea, a doctoral student in the Center for the Study of Higher Education at the University of Michigan, has worked as my research and editorial assistant. She has done yeoman service. So also have Mrs. Patricia Barr and Miss Dianne Stribley in handling the secretarial responsibilities.

Stephen H. Spurr

February, 1970

1. Academic Certification and Degree Structures

An institution of higher learning has two broad functions: one is the education of its members, and the other is their certification. In the analysis of degree structures in American higher education, we are primarily concerned with the latter. Certification, however, represents only the form and not the substance of education. Our treatise has significance only to the extent that the forms of certification record with reasonable accuracy the accomplishments of education.

ACADEMIC CERTIFICATION

The sine qua non of academic certification is that it represents the evaluation of a student's accomplishment by a competent and objective second party. The value of certification is governed by the confidence that society, both in its formal institutions and in its subjective acceptance, places in those who examine student accomplishment. In most situations this confidence is maximized if the certification is carried out formally by groups of individuals, themselves highly selected by reason of relevant training, experience, and demonstrated objectivity. Traditionally, senior faculty members or scholars of equivalent rank, whether within or without a particular institution, have best satisfied these criteria. Other students, lay governing boards, and external political bodies have not. It follows that academic certification by such groups is of little value, and this is indeed the case for honorary degrees bestowed by the lay boards of American universities[1] and for ranks established by political bodies. Stu-

[1] We use the word *university* in two senses: to denote present institutions of higher education in the United States in general and to identify complex institutions having several constituent schools and colleges. The term *college* is used to denote American institutions of higher education in general before the Civil War, subsequent independent liberal arts institutions, and major units within universities. We should also bear in mind that the name *college* is given to secondary schools in many other parts of the world.

dents themselves are not considered by the general public qualified to certify other students of comparable experience and training as to their academic or professional competence. It is unlikely, therefore, that certification by students will obtain any wide acceptance in our social structure.

The academic credentials of students in our institutions of higher education are generally certified by examiners appointed and qualified by one of four patterns: (1) by the faculty who taught the students, (2) by external examiners appointed by this faculty, (3) by external examiners appointed by established professional or scholarly bodies, and (4) by external examiners appointed by the state. These groups are not mutually exclusive. For example, professional associations may accredit professional programs in universities, and thus bind themselves to accept the certification by the university of professional accomplishments as qualifying the student for at least the first level of professional status. Similarly, states may delegate to professional associations the legal authority to admit applicants into professional status.

Certification of past academic accomplishment through the faculties and governing boards of universities is formalized through the awarding of academic degrees. The examiners may be internal in that they are members of the faculty recommending the degree or external in being selected from other faculties and other institutions. In the United States, primary reliance is placed upon internal examiners although a faculty examiner from another academic department is usually included on doctoral committees. The recommendation of the particular department or program, however, is subject to review by the school or college faculty as a whole and at least nominally by the governing lay board of the institution. Variants to the practice of internal examination occur at Swarthmore where external examiners are used to evaluate undergraduate honors achievement and at Hampshire where a separate director of examinations will have responsibility for the certification function. In Great Britain, external examiners are widely used. In both the United States and Great Britain, recognition of accomplishment, not only in the faculties of arts and letters but also in the professional schools, is through the form of academic degrees which properly record past academic accomplishment. They do not, except through ratification by professional societies or the state, license an individual for future professional work.

In contrast, certification by professional societies or governmental bodies exists primarily to qualify an individual for professional employment, not to measure past academic progress. Success is not marked by academic degrees but by such certification as is provided by admission to the bar, licensure to practice medicine and surgery, registration as an engineer, or membership in the AIA (American Institute of Architects).

In the United States, the degree is almost always taken by university students, and its award is often a prerequisite for admission into a higher academic program, for entrance into a profession, or at least for the right to take the examinations for entrance into a profession. This is not the case in continental Europe where, in many fields, a student attends an institution of higher education not to gain an academic degree but to qualify himself to take a state examination for admission into a profession, frequently as an employee of the state. There, the degree is frequently omitted, and certification by the governmental body is deemed sufficient to mark the end of formal education.

TERMINOLOGY There is little consistency in the usage of the various terms marking formal certification. We must therefore make some effort to standardize terminology.

The term *degree* is widely used in institutions of higher education both in a general and a specific sense. In the former, it refers to any formal certification of academic accomplishment by the governing faculty that is ratified by the governing board of the institution of higher education. In the latter, it is restricted to those certifications that mark the completion of programs extending over several years under the supervision of the traditional faculties and therefore of "university" quality as opposed to "technological" or "vocational quality." A distinction is often made between fully accepted academic programs for which a degree is awarded and others which are recognized by a certificate.

Besides the terms *degree* and *certificate,* the word *diploma* is also used, sometimes indiscriminately as a synonym and sometimes in a specific sense. Technically, the diploma is the document testifying to the degree or to the certification, and this is its usual sense. To a limited extent, however, the work is also used as a title for a specific academic award in the university, especially in such European countries as France and Germany. It also, of course, identifies the certificate of secondary school graduation in the United States.

We may take, then, the following selected definitions:

Degree: An academical rank or distinction conferred by a university or college as a mark of proficiency in scholarship (Oxford). A grade or rank to which scholars are admitted by a college or university in recognition of their attainments (Merriam-Webster).

Certificate: A formal recognition conferred by a university or college on the completion of a course of study of lesser length or stature than those recognized by the award of a degree. A document certifying that one has met the requirements of a course or school or passed a final examination (Merriam-Webster).

Diploma: A document conferring some honour, privilege, or license; especially that given by a university or college, testifying to a degree taken by a person, and conferring upon him the rights and privileges of such degree, as to teach, practice medicine, etc. (Oxford). A document bearing record of graduation from, or of a degree conferred by an educational institution (Merriam-Webster).

Following these definitions, the distinction between *degree* and *certificate* will be a relative one, distinguishing the more formal and prestigious recognition from the less. This is in accordance with common practice at American universities. At the University of Michigan, for example, a student may earn the master's or doctor's *degree* in Slavic languages and literatures in contrast to another student who may earn a *certificate* in Russian studies while working on a doctorate in economics or political science. Similarly, the student taking the combined four-year curriculum in liberal arts and dental hygiene receives the A.B. *degree* in dental hygiene, whereas the student taking only a two-year professional course receives the *certificate* in dental hygiene. A certificate may, moreover, simply signify attendance rather than academic accomplishment and in this sense is widely used in American universities to satisfy the needs of foreign students who are not degree candidates and of short-course participants who are not subject to evaluation.

RIGHTS CONFERRED BY CERTIFICATION We have made the point earlier that the American academic degree certifies past accomplishment while professional and governmental licenses grant future rights of professional practice. This distinction is fairly clear in American practice, but it is not always so in Europe.

In the United States the high school diploma does not guarantee admission into college; the baccalaureate does not confer the right to attend graduate school; and the law degree does not admit its holder to the bar. Each degree or certificate records academic accomplishment to date. It may be the prerequisite to admission to the next higher academic program or to professional status, but such goals are attained only through a separate admissions procedure.

The distinction is important and wise. Historically, however, academic degrees conferred greater rights. In the medieval university, the act of conferring the degree carried with it the granting of the right to practice one's profession. The Doctor of Theology had the right to preach; the Doctor of Medicine and the Doctor of Law to practice; and the Master of Arts to teach. This latter practice persists in Germany today where the *Habilitation* granted by the university to the advanced scholar confers upon him the formal *venia legendi* (the right to teach) and is the necessary qualification for appointment as professor. Much the same applies to the French *doctorat d'État* which qualifies one for senior teaching appointments in faculties of letters and sciences.

The duality of a certification serving both as a leaving certificate for the just completed academic program and as an admission certificate for the next higher academic program is at the core of much of the university problem in continental Europe. In both the United States and Great Britain, university entrance is competitive and selective. Consequently, universities themselves have control over their size. In France and Germany, by contrast, the leaving certificate for those secondary schools that prepare for university entrance guarantees admission to the university. Thus, the French student with the *baccalauréat* and the German with the *Abitur* has the right to attend the university. As populations expand and as pressures for the democratization of higher education result in broader opportunities, the numbers attending the university are reaching unmanageable proportions. True, only a small percentage of the youth in these countries are admitted into the university-preparatory *lycée* or *Gymnasium,* and a large percentage even of these fail to obtain their leaving certificates. Nonetheless, the universities in France and Germany are unequipped to handle those that do. Laboratory science departments and professional schools such as the *grandes écoles* of France have the right to impose *numerus clausus,* i.e., to limit enrollment. The net result, however, is to overload the humanities and social sciences, a factor which contributes to student dissatisfaction and disorders.

Our concern here, however, is with degree practice and these illustrations are provided simply to emphasize the fact that the American practice of separating the certification of past academic accomplishments through the award of academic degrees and certificates from the admission process into higher academic programs or into professions is a good one, and one that should be continued at all cost. At the two-year college level, as well as at the four-year institutions, admissions, including the right to control numbers, should be in the hands of the institution.

DEGREE STRUCTURES   Degree structures may be defined as general categorizations of curricula leading to specific academic degrees. The four-year undergraduate curriculum in the liberal arts leading to the Bachelor of Arts (B.A.) or Bachelor of Science (B.S.) is such a degree structure. So, too, is the two-year, postbaccalaureate program leading to the Master of Business Administration (M.B.A.) or the three-year, postbaccalaureate program leading to the Doctor of Medicine (M.D.) degree. Such are the elements of the system of higher education under scrutiny in this study. Put together they determine the shape of higher education. Any basic changes in the structure of higher education involve a reconsideration of degree programs as identified by (1) the normal period of study, (2) the general curriculum requirements, and (3) the title of the degree awarded.

From the viewpoint of the student, degree programs form the structure of higher education. Whereas the faculty tend to see higher education as being organized in terms of administrative units such as institutions, schools and colleges, departments, research institutes, and the like, students are more apt to view it in terms of a series of program choices identified by academic degrees rather than by organizational units. Through a better conceptualization and ordering of these choices, it should be possible to improve the flow of students through the system.

Academic degrees are not important in themselves, but they do serve to characterize simply and directly an academic program in terms of generally accepted admission standards, curriculum, duration of effort, and level of accomplishment. In this study, therefore, we shall not be overly concerned with the nomenclature and precise definition of academic degrees. The name of the degree is relatively unimportant as long as it has an accepted interpretation. The important thing is that the package is correctly labeled. It is not really important, for example, whether the three-year, postbaccalaureate professional training in law is rewarded with the LL.B. or with the J.D. Both degree titles identify the basic professional education of the individual possessing either degree.

While a degree title provides a generic label, it is not ordinarily sufficient in itself to describe a student's accomplishment. The complete label includes the name of the institution at which the degree was earned, the year, and the field of specialization in which it was earned. The academic transcript of the student indicating the particular courses elected and his academic performance in them must be studied for detailed evaluation. These quantitative measures along with the subjective evaluation by faculty form the basis for the conventional evaluation of academic training, performance, and capability. Nevertheless, the academic degree represents the broadest categorization of the student's achievement and serves to describe in general terms the basic academic programs of American higher education.

2. The Development and Nomenclature of Academic Degrees

The concept of academic degrees originated in the thirteenth century at the two original universities—Paris and Bologna. The present western European and American degree structures can be traced directly and with remarkably little change from these beginnings.

ORIGIN OF ACADEMIC DEGREES

According to Roman law as understood in the Middle Ages, every trade or profession had the intrinsic right to form itself into a *collegium* and to elect magistrates of its own. By the middle of the twelfth century, teachers and students began to aggregate in Bologna and Paris and to form themselves into guilds.[1] A guild or *universitas* of doctors (from the Latin *doctorem,* a teacher) seems to have existed from about the year 1160 in Bologna. In 1215, we have records of a new book being read there before the "University of Professors of the Civil and Canon Law." The system of degrees at Bologna is known to have been fully established before 1219. At Paris, the first trace of a rudimentary guild of masters (from the Latin *magister*) dates from about 1170–1175 according to Rashdall, and the earliest written statutes regarding it date from about the year 1208.

In the thirteenth century, Bologna was a center for the study of civil and canon law and its teachers were called *doctors;* while Paris was preeminent in the study of arts and its faculty were termed *masters.* These titles were conferred by the respective guilds or faculties on students who had completed their studies,

[1] The standard English-language work on medieval universities, on which this section is largely based, is the second edition of Rashdall (1895) edited by Powicke and Emden (1936). Paperbacks of shorter treatises currently available are those of Haskins (1923) and Schachner (1938). A fascinating early treatise is that by Malden (1835).

9

passed the necessary examinations, and had been formally admitted to the guild of teachers. Taking the degree in its earliest form, therefore, meant being admitted into the faculty of the university by the faculty.

In the Middle Ages, the three titles *master, doctor,* and *professor* were synonymous. At Paris and later at Oxford, *master* was the prevailing rank although the term *professor* was frequently used. At Bologna, the common title was *doctor,* a usage that spread throughout Italy and into Germany. Until modern times, therefore, the German *Doctor of Philosophy* was essentially equivalent to the English *Master of Arts.*

Masters and doctors of Paris, Bologna, and Oxford were early recognized as having the right to teach anywhere without further examination *(ius ubique docendi).* When Gregory IX founded a *studium generale* (university) at Toulouse in 1229, he followed his action with a papal bull in 1233 which declared that anyone admitted to mastership in that university was automatically qualified to teach in other universities. Thus, the right of medieval faculties to convey the privilege of mastership received international sanction Gradually, the special privilege of conferring the *ius ubique docendi* became accepted as being conferred on universities by papal or imperial action.

The titles of *master* and *doctor* conveyed the full right to teach. At Bologna, however, control of the university early fell into the hands of the students with the result that the *doctor,* or teacher, became shorn of his prerogatives and the title came not to represent an office but merely an honorary distinction. In short, it became a degree. The same transformation took place with *master,* the term coming to represent a degree rather than a title except in the colleges of Oxford and Cambridge. In contrast, *professor* has consistently remained a title and has come to signify universally senior rank as a teacher.

A bachelor was originally a student allowed to teach in a master's school—a teaching assistant as it were. While ordinary lectures in law at Bologna were reserved to doctors, advanced students were authorized to tutor or lecture in limited areas and became known as *bachalari.* The term seems to have been applied after perhaps four or five years of study while the full doctorate required seven or eight. At the University of Paris, by the last part of the thirteenth century the *baccalauréat* had become in fact an inferior degree marking the completion of the first period in which the student devoted himself completely to his studies and the admission to the second phase during which he undertook limited teaching simultaneously with advanced studies. The act of determination, or qualification for the bachelorship, involved a formal disputation in grammar and logic with a master, an examination by a faculty board, a ceremony consisting of the determiner's putting on his bachelor's *cappa* (student gown) and taking his seat for the first time among the bachelors, and usually a feast with wine provided by the successful candidate. From the symbolism of the feast of Bacchus and the laurel wreath of victory comes the term *baccalaureate.* The term *bachelor* is from the old French *bacheler,* young man or squire, which in turn is from the medieval Latin *baccalaris,* farmer or tenant. Thus, *baccalaureus* may be a pun on *baccalaris* as well as having its own symbolism.

In France, the period of study for the bachelor's degree gradually became shorter and the second period of study leading to the *license* or master's degree became longer until at present the *baccalauréat* has become the secondary school leaving certificate and the *license* has become the first university degree. In England, the reverse occurred, with greater and greater emphasis being placed upon the Bachelor of Arts and the gradual reduction of the Master of Arts to a formality as at Oxford and Cambridge today. In Germany, the bachelorship gradually disappeared with the result that the doctorate became the first earned degree.

DEVELOPMENT OF AMERICAN DEGREE USAGE From the founding of Harvard in 1636 to the Civil War period, American higher education was based upon the English college model and the baccalaureate was the only earned degree awarded.[2] The Bachelor of Arts (B.A.) was awarded for the completion of usually a four-year and always a strictly prescribed classical curriculum. Until well into the nineteenth century, students came to college with little secondary school background and at an earlier age than at present. The B.A. in this earlier period, therefore, represented accomplishment roughly equivalent to that provided by a good high school or preparatory school now. These practices are reflected by the fact that today the term *college* persists in England and other European countries to identify a secondary school, and

---

[2] For general histories of the development of American higher education, see Brubacher and Rudy (1958) and Rudolph (1962). Hofstadter and Smith (1961) reproduces many relevant source documents.

the aforementioned use of the term *baccalauréat* identifies the leaving certificate in French secondary schools.

The Bachelor of Science (B.S.) degree was introduced by Harvard in 1851, followed by a Bachelor of Philosophy (B. Phil.) degree established by Yale in 1852, to recognize the completion of a three-year science program in contrast to the traditional and higher-status four-year classical curriculum.

From 1636 to the Civil War, the Master of Arts (M.A.) was awarded *in cursu* (which should be translated in this case "as a matter of course") to all holders of the B.A. who paid fees for three or so years and remained more or less out of trouble. This pro forma master's degree was gradually abandoned in the United States over the period 1869-1893, although it still persists at such English institutions as Oxford and Cambridge.

The German influence on American colleges (Thwing, 1928) resulted directly in the introduction of formal academic studies beyond the baccalaureate (Storr, 1953) and the transformation after the Civil War of the major American colleges into universities.

In 1815 and the years immediately following, four young Americans enrolled at the University of Göttingen and returned to Harvard professorships. Edward Everett, George Ticknor, George Bancroft, and Joseph Green Cogswell all had distinguished careers and markedly influenced the academic thinking of their time. Everett later became president of Harvard and Ticknor its major early apostle of reform.

The American university on a combined English-German model was conceptualized by Henry Philip Tappan in 1851. Although he was only partially successful in transforming the University of Michigan to this model during his tenure as president (1852-1863), his model of a higher university to be fed from the American colleges is worthy of quote (Tappan, 1851):

We would constitute four Faculties, a Faculty of Philosophy and Science, a Faculty of Letters and Arts, a Faculty of Law, and a Faculty of Medicine. Under these should be comprised a sufficient number of professorships to make a proper distribution of the various subjects comprehended under the general titles. These professorships should be endowed to an extent to afford the incumbents a competency independently of tuition fees. The necessity of such endowments must be obvious when we reflect that studious men require undisturbed minds, and that there are branches of knowledge which the interests of the world demand to have taught—such as Philology, Philosophy, the higher Astronomy, Mathematics, and Physics, while at the same time the number of students will be comparatively few. . . .

By the *Academical* Members, we mean those who shall be admitted upon examination, or upon a Bachelor's degree from any College, and who shall enroll themselves as candidates for the University degrees.

These degrees may be of two grades. The lower grade may comprise Master of Arts, Doctor of Philosophy, Doctor of Medicine, and Bachelor of Laws, Doctor of Theology, and other degrees to mark a high and honorable advance in Medicine, and in Philosophy, Science, Letters and Art.

Those of the first grade to be awarded after three or four years study, and upon examination. Those of the second grade to be awarded as honorary degrees to men distinguished in the walks of life for their attainments and professional eminence, and to individuals who remain for a still longer term of years connected with the University in learned pursuits. It is, of course, understood that the provisions of the University are to be such as to enable students to pursue favorite branches of science, or learning in general, for an indefinite term of years.

One concurrent effect of this organization would be to elevate the character of Academical degrees, by making them the expression of real attainments, and honorable badges of real merit.

Symbolic of the formalization of postbaccalaureate education was the establishment of the earned Master of Arts degree (termed *pro meritis* in contrast with the automatic Master of Arts *in cursu*) at Michigan in 1853 (first awarded in 1859) and the introduction of the earned Doctor of Philosophy program at Yale in 1860 (first awarded in 1861).

The American university finally was realized with the establishment of the Johns Hopkins University in 1876 (Hawkins, 1960; Cordasco, 1960) and the University of Chicago in 1890 (Storr, 1966). Their primary emphasis upon graduate studies, coupled with parallel developments at the major existing universities (Ryan, 1939; Bean, 1958), resulted in the rapid ascendancy of the Ph.D. as the ultimate goal of formal education. By the turn of the century, the doctorate had become an almost mandatory qualification for professorial appointment in the leading universities (Veysey, 1965) in most fields other than the humanities.

The increasing relative importance of the master's and doctor's degrees despite the sharply increased number of bachelor's degrees awarded in the United States since 1861 is detailed in Table 1, in which the estimated grand total of degrees awarded at the three general levels are given at periodic intervals. Earned degrees by fields of study for 1965-66 are summarized in Table 2.

Year	Bachelor	Master	Doctor
1861	n.a.	n.a.	3
1872	n.a.	794	14
1880	n.a.	879	54
1890	15,539	1,015	149
1900	27,410	1,583	382
1910	37,199	2,113	443
1920	47,326	4,279	615
1930	111,411	14,629	2,299
1940	186,500	26,731	3,290
1950	433,734	58,219	6,633
1960	394,889	74,497	9,829
1966	524,117	140,772	18,239

n.a.: not available.
SOURCE: U.S. Office of Education.

DEGREE NOMENCLATURE

The number of named degrees is excessive. The problem was already acute toward the end of the nineteenth century (Wooton, 1883; Thomas, 1898), and by 1960 the number of degree titles recorded in the United States had risen to 2,400, of which two-thirds were still in use at that time (Eells and Haswell, 1960). The present confused state of degree nomenclature has been well summarized by Eells (1963) and criticized by Whaley (1966). A few words on current practices and trends, however, may serve to forward a rational approach to American degree nomenclature.

Earned Degrees

General agreement exists on the several degree levels and their appropriate general designations.

The *associate's* degree is universally used for the successful completion of two years of undergraduate studies in college whether in liberal arts or in technical and vocational subjects.

The complete four-year undergraduate program leads to the *bachelor's* degree.

The first postbaccalaureate or graduate degree, representing not less than one nor more than two years of full-time study beyond the baccalaureate is recognized with the *master's* degree.

Planned academic programs that involve at least one year beyond the master's but which do not qualify as doctoral programs are of increasing importance, but no single degree designation has received widespread acceptance. The most commonly used terms are *candidate* or Master of Philosophy in the arts and sciences, *specialist* in education, and *engineer.* Some professional doctoral programs (Doctor of Pharmacy and Doctor of Optometry) and certain current proposals for the Doctor of Arts fall into this general category in that they normally require six rather than seven or more years of study past secondary school.

The *doctorate* requires a minimum of three years (frequently more) of full-time graduate study and the demonstration by the student of the capacity to do independent work. Such effort may take various forms. The Doctor of Philosophy recognizes completed research; the Doctor of Musical Arts, musical composition or performance; the Doctor of Medicine, clinical competence; and Juris Doctor, the knowledge and capacity to analyze legal problems.

To the broad degree name, accepted American practice adds a second designation indicative of the faculty, school, or college under which the studies are carried out. The term *arts* may be applied to the entire spectrum of liberal arts or be restricted to the humanities and social sciences as opposed to the natural sciences. *Science* may be applied to both theoretical and applied natural science or be restricted to the former. In contrast, *philosophy* is used in the broadest sense as embracing both the arts and sciences.

The practice exists in many institutions of further compounding named degrees by adding a second modifier to indicate the name of the department or field of specialization in addition to the name of the school or faculty. Thus, an institution may offer a Master of Science in Electrical Engineering. This is poor practice as it leads to an unending multiplicity of degree names. The field of specialization may better be cited on the diploma without creating a separate degree for each such named field.

Honorary Degrees The generally accepted principle in the United States is that the same degree title should not be used for honorary *(honoris causa)* as for earned academic degrees.

The B.A. and the M.A. unfortunately are still awarded occasionally as honorary degrees in the United States. The granting of the Ph.D. as an honorary degree, however, was largely stamped out through concerted efforts by the academic community beginning in 1881 and extending into the twentieth century.

Several professional doctorates, however, are awarded by some institutions as earned and by others as honorary degrees. The

TABLE 2 *Earned degrees conferred by field of studies in the United States 1965–66*

Field of study	Bachelor's degree		First professional degree	
	Number	Percent	Number	Percent
Arts and sciences	242,227	46.2	64	.2
Natural science	85,220	16.2	42	.1
Social sciences and humanities	157,007	30.0	22	.1
Agriculture	5,730	1.0		
Architecture	2,401	.4	198	.6
Business	63,500	12.1		
Education	118,399	22.5	22	.1
Engineering	35,815	6.8		
Fine arts	9,871	1.8		
Forestry	1,443	.2	23	.1
Health professions				
Dentistry			3,264	10.4
Medicine			7,720	24.5
Nursing	7,831	1.4		
Pharmacy	3,311	.6	452	1.4
Other	3,912	.7	1,817	5.8
Home economics	5,724	1.0		
Journalism	3,131	.5		
Law	245	.0	13,442	42.7
Library science	619	.1	23	.1
Music	3,537	.6	28	.1
Religion	4,036	.7	4,443	14.1
Social work	1,664	.3		
Others	10,721	2.0		
ALL FIELDS	524,117	100	31,496	100

SOURCE: Adapted from U.S. Office of Education, *Earned Degrees Conferred, 1965-66,* Washington, D.C., 1966.

Doctor of Science (D.Sc.), awarded by 221 institutions as an honorary degree, is given by 8 as an earned degree identical in rank with the Ph.D. This practice is particularly unfortunate since the D.Sc. in England, other British Commonwealth countries, the U.S.S.R., and elsewhere is the highest earned doctorate, substantially above the Ph.D. in measurement of maturity and scientific accomplish-

Master's degree		*Doctor's degree*	
Number	*Percent*	*Number*	*Percent*
,491	29.5	10,776	59.0
,899	12.0	7,028	38.5
,592	17.5	3,748	20.5
,363	1.0	537	2.9
381	.3	9	.0
,988	9.2	387	2.1
,478	35.9	3,063	16.8
,678	9.7	2,304	12.6
,789	1.3	72	.4
303	.2	51	.3
863	.6	1	.0
187	.1	78	.4
,817	1.3	172	.9
740	.5	54	.3
523	.4	15	.1
780	.6	29	.2
,916	2.8	19	.1
,695	1.2	164	.9
,946	1.4	333	1.8
,912	2.8	64	.4
,922	1.4	111	.6
,772	100	18,239	100

ment. It is no wonder that foreign students in the United States will opt for the D.Sc. rather than Ph.D. if given the alternative.

Other doctorates given both as honorary and earned degrees are Doctor of Music (102 institutions granting as honorary and 3 as earned), Doctor of Engineering (47 honorary and 7 earned), Doctor of Education (22 and 74), Doctor of Sacred Theology (19 and 7), and Doctor of Business Administration (11 and 10) (Eells and Haswell, 1960). It would be highly desirable to develop generally accepted pairs of doctoral titles, one for the honorary and one for the earned degree, in each of these and other major professional fields.

Special types of honorary degrees are the M.A. *privatim* given by Yale to all its full professors who have not already received a higher degree from Yale, and the B.A. and M.A. *ad eundem* formerly given by Harvard, Yale, and Wesleyan on application to holders of comparable earned degrees from sister institutions.

Spurious Degrees Mention should at least be made of the fact that degrees could formerly and may still be purchased without meeting any academic standards or without attending an institution. Wooton, in describing American education in England in 1883 wrote:

In the United States of America the sale of degrees is maintained to the present day. There are unchartered bodies granting these titles with and without prior examination. There are chartered institutions only too happy to sell spoilt parchment at about 60 dols. the foot, and such venal bodies are not rare, but are to be found in large numbers scattered over the States of the Union.

He went on to suggest that the practice is not greatly different from English practice in granting the master's and the doctorate:

The Doctorate, at the greater number of universities of the United Kingdom, is merely a receipt for so much money paid, the examinational tests ending with the Bachelorship. Many other degrees are granted in a similar manner.

As late as 1959, one could purchase in the United States the degree of Doctor of Psychology for $100, Doctor of Metaphysics for $150, Doctor of Divinity for $200, and Doctor of Philosophy for $250 (Eells and Haswell, 1960). The pecking order established by the monetary considerations is of interest.

RECOMMEN-DATIONS Following the principles outlined above, we present in Table 3 a suggested simplified pattern of degree names and abbreviations. These are based upon prevalent usages identified by Eells and Haswell (1960), modified by the application of principles developed by the Council of Graduate Schools in the United States and influenced by current trends in professional degree nomenclature.

TABLE 3 *Recommended simplified degree nomenclature*

Faculty or school	Associate, 2	Bachelor, 4	Master, 5-6	Intermediate, 6-7	Doctor, 7 plus	Honorary
	Levels and number of years of full-time study past secondary school					
Liberal arts	A.A.	B.A.	M.A.	L.Phil.[1]	Ph.D.	L.H.D.[2]
Natural science	A.S.	B.S.	M.S.	L.Phil.[1]	Ph.D.	D.Sc.
Agriculture	A.Agr.	B.S.Agr.	M.Agr.	L.Phil.[1]	Ph.D.	D.Agr.
Architecture		B.Arch.	M.Arch.		D.Arch.	
Business administration	A.B.A.	B.B.A.	M.B.A.	L.Phil.[1]	Ph.D.	D.B.A.
Dentistry					D.D.S.[3]	
Education						
Professional	A.Ed.	B.Ed.	M.Ed.	Ed.S.	Ed.D.[4]	Ped.D.[5]
Liberal arts	A.A.	B.A.	M.A.	L.Phil.[1]	Ph.D.	L.H.D.[2]
Engineering						
Professional	A.E.	B.S.E.	M.E.	Eng.	Ph.D.	D.Eng.
Science	A.A.S.[6]	B.S.	M.S.	L.Phil.[1]	Ph.D.	D.Sc.
Fine arts	A.F.A.	B.F.A.	M.F.A.			D.F.A.
Forestry	A.F.	B.S.F.	M.F.	L.Phil.[1]	Ph.D.	D.F.
Law					J.D.[7]	LL.D.
Library science		B.L.S.	M.L.S.		D.L.S.	L.H.D.[2]
Medicine					M.D.[3]	Med.Sc.D.
Music	A.Mus.	B.Mus.	M.Mus.	L.Mus.A.	A.Mus.D.	D.Mus.
Nursing	A.N.	B.N.	M.S.N.			
Pharmacy		B.S.Pharm.	M.S.Pharm.	Pharm.D.	Ph.D.	
Public administration		B.P.A.	M.P.A.		D.P.A.	LL.D.
Public health			M.P.H.		D.P.H.	
Social work			M.S.W.		D.S.W.	
Theology, divinity					B.D.[8]	D.D.

[1] Licentiate in Philosophy or other generally acceptable new name.
[2] Doctor of Humane Letters.
[3] Advanced professional-scientific work leads to M.S. and Ph.D.
[4] Also Ph.D. in research areas.
[5] Doctor of Pedagogy.
[6] Associate in Applied Science.
[7] Higher professional degrees are Master of Laws (LL.M.) and Doctor of Juridical Science (S.J.D.).
[8] Higher professional degrees are Master of Sacred Theology (S.T.M.) and Doctor of Theology (Th.D.).

Five general degree levels are recognized. The first three are consistently named as *associate, bachelor,* and *master.* The fourth, covering intermediate graduate degrees, is in a state of development and therefore of flux. The term *specialist* is accepted in professional education and *engineer* is standard in that field. In the liberal arts, *candidate* has the widest current usage although *licentiate* has much to recommend it (Chapter 8). The fifth and highest level is *doctor.* Law schools are rapidly moving from the Bachelor of Laws to the Juris Doctor at this level, and theological seminaries are considering a similar move from the Bachelor of Divinity to a doctoral degree.

In those fields where the first professional degree is the doctorate, the need exists for higher scientific or professional degrees. In medicine and dentistry, the path from the professional doctorate in science is recognized by the M.S. and the Ph.D. Advanced clinical accomplishment is recognized through certification by specialty boards established by the profession rather than by academic degrees. In law, advanced professional degrees are the Master of Laws and the Doctor of Juridical Science. In theology, they are Master of Sacred Theology and Doctor of Theology.

An attempt has been made to suggest a limited number of honorary degrees in an effort to reduce the absurd number in use and to avoid using earned degree titles for honorary degrees and vice versa. There is much merit in deciding whether or not such professional degrees as Doctor of Architecture, Doctor of Business Administration, and Doctor of Fine Arts should be restricted to the earned or to the honorary classification. Whichever is done, a different name should be developed for the parallel doctorate for the other usage. Some effort at such preliminary classification is attempted in Table 3.

3. A Theory of Academic Degree Structures

The principle of academic certification through the award by a faculty of academic degrees, regardless of their names, has been an accepted part of our social structure since the thirteenth century. Shakespeare, as usual, said it well, putting the words into the mouth of Ulysses *(Troilus and Cressida,* Act I, Scene 3):

O, when degree is shaked
Which is the ladder of all high designs,
The enterprise is sick! How could communities
Degrees in schools and brotherhoods in cities,
Peaceful commerce from dividable shores,
The primogenitive and due of birth,
Prerogative of age, crowns, sceptres, laurels,
But by degree, stand in authentic place?
Take but degree away, untune that string,
and hark, what discord follows!

Our task is not to say it again, or even to detail the elaborate degree structures and the programs which they codify in American higher education, but to concentrate upon the basic principles, to outline the system, and to propose modest changes that might conceivably be acceptable to the academic community and that might improve somewhat the working of the system itself.

THE IDEAL Degree structures should be flexible enough to facilitate the student's finding a place in the system of higher education appropriate to his current interests and abilities. Additionally, he should have the opportunity of movement consonant with the development of his motivation, abilities, and performance. His eventual accomplishment should not be unduly restricted by the circumstances of his genetic constitution or his environmental background, by his previous educational opportunity, or by his early performance in educational tests. The system should, in other words, provide recurring opportunities so that no one failure should permanently stop the student's progress.

In short, the ideal degree structure should provide for a continuum of choice of career goals and a continuum of choice of institutions, programs, and curricula within programs through which these career goals can be pursued. Too much effort has been expended upon the definition and establishment of mutually exclusive classes of institutions and discrete nonoverlapping programs within these institutions. Academic programs and the degree structures that characterize them can most logically be classified and defined in terms of their place in a continuous interwoven system rather than as discrete mutually exclusive classes. To the extent that we can find a logical classification and a manner of speaking that will so identify academic degree structures, they are apt to remain viable and flexible.

This theme is contradictory to much of the American literature on degree structures. Many critics abhor generalized degrees that are but imperfectly characterized in terms of curriculum, duration of effort required, and academic performance expected. Such critics are apt to propose the establishment of new academic degrees which would be earned following the completion of a restrictive curriculum by a carefully defined and separately admitted student body. Many such programs have been suggested; several have been tried; few have been effective. American educators and students alike have resisted pressures to separate students into discrete units, perhaps because of an instinctive feeling that to do so is to place unnecessary limits on the student's future academic training and professional career. Given the choice, the student will normally opt for the generalized Bachelor of Arts rather than for a highly specific professional bachelor's degree, such as the Bachelor of Chemistry, because of the wider range in choice of career development available to the holders of the generalized degree. And who wouldn't prefer the Master of Arts to a degree entitled Master of Arts in Teaching College Psychology? Where degree structures have been sharply defined, made mutually exclusive, and limited to specific segments of the student population, they have tended to wither on the vine for want of students and reform. Our basic degree structures in the liberal arts have remained highly variable and poorly defined. For these very reasons they have also remained more flexible and more capable of evolution. If our aim is indeed to provide the student continua of choice and opportun-

ity, we should constantly seek in the identification and characterization of our degree structures a form of logic and a manner of
speaking that will permit these developments.

In countries like England, France, Germany, and Italy the student's performance on his matriculation examination may determine once and for all the limits of his subsequent career. Similarly,
his performance at college may determine his subsequent prospects.
The student at Oxford who takes first-class honors moves from
that moment on into quite different channels than those available
to the man from the same institution with a pass degree. In America, on the contrary, we have been successful in providing the student opportunities to accomplish at a later stage what he failed to
accomplish earlier. The high school graduate who cannot get into a
prestige private institution can still go to a respectable state university. If he cannot get into that, the developing system of public
two-year colleges provides an academic opportunity for him to
progress at his own speed so he can move into a four-year college
at the junior-class level. The student who begins in a community
college may well end up with a Ph.D. or professional doctorate
from a prestige institution. Similarly, graduation from an Ivy
League institution is no sure indicator of success. Our system is
indeed flexible.

We should define our system of higher education in terms of
academic degree structures so that each becomes a natural part
of a fluid and interconnecting system. Our aim should be to keep
our degree structures few and broadly defined so as to facilitate
the movement of the student within the system and to bring him as
close as possible into accordance with his potentialities. To the
extent that we improve our simple and fluid degree structures, we
can consciously plan to keep our system adaptable and evolutionary. If, on the other hand, we allow our degree structures to become
more discrete, mutually exclusive, and inevitably more numerous,
we are apt to limit the opportunities of students to maximize their
educational experiences and to change their degree goals as they
themselves mature and develop.

SUCCESSFUL AND UNSUCCESS- FUL DEGREE STRUCTURES Much of the criticism of American degrees is leveled at a relatively
few titles. The level of criticism in the twentieth century may be
used as an inverse indicator of the relative success of a degree and
the degree structure it represents. The characteristics of successful
and unsuccessful degrees provide clues to principles that can be
applied to evolve a more satisfactory system of degree structures.

Starting with the unsuccessful degrees, much criticism has been leveled against the master's program in the liberal arts. The Master of Arts and Master of Science degrees are too often awarded for the mere accumulation of additional credits, including many representing work of only undergraduate caliber. They too often embody no academic program. And they are often awarded as a consolation prize to those who cannot continue on for the doctorate.

The Doctor of Philosophy degree has been equally subject to severe criticism on a wide range of counts. Once given solely to recognize demonstrated research ability and scholarship in the liberal arts, it now represents merely certification for employment in colleges and research organizations in almost any field of specialization. The Ph.D. program is notoriously inefficient both in drag-out of time and in dropout of students. Hundreds of pages of criticism have been leveled against the Ph.D. in recent years. Very little has been achieved.

Among the professional degrees, the Doctor of Education (Ed.D.) is widely considered to be a second-class degree. On quite different counts, the physician-training program is considered by many to require an inordinate length of time, especially when the total span of a physician's training is measured from university entrance to ultimate qualification as a practicing specialist. The Doctor of Medicine (M.D.) program has created concerns within the medical profession as being unnecessarily rigid and is being reexamined at many medical schools. We may add the M.D. and the Ed.D., therefore, to the M.A. and the Ph.D. as degrees that require reappraisal and may look to the characteristics of these degrees in an effort to discern improvements in our educational system that might be brought about by the establishment of alternative degree requirements.

Moving to the successful degrees, the liberal arts baccalaureate (B.A. or B.S.) heads the list. Virtually all students take it. It is a respectable degree. The literature on it is remarkably free of criticism. There seems to be an almost universal acceptance of its general characteristics. The duration of study is four years. All students must select from a broad spectrum of general education or distribution requirements. In addition, they must accumulate a concentration in a specific subject. The Bachelor of Arts and the Bachelor of Science degrees cover a wide range of choice and quality of effort but remain standard degrees. Even the experimental and avant-garde colleges offer the B.A. degree. They continue to require essentially a four-year program involving both concentration and distribution in liberal studies. With the improvement of secondary education and the introduction of standardized methods of advanced placement, the duration of the baccalaureate program may readily be reduced for qualified students. The four-year curriculum, however, remains the standard. Curriculum discussions are constantly going on in innovative institutions around the country but, in almost all instances, there is an implicit assumption that the revised curriculum will involve a judicious mixture of general education on one hand with specialization on the other. In short, the four-year baccalaureate is a generally accepted degree structure, and one which we can well use as a model of success.

At the graduate level there is relatively little criticism of a number of major professional master's and doctor's degrees. Such master's degrees as the Master of Business Administration, Master of Social Work, and Master of Forestry represent formal professional programs open to holders of the baccalaureate that seem generally to meet the needs of the students and the professions they serve. Similarly, there is general acceptance of the broad features of the modern law program leading to the LL.B. or J.D. The same may be said for a number of professional doctorates such as in dentistry (Doctor of Dental Surgery), veterinary medicine (Doctor of Veterinary Medicine), and public health (Doctor of Public Health). As with the B.A. and B.S. degrees, faculty and student discussions in these professional areas tend to be concerned with internal modification rather than with criticism of the degree structure itself. One may well ask what characterizes these degrees that makes their reception so different from that accorded the master's and the doctor's.

HYPOTHESIS   The B.A. program may well be as successful as it is because it offers a wide range of opportunity under a single degree title to which virtually all students aspire and which opens a wide variety of doors for those who succeed. In contrast with several of the less successful degrees, there is no connotation that the B.A. is a terminal degree, a washout degree, or a consolation prize for those who cannot go on. Many students indeed decide not to go on with their higher education, having achieved a level of academic exposure and career training which satisfies their needs. Others choose professional programs leading to advanced professional degrees. Still others are accepted for graduate study in liberal arts graduate programs—ranging widely in the field of specialization, in the prestige of the institutions offering them, and in the difficulty of the individual graduate program. In short, the B.A. represents a broad degree gate, offering a wide range of noninvidious choice to a wide range of students. It is a gate through which everyone passes regardless of whether they are going into the outside world, into professional schools, or into graduate study in the liberal arts. The generalized baccalaureate permits a progressive choice of career opportunities and provides reentry possibilities for those who wish to change their field as their interests, talents, and motivations develop. Perhaps other degree programs in the liberal arts would be more generally accepted if they offered progressive, noninvidious choices within a reasonable time span.

GENERAL PRINCIPLES Following this line of reasoning, we suggest a number of principles around which we shall develop a proposed system of degree structures:

First, the number of different degree titles should be kept as low as possible, allowing for substantial variation within each as regards subject matter, emphasis, quantity, and even quality of effort. The wider the degree gates the better. At each level, each degree title recognized should denote clearly separable curricula. Separately named professional degrees are both inevitable and desirable, but these, too, should be limited in number.

Second, degree structures should be flexible in time required for the completion of the academic program in order to encourage acceleration, but should have rather specific overall time limits in order to discourage too attenuated an effort. The typical Bachelor of Arts program provides an excellent model in that, with advanced credit or accelerated study, the bright student has no problem completing the baccalaureate in three years or less. Any steady, hard-working student of moderate ability, however, can complete the baccalaureate by carrying a normal academic load for four academic years. Similar opportunities for acceleration combined with a standardized maximum duration could well be applied to master's and doctoral programs.

Third, each degree should mark the successful completion of one stage of academic progress without implication or prejudgment as to a student's capacity to embark on following stages. All but the highest degrees are terminal for some students and intermediate for others. The important thing is that the student be able to make a noninvidious decision upon completion of one stage of his academic career as to whether he will stop or delay his formal education at that point, move into a professional curriculum, or move into an advanced liberal arts curriculum. His choices should be progressive rather than retrogressive. The latter can only lead to implications that the student has failed or that he has been forced into a second-track program because of his academic limitations. Although different admissions criteria may be used to choose the students best qualified for each of the alternative progressive steps, such criteria should emphasize the matching of the student to the specific program and not be based simply upon overt differences in the academic performance of the student at his previous stage.

Fourth, degree structures should be so interrelated that the maximum opportunity exists for redirection as the student's motivation, interests, and intellectual achievements permit. Basically this means that students electing a professional program on college admission, at the bachelor's stage, the master's stage, or the doctor's stage, should not be prohibited or restricted from moving back into advanced liberal arts work should their capacities and interests dictate. The students who elect a program leading to a professional bachelor's in engineering, a master's program in business, or a doctor's program in medicine all should have the opportunity of ending up with the doctor's degree. Their respective professional training programs provide different but worthwhile backgrounds for a research and scholarly career as compared to the alternative backgrounds they could have obtained in liberal arts training. Conversely, the student ought to be able to move into professional training either at the bachelor's level, the master's level, or the doctor's level in accordance with the practice of the particular profession.

Fifth, the various components of the educational experience are not optimally separable into different time periods. While there is general acceptance that the student trained both in the general liberal arts and in a specific field of concentration or in a specific profession is more desirably educated than either the pure generalist or the pure specialist, it is by no means clear that one phase of education should be separated in time from the other or, if so, which should precede which. To be specific, it is not desirable to confine general liberal arts education to the first two years and subject-matter specialization to the last two years of undergraduate study. In many cases, it is better to allow the student who is preoccupied with a given line of study to follow this line vigorously in his first exposure to the university, as long as his program will be balanced out before he finishes. One consequence of this principle is that there continues to be merit in providing integrated four-year undergraduate programs on a university campus rather than farming out the first two years to a junior college system. Another is that opportunities should be provided for joint liberal arts-professional programs taken concurrently rather than in series.

LEVELS OF ACADEMIC ACCOMPLISHMENT In discussing the application of these principles, we shall first deal separately with each of the six general degree levels prevalent in American higher education. The first, or associate level, recognizes the completion of the underclass or first two years of undergraduate effort. The second, the bachelor level, records the completion of undergraduate experience after four years. The third is the master level; the fourth the intermediate graduate stage; the fifth the doctorate, and the sixth postdoctoral or higher doctoral recognition. Each will be discussed in separate chapters.

4. Secondary School–University Articulation

University degree structures and the academic programs they represent are constructed on the base of the maturity, intellectual capabilities, and previous education of the students who enter the system. The present system of higher education in the United States is designed to train young men and women who, at the average age of 18, have had 12 years of education. Whether or not they spend 8 years in elementary and four years in secondary education or whether they follow the 6-3-3 program with an intermediate or junior high school phase, their general preparation is comparable. Four-year institutions, ranging from some private institutions which select a limited number of highly qualified students on multiple criteria to large public institutions which have only moderately difficult admission standards but which do close their doors when their freshmen quota has been filled, usually practice selective admission. Public community colleges, in contrast, attempt to help all interested students in the postsecondary age group within the limits imposed by their facilities and offerings.

DEVELOPMENT OF CURRENT ADMISSION PRACTICES The practice of starting higher education at about 18 years of age after 12 years of schooling is only around a century old. When our first colleges were founded, they recruited much younger students whose previous training had been for the most part a year or two in a preparatory school or simply tutoring in Greek and Latin by the local minister. The only entrance requirements were Greek and Latin until arithmetic was added (by Yale in 1745 and Harvard in 1807), followed by geography (Harvard, 1807) and English grammar (Princeton, 1819). Algebra, geometry, and history also were added prior to the Civil War. Students as young as 14 but commonly 15 or 16 were admitted. Clearly, the American college prior to the Civil War was a secondary school by modern standards, both in terms of subject matter taught and in the age of its student body. As Andrew Fleming West (1900) put it:

Up to the close of the civil war [1861-1865] it [the American college] was mainly an institution of secondary education, with some anticipations of university studies toward the end of the course. But even these embryonic university studies were usually taught as rounding out the course of disciplinary education, rather than as subjects of free investigation.

The last half of the nineteenth century in the United States saw the strengthening of secondary education, both in the development of college preparatory schools along the Eastern Seaboard and the emergence of public high schools, most notably in the Midwest and Far West. During this period, the average age for beginning higher education moved up rapidly to the present level of 18, and increasingly stringent academic requirements were imposed for university admission. Beginning with the University of Michigan in 1870, Midwestern universities accredited high schools which presented adequate college preparatory programs. Regional standardization of entrance requirements developed through such agencies as the New England Association of Colleges and Preparatory Schools and the North Central Association (1894). The New York State Board of Regents and the College Entrance Examination Board (CEEB) provided standard examinations which influenced the raising and standardizing of college preparatory studies in secondary schools. The net result has been still to bring the students from high school into college at the average age of 18, but at an increasingly higher level of preparation. Considerable material taught in our universities a decade or two ago is now taught in secondary schools.

Much the same trend developed in England where the undergraduate university program was reduced from four to three years. That this didn't take place in the United States despite abortive efforts, detailed in Chapter 6, would seem to be largely due to the fact that English universities accepted only the very ablest youth. In contrast, American universities since the Civil War have increasingly accepted the premise that most, if not all, young men and women have the right to at least begin college if they present a satisfactory high school record in a college preparatory course. The retention of the fourth undergraduate year in the United States permits the equalization of opportunity for students having a wide range of basic intellectual ability and coming from a wide diversity of secondary school experiences.

PRESENT ADMISSION REQUIRE- MENTS

Present admission requirements for American undergraduate programs are fairly well standardized. Almost all four-year institutions require the successful completion of a four-year secondary school program, the presentation of 15 to 16 units (each equivalent to a year of high school study) primarily in academic subjects, and for most selective institutions, the taking of college board SAT verbal and quantitative aptitude examinations. College boards were established at the turn of the century to serve the common admissions needs of Eastern universities (Fuess, 1950; Bowles, 1967). As many four-year institutions have moved more and more into selective admissions, a student's performance on these examinations has become one of the factors assessed by most admissions offices. In their present form, the examinations are primarily intelligence and aptitude tests utilizing a knowledge of English vocabulary and basic mathematical skills. Despite the prevalence of their use, most universities continue to place equal reliance upon the student's secondary school transcript, subjective recommendations, and personal interviews.

In summary, the present-day American student spends four years in high school and enters college at the average age of 18 (plus or minus a year) looking forward to four years of undergraduate study before earning the baccalaureate. It is true that the student may reduce the length of this latter period through advanced placement on matriculation, that he may accelerate by taking a heavier than normal load of courses, or may decelerate by taking less than a normal load. Nonetheless, there is little flexibility in the mode of transition from secondary school to college or to the time span assigned to each experience.

EFFORTS TO CHANGE ARTICULATION

The century-old pattern in the United States of 12 years in school followed by 4 years as an undergraduate creates no particular problems when the baccalaureate terminates formal education and marks the beginning of a career for the young man or woman of 22. As formal postbaccalaureate education has become more and more prevalent, however, we have become more and more concerned with duplicative and unnecessary elements in the secondary school and university articulation. While the student formerly entered the job market at 22 with the B.A., he is now apt to be delayed up to another 10 years if he must qualify himself with the Ph.D. or comparable professional degree. For instance, students normally take time out for work or military service and begin graduate study at an average age of 24. The master's degree requires an average of two additional years, bringing the average age to 26. The doctor's degree adds at least two more years of study, and a period in which an acceptable thesis is prepared. This period is usually prolonged by time added for employment, either for financial support or experience. The average Ph.D. is thus 32 when he has his diploma in hand.

Efforts to improve these situations by reducing the age at college entrance or by reducing the period of undergraduate study itself have not been successful. Yet, a number of innovations have been proposed or attempted. These fall into three general categories: (1) the compression of the term of baccalaureate study from four to three years, (2) reduction of the length of preuniversity education from 12 to 11 or even 10 years, and (3) the establishment of a separate "collegiate" institution to serve students between secondary school and the university. To these, we may add consideration of the possible desirability of a hiatus between secondary school and the university.

The Three-year Baccalaureate

We have already noted that in England and Wales, the B.A. program was shortened from four to three years during the nineteenth century. Efforts to achieve a similar reduction in America were also made during the nineteenth century. In 1851, Harvard established a three-year science curriculum leading to the Bachelor of Science degree, and the following year Yale followed suit, naming its three-year degree Bachelor of Philosophy. Both were considered second-class degrees, however, in comparison to the dominant four-year Bachelor of Arts program. Later in the century, President Eliot of Harvard argued long, but in vain, for a general three-year B.A. program. As late as 1905, he wrote:[1]

The argument in favor of a three years' course for the degree of Bachelor of Arts rests on three assumptions. It assumes (1) that a boy who has had good opportunities may best leave his secondary school at the age of eighteen, because the average boy is then ready for the liberty of a college or technical school; (2) that a young man who expects to follow a profession ought to enter on the practice of that profession by the time he is twenty-five, or at least twenty-six years of age; and (3) that a young man who is going into business after obtaining a college training may most advantageously enter on that business at twenty-one or twenty-two years of age.

[1] Letter of President Eliot to the Associated Harvard Club, May 13, 1905, quoted by Thwing (1906, p. 425).

If these assumptions can be denied, the argument for the three years' degree falls.

Although Eliot encouraged well-prepared and professionally motivated students to complete their Harvard undergraduate preparation in three years, he was successful with only 36 percent of the class of 1906 (Rudolph, 1962).

Johns Hopkins opened its undergraduate program in 1867 with more exacting admissions standards than those of Harvard and Yale. It reduced the normal time span for the baccalaureate from four years to three soon after opening, but fell into the pattern of a preliminary year at the university before matriculation, and formally fell back into a four-year program in 1907 (Hawkins, 1960).

The other major effort to reduce the length of undergraduate study in the nineteenth century was Columbia's professional option plan which permitted able students to enter any of its professional schools except law after two or three years of undergraduate study. Between 1892 and 1902, one-quarter of the student body at Columbia followed this option (Brubacher and Rudy, 1958). Although many American colleges and universities continued to offer similar options, both on an intramural and on a transfer basis, the percentage of students choosing to cut a year of their undergraduate experience is not large.

A more recent development is the advanced placement program which originated in 1952 with 7 preparatory schools agreeing to offer college-level courses in 1953-54 and 12 colleges agreeing to grant advanced standing to students who performed creditably in the courses and on the examinations (Radcliffe and Hatch, 1961). Under its present form, students who have done advanced work in secondary school or who have otherwise been similarly educated may qualify for advanced college placement, college credit, or both by attaining high scores on the CEEB Advanced Placement Examinations. These are given in such subject-matter fields as literature and English composition, American history, European history, French, German, Latin, Spanish, mathematics, biology, chemistry, and physics. Essay questions predominate. At Harvard, Princeton, and Yale, among others, any student who reaches requisite levels in three or more subjects may be considered for admission with full sophomore standing and may shorten his course by a full year. Relatively few do so, however. While advanced placement has been quite successful in improving the articulation between secondary school and the undergraduate program, it has served generally to exempt the student from taking specified introductory courses as an underclassman but not to shorten the student's undergraduate career.

The case for a three-year bachelor's program has recently been revived by Woodring (1968) who has suggested that it be confined to liberal arts only and that it be followed by a two-year master's program whether (1) in professional fields, (2) in the various academic disciplines, or (3) to qualify teachers.

All in all, though, it may be said that, despite many efforts to formalize a three-year baccalaureate program, and despite the fact that able students can readily accelerate and complete the baccalaureate today in three years through advanced placement and summer study, the American student by and large has opted for the four-year undergraduate experience. Where accelerated or shortened programs have been tried, faculty opposition has also generally contributed to their demise.

Shortened Primary and Secondary Education

Although a detailed consideration of the first 12 years of American education is beyond the scope of this present work, we should at least note that many of its critics have pointed out that there is much redundancy and opportunity for compression in it. William Rainey Harper, the first president of the University of Chicago, was one who suggested that secondary education begin with the eighth rather than with the ninth grade and that at least one year be lopped off the period prior to entry to upper-division university work (Brubacher and Rudy, 1958). In a contemporary experiment, St. Louis University is experimenting with a pilot program in which students will begin high school with the eighth rather than the ninth grade, take advanced placement courses for guaranteed university credit while still in high school, and receive their baccalaureate after three years in the university. The program will thus cut two years off the average time for completion of the baccalaureate.

The Intermediate Collegiate Institution

The concept of a separate institution at the "collegiate" level between the secondary school and the university is an old one. Suggested as the appropriate means of providing a broad liberal arts education prior to specialization at the university level, it has its origins in the better features of the English sixth form, the French *lycée,* and the German *Gymnasium* and the relationship they bear to the universities of their respective countries. Henry Philip Tappan, in his inaugural address at the University of Michigan in 1852, was the first to suggest the transfer of the general education aspects of the university program to the high schools (Eells, 1931). The separation of the two functions became a reality with the opening of the University of Chicago in 1892. There, freshman and sophomore work was offered in a separate "academic" college, a unit that was renamed junior college in 1896. Furthermore, Chicago began encouraging the offering of parallel work in local high schools. Joliet Junior College, established in 1902, was the first public community college and the progenitor of this major class of institutions of higher education.

While two-year colleges have grown enormously in numbers and in services rendered, they have provided only an alternative track from high school to the university and one of secondary importance as far as numbers of students reaching the university is concerned. They may have provided better articulation between secondary school and the university for many, but they have not, in general, shortened the total time required for a university degree.

Further innovations along the line of an intermediate collegiate institution have been proposed and even tried. Robert M. Hutchins, president of the University of Chicago from 1929 to 1945, attempted to create a college which would combine the last two years of high school with the first two years of college and which would offer the bachelor's degree. Students could be accepted into the College at Chicago prior to high school graduation and could move through as fast as they could pass their examinations. The experiment was exciting, and many of the students in it did well. Eventually, however, widespread opposition won out and the College at Chicago lapsed back into a traditional four-year postsecondary program. As Brubacher and Rudy (1958) put it:

The forces of tradition, however, were not to be dislodged easily. Opinion generally rose to the support of the traditional four-year college in fear that the proposed four-year college, even if it did not curtail intellectual objectives, would lack the time to develop deep social and moral values formed by the social attrition of undergraduate life and long associated with the college in both England and the United States. America easily accepted a graduate school of the German model atop their college, but they resisted partitioning their college to assimilate their high school to a German Gymnasium.

The merits of the general Chicago plan have resulted in persistent interest in the potential of a separate collegiate institution. In 1967, F. Champion Ward, former dean of the College at Chicago (1947–1954), suggested an 11–3–3 program, ending secondary schooling after a total of 11 years of education, followed by 3 years in a collegiate institution, and 3 years of graduate work in a university. His collegiate institutions would include both upgraded junior colleges of arts and sciences and also the general category of four-year independent and university colleges, which would reduce their first course of study by one year. Carl Kaysen has suggested a similar plan, in which high school would end with the eleventh grade and be followed by a three-year collegiate program leading to the bachelor's degree. Whereas Chicago stressed the classical liberal arts education, Kaysen would have his colleges offer much broader educational opportunities including both pre-university and terminal technical programs.

A Hiatus between Secondary School and the University The implicit assumption of most attempts to improve the secondary school-university articulation is that it is desirable to reduce the overall period of formal education either by the encouragement of acceleration or by the shortening of the normal academic program. The reverse of the coin is that the opposite course may in fact be desirable, that there is much to be said for encouraging or even requiring a youth to spend a year or two outside of school to experience the outside world, to get out of the academic rut, to mature, and to develop his own motivation. Although this hiatus may profitably occur at any time within the period of higher education, the most logical places for it are between programs, especially between secondary school and the undergraduate experience. Paul Goodman (1962) puts the case succinctly:

First, suppose that half a dozen of the most prestigious liberal arts colleges . . . would announce that, beginning in 1966, they require for admission a two-year period, after high school, spent in some maturing activity. These colleges are at present five times oversubscribed; they would not want for applicants on any conditions that they set; and they are explicitly committed to limiting their expansion.

By "maturing activity" could be meant: working for a living, especially if the jobs are gotten without too heavy reliance on connections; community service, such as the Northern Student Movement, volunteer service in hospital or settlement house, domestic Peace Corps; the army — though I am a pacifist and would urge a youngster to keep out of the army; a course of purposeful travel that met required standards; independent enterprise in art, business, or science, away from home, with something to show for the time spent.

The purpose of this proposal is twofold: to get students with enough life-experience to be educable on the college level, especially in the social sciences and humanities; and to break the lockstep of twelve years of doing assigned lessons for grades, so that the student may approach his college studies with some intrinsic motivation, and therefore perhaps assimilate something that might change him. Many teachers remember with nostalgia the maturer students who came under the GI-bill, though to be sure a large number of them were pretty shell-shocked.

A subsidiary advantage of the plan would be to relieve the colleges of the doomed, and hypocritical, effort to serve in loco parentis on matters of morality. If young persons have been out working for a living, or have traveled in foreign parts, or have been in the army, a college can assume that they can take care of themselves.

University counselors have long known that one of the best ways of salvaging a student who has lost his interest in higher education and who is emotionally or academically at odds with the institution is to encourage him to take a year or two off with the promise of readmission on his return. Flexibility in lengthening the college career is just as important as flexibility in shortening it. One of the causes of student dissatisfaction and the wave of anti-intellectualism on our college campuses today is that the fear of the draft keeps many students on campus who do not want to be there, who find their continued academic servitude unsatisfactory and irrelevant, and who quite naturally turn against the university as a symbol of the repressive establishment. Greater opportunities to leave the educational track for a year or two without penalty, whether on an individual voluntary basis or as part of the plan Goodman suggests, are obviously highly desirable.

UNIVERSITY ADMISSIONS IN WESTERN EUROPE A brief look at the secondary school-university articulation in England, France, and Germany is relevant in that it serves to clarify the distinction between secondary school leaving and university admission. In the United States, the two are generally quite separate. In only a few states does the earning of a high school diploma guarantee admission into the state university system. Where this does occur, a high percentage of those admitted are inevitably weeded out in the first undergraduate years.

In England, the first period of secondary education or "main school" usually lasts four or five years after entry, during which time the student prepares for and takes ordinary (O-level) examinations in each of perhaps eight subjects. This is followed for a limited number of university-oriented students by the sixth form. After two or more usually three years, the student takes a series of A-level examinations. An honors grade in three such examinations is required for university entrance. The normal age of university entrance is 18. Since those few students (perhaps 5 to 6 percent of the age group) who are successful in getting into a university have crammed for their A-level subjects for many years, they have a substantially greater knowledge of those particular subjects than comparable American students, albeit at the expense of a narrower education in other respects. University admission in England is handled centrally, students being assigned to a particular university insofar as possible in accordance with their own priorities.

In France, the *baccalauréat* examination serves both as a school leaving and as a university entrance examination. Taken on the average at the age of 18, its passage confers the right to enroll in a university or to take competitive examinations for admission to the *grandes écoles.* Since 1965, when the first part of the *baccalauréat* was eliminated by the Ministry of Education under political pressures for a democratization of the system, the failure rate has been greater than anticipated and has created political problems. Less than one-third of the age group take secondary school programs aimed at this examination and only one-half of these pass. Even so, the French universities do not have the facilities to handle the 15 to 16 percent of the 18-year-olds who, by passing this examination, are automatically qualified to enter the university.

The German system is similar to the French but less chaotic. Only limited numbers of students are accepted into the *Gymnasium* and an even smaller percent obtain their *Abitur* or leaving certificate which guarantees university admission. About 7 percent of the age group, therefore, is enrolled in the university. This, too, creates serious overcrowding, especially in the faculties of philosophy and the arts where there are no restricted enrollments *(numerus clausus).*

The broad problem of access to higher education has been explored for UNESCO by Bowles (1963); a second volume details the situation in 12 selected countries. Mayer (1968), more recently, has reviewed the college admissions problem from the particular standpoint of international transfers and has recommended the establishment of international admissions standards.

RECOMMEN-
DATIONS

In reviewing both the general picture of articulation between secondary and higher education and the specific problem of university admissions, it seems apparent that the clear separation in the United States between secondary school leaving and university admissions is much more satisfactory than the practices of western Europe. In England, the sole reliance upon national examinations makes for great rigidity in the system and the denial of opportunity to all but those who were able to achieve high academic performance throughout their teens. In France and Germany, the *baccalauréat* and *Abitur,* granting as they do the right to attend the university, have deprived the universities of the right to maintain quality by restricting enrollment. Our system has much to recommend it, embodying as it does multiple standards of CEEB examination, high school transcript, recommendation, and interview and providing an alternate route through the junior college for those unable or disinclined to begin the freshman year at the university. We see no reason to recommend basic changes in our university admission practices.

Despite the theoretical advantages of the concept, the collegiate institution separate from and antecedent to the university does not seem to be practical. Most universities feel strongly that they must retain a full four-year undergraduate program, academically to permit selected students to profit from a full exposure to university-level instruction and economically because it is the mix of underclassmen that makes graduate programs viable under the conditions that control university finance today. The pragmatist must settle for the present system of coordinated four-year and two-year undergraduate programs with ample opportunity for transfer.

There is much to be said for cutting from one to two years off the total time span required for the baccalaureate. It would be nice if qualified students could enter the university after the eleventh grade routinely or at least far more commonly than is now the case. Equally desirable, and much more immediately practicable, would be an expansion of the advanced placement program on terms which allow the student to obtain university credit toward a degree as well as advanced placement in a course sequence. There seems to be no valid reason why the student bound for graduate or professional school should not enter the university at 17 instead of 18 and receive his bachelor's degree at 20 or 21 instead of 22.

5. The Associate's Degree

The completion of two years of postsecondary education is marked when formally recognized, with the title *associate*. The term is used to mark both the completion of the first two years of a four-year baccalaureate program and of a terminal two-year vocational or technical course. The completion of courses of shorter duration is normally documented by an untitled certificate.

HISTORY The title or degree of associate has been sporadically used in Great Britain since 1873. In the United States, where it has its greatest usage, it originated at the University of Chicago. When this institution was opened in 1891, it awarded certificates on the completion of the first two years of undergraduate study which were offered in what originally was termed the "academic" and later renamed the "junior" college. The certificate was converted into a degree in 1899, and the titles *Associate in Arts, Associate in Literature,* and *Associate in Science* were first awarded to 83 students in 1900. A total of 4,462 such degrees were awarded between this date and 1920 when the University of Chicago discontinued the use of the degree in this sense. It revived it as an external degree, however, during the period 1931-1942 to recognize high school students who passed a series of seven comprehensive examinations given by the university (Eells, 1963).

As external junior colleges were organized to feed students into the senior colleges of the University of Chicago, they adopted the associate's degree. The first was Lewis Institute (later merged into Illinois Institute of Technology) in 1901. The concept of the associate's degree was adopted by Stephens College in Missouri in 1912 and by the Junior College of Kansas City in 1916. Harvard used the same title from 1910 to 1933 in quite a different sense to recognize completion of a four-year extension program, a practice also adopted by Radcliffe and Tufts.

Today, the associate's degree is conferred by virtually all junior and community colleges as a universal two-year degree. It is also used for the same purpose by at least 150 four-year institutions for certain two-year programs (Eells and Haswell, 1960).

The most common associate's degree title is *Associate in Arts,* given by 404 two-year colleges in 1959 and representing 73 percent of all associate's degrees awarded by these institutions that year (Eells, 1963). Other titles in common usage were *Associate in Science* (14 percent), *Associate in Applied Science* (5 percent), *Associate in Business Administration* (3 percent), and *Associate in Engineering* (2 percent).

The U.S. Office of Education began to collect national data on associate's degrees and other formal awards below the baccalaureate for the first time in 1965-66 (Brinkman, 1969). The total number of associate's degrees granted both for transfer and terminal programs was 111,740 in 1965-66 and 139,731 in 1966-67. The Associate in Arts accounted for over 60 percent of all degrees, with Associate in Science comprising about 20 percent, and all other degrees constituting the remainder.

Approximately two-thirds of all associate's degrees are granted by public two-year institutions. The breakdown of number of degrees granted by type of institution in 1966-67 is as follows:

Public two-year	94,693
Private two-year	24,458
Public universities	7,224
Private universities	1,525
All other four-year public	8,220
All other four-year private	3,611
TOTAL	139,731

In interpreting these data, it should be remembered that many technical or semiprofessional curricula of at least two but less than four years and virtually all such curricula under two years in length are recognized by certificates rather than by degrees.

By states, California led with 32,743 associate's degrees in 1966-67, followed by New York with 19,630, and Florida with 11,052.

Responsibility for postsecondary curricula shorter than four years has been moving rapidly from four-year colleges and universities to the community colleges. Approximately a million students are currently enrolled in two-year colleges, and the numbers are expected to increase dramatically over the next decades. The development of the junior college system in its earlier years has been summarized by Eells (1931). Its present status, institution by institution, is obtainable from *American Junior Colleges* (Gleazer, 1967).

The statistics of Brinkman (1969) provide the number of awards given in different curricula in 1966-67 and are indicative of the scope and relative importance of occupational curricula (as distinct from academic transfer curricula) of less than four years in length in both two- and four-year colleges (Table 4).

SUGGESTED
UNIVERSAL
USAGE
Students going the community college route today will earn the associate's degree on successful completion of either a two-year liberal arts program or of a comparable vocational or technical curriculum. In contrast, students going immediately into a four-year undergraduate program will not normally receive this recognition. The net result of this dichotomy is that the degree, although useful and accepted, does not have the relative status or prestige that the baccalaureate degree has at its level. Indeed, it has a certain second-class implication in that it implies that its holder, whether voluntarily or necessarily, chose the "easy-in, easy-out" two-year college program rather than aspiring at the beginning toward the baccalaureate.

Nonetheless, it would seem that the associate's degree does indeed have a place, particularly in view of the burgeoning role being played by the two-year colleges throughout the United States. We now have a million students in our junior and community colleges. Cartter and Farrell (1965) predict that we shall have 2 million by 1980, over 3 million by 1990, and over 5 million by the year 2000.

If we accept the premise that the two-year college and, consequently, the associate's degree are here to stay, it would seem desirable to require the associate's degree en route to the baccalaureate just as we shall recommend that the master's degree be required en route to the doctorate. By so doing, all students would automatically pass through the associate's degree level, thereby endowing that step on the academic ladder greater status and prestige than is the case when it is associated primarily with the community college movement. Then, the associate's degree could no longer be interpreted as a mark of a second-track academic career,

TABLE 4 *Numbers of awards granted on completion of subbaccalaureate occupational curricula, 1966–67**

Field of study	Length of program	
	At least 1 but less than 2 years	*At least 2 but less than 4 years*
Engineering technology	3,341	17,882
Electrical	1,125	6,372
Mechanical	433	3,092
Architectural and building	120	1,844
Industrial	390	1,221
Civil	52	1,056
Other	1,221	4,297
Agriculture	111	1,680
Health services	4,710	9,418
Nursing diploma	265	4,661
Practical nursing	3,231	591
Dental hygiene	12	1,602
Dental assistant	625	422
Other	577	2,142
Scientific data processing	58	951
Business and commerce	1,839	16,318
Secretarial	3,276	9,531
Educational	336	7,387
Fine, applied, and graphic arts	220	3,932
Police technology and law enforcement	269	1,181
Other	1,814	16,476
TOTAL	15,974	84,756

*The table does not include two-year liberal arts awards. Not all programs listed are recognized by the associate's degree.

SOURCE: Adapted from Brinkman, 1969.

but would rather represent the successful completion of the first phase of higher education.

By bracketing together all who reach the two-year level with the associate's degree, whether on the completion of an academic or in a technical-vocational program, all successful students at this point will share "the prestige and recognition and the sense of satisfaction and completion that comes from the possession of a college degree" (Eells, 1963). Furthermore, such a procedure would provide the same safety net for students in four-year colleges that already exists in two-year colleges. In four-year colleges, attrition is 40 to 50 percent, and much of it is due to factors other than academic performance (Summerskill, 1962). Were the associate's degree required en route, many of these would be in a position of having successfully completed the associate's program rather than being identified as college dropouts.

Were the associate's degree to be universally required en route to the baccalaureate, it would be desirable to so categorize the requirements for the degree that it could be earned in transit and that no additional effort or work would be required by the student planning to continue on to the baccalaureate over that which would would be required for the baccalaureate alone. The present two-year college requirement is based upon the completion of an academic program requiring two academic years of full-time effort, usually 60 semester hours or 90 quarter hours in length, with a passing, or C, overall average. Such a requirement is readily applicable to the four-year college in that any student completing two academic years work with a C average can readily be given the associate's degree provided that he has met specified curriculum requirements. These curriculum requirements could well be the completion of the general education or distribution requirements normally established as a part of the baccalaureate degree program.

In addition, however, the possibility exists of using the associate's degree to stimulate the qualified student to move more rapidly through his undergraduate program into graduate education. Whereas the two-year requirement can serve as a useful maximum qualifying students to move from the associate's to the baccalaureate level at the end of two academic years of full-time effort, the degree can also be used to measure the successful qualification of the undergraduate student for baccalaureate or upper-division effort on grounds of academic performance rather than credits earned. This alternative use of the associate's program is increasingly desirable because of improved academic programs at the secondary school level and the development of standardized advance placement procedures throughout the United States. If, indeed, the associate's degree can be characterized as representing the qualification of the student to undertake academic effort at the upper-division level because of his demonstrated competence in general studies, then provision should be made for the early satisfaction of these requirements so that the student can move to upper-division work early in his collegiate career. Perhaps we could even consider the extreme of allowing the student to meet the requirements for the associate's degree through a high level of performance on advanced placement and other college entrance examinations. Conceivably the student performing exceptionally well and demonstrating a broad breadth of competence on these examinations could be admitted immediately as an upper-division student and be given the associate's degree either solely on the basis of his entering examinations or upon the successful completion of a term or two of collegiate work added to his examination performance

In other words, the associate's degree should be defined as certifying the successful completion of the general education or broad exposure to lower-division undergraduate work. This requirement could be met in as little as one-half to one academic year by the brilliant student and in a maximum of two academic years by the steady and persistent student. Such a use for the associate's degree in the four-year undergraduate program might well stimulate a shorter total period of effort from high school graduation to the baccalaureate. In effect, this definition of the associate's degree would impose a maximum period of two years on the baccalaureate. Students qualifying at the associate's level on the basis of early performance could thereby cut up to two years off the total amount of time required for the baccalaureate.

The proposal to require the associate's degree en route to the baccalaureate in all academic institutions is made with some trepidation and only in the dual belief that, first, the associate's degree is here to stay because of the important and rapidly growing two-year college movement and, second, any collegiate degree, to be fully respectable, must be a general degree taken en route by virtually all students climbing up the academic ladder.

There is a real danger inherent in this proposal, however, and that is the effect it might have encouraging baccalaureate institutions to segregate the general education or distribution aspects of the undergraduate curriculum into the first two years and the specialization or concentration aspects of the same curriculum into the upper class or last two years. As we have already pointed out, this distinction is generally not desirable. Should institutions adopt the concept of the required associate's degree, it would be hoped that they would allow considerable leeway in permitting both early specialization and later general studies for appropriate students. There is no reason why this cannot be accomplished within the framework of an undergraduate program which provides for all students passing through the associate's gate en route to the baccalaureate portal.

If the associate's degree were to be required en route to the baccalaureate and awarded routinely to all students in four-year as well as two-year institutions, it follows that the initial admission to college should be for the associate's program only and that students would have to be readmitted for the baccalaureate on completion of the first phase of their studies. This procedure has merit in that it would enable each four-year institution to program the number of upper-division students separately from those in the lower division, and to create a common pool of applicants for the upper-division program leading to the baccalaureate in which two-year college transfers would have an equal opportunity to compete with those in the lower division already on campus. From the standpoint of the student, too, the procedure has psychological value. Many of those students who under our present system end up as college dropouts would be in the position of having "decided"— acknowledging that the decision may be voluntary or involuntary— not to continue with the bachelor's program at that particular time.

Actually, there is precedent for readmission to college for concentration studies after completion of the general education phase. It exists in such institutions as Minnesota, Michigan State, and Florida where the student may pass through a lower-division general college en route to upper-division work in a variety of different colleges on the same campus. It also exists in multicampus institutions where the first two years of college work are offered on a number of regional campuses as well as on the main campus, but where the upper-division work is concentrated at a central location. Furthermore, at some institutions such as Swarthmore, students must apply to and be accepted into the individual concentration programs of their choosing. The innovation of admitting high school graduates for the associate's program only and requiring readmission for the bachelor's program after not less than one or more than two years of academic study, therefore, has much to recommend it and should not be difficult to introduce. We urge its adoption.

DEGREE OR CERTIFICATE In the community and junior colleges, the associate's recognition is in the form of a degree. This is entirely appropriate in such institutions where the associate's level marks the completion of the full academic program offered by the institution. Considerable opposition, however, may be expected to any effort to introduce recognition of the associate's stage into four-year baccalaureate institutions. Whereas most community and junior colleges offer the associate's degree, the degree is offered by only a relatively few baccalaureate institutions and usually on the completion of special two-year programs. If a serious effort should be made to introduce this recognition for all students in baccalaureate institutions, there is considerable merit in introducing it as a certificate rather than as a degree. Such an action recognizes the fact that this stage, at least in the baccalaureate institutions, is less well established and accepted than the stages authenticated by degrees. From a practical standpoint, the concept of an associate's *certificate* is probably more salable to the faculty of a typical complex university than that of the associate's *degree.*

6. The Bachelor's Degree

We have already seen that the bachelor's degree or baccalaureate originated at our first universities (Bologna, Paris, and Oxford) in the thirteenth century as a formal certification of the right of the advanced student to participate to a limited extent in college teaching. The present use of this degree in higher education is largely confined to English-speaking countries where it is granted upon completion of the basic three- or four-year undergraduate course of study.

In England and Wales, the bachelor's degree was long awarded only in the sciences and the arts and upon three years of specialized study. Recently, the degree there has been opened up to students in engineering and applied science with the raising of the colleges of advanced technology to university status. Furthermore, there is considerable experimentation in broadening the course of baccalaureate study within the universities themselves. In the United States, the degree is universally based upon a four-year program and is awarded not only in the liberal arts but also in a wide variety of professional and mixed liberal arts-professional areas.

TYPES OF BACHELOR'S DEGREES Our concern here is primarily with the four-year baccalaureate courses of study in the liberal arts. These are the standard Bachelor of Arts (B.A.) or Bachelor of Science (B.S.) programs offered by independent liberal arts colleges and, within the university, by the college which may simply be designated with the definite article or by such modifiers as liberal arts; arts and science; literature, science and the arts; or science, arts, and letters. In the United States, in contrast with Western Europe, the faculties of arts and science have traditionally been combined, although the present trend at a number of institutions is to separate them not into two

49

but into three or four faculties or colleges concerned with humanities and the arts, social and behavioral sciences, and natural sciences (biological and physical). Nearly 50 percent of bachelor's degrees are taken in these traditional areas of university study.[1]

The bachelor's degree is also awarded by professional school faculties on the completion of four-year undergraduate programs in education (24 percent of all baccalaureate degrees), business administration (12 percent), engineering (7 percent), fine arts (4 percent), and a wide variety of undergraduate-professional as contrasted with graduate-professional fields. Where the curriculum embodies more or less the same distribution requirements as the comparable liberal arts baccalaureate on the same campus, and where a reasonable amount of liberal arts content is included in the field of concentration, the B.A. or B.S. is commonly given. Through the device of borrowing these standard degrees from the liberal arts faculties, the undergraduate-professional schools may emphasize the liberal and preprofessional content of their bachelor's programs and perhaps add luster to them by association. In contrast, where the bachelor's program is clearly professional in content and intent, professional bachelor's degrees are more appropriate. Among the most common and the best established are Bachelor of Science in Education or Bachelor of Education; Bachelor of Music or Bachelor of Science in Music; Bachelor of Business Administration or Bachelor of Science in Business Administration; Bachelor of Science in Engineering; and Bachelor of Fine Arts. As we have already indicated, the simpler form is preferred. These professional bachelor's degrees will only be given incidental attention in the present study, not because they are unimportant, but rather because most of what may be said about the liberal arts baccalaureate applies in principle to them.

We should note at this point that the title *bachelor* is used to a limited extent in other senses than the common one of identifying an on-campus four-year undergraduate curriculum. In some professions, the bachelorship identifies the first professional degree, awarded after one to three years of postgraduate study. Such are the Bachelor of Laws and Bachelor of Divinity, both of which require three years of graduate professional study. The first, however, is rapidly being supplanted by the synonym Juris Doctor. A similar

[1] U.S. Office of Education, *Earned Degrees Confered 1965-66*, Washington, D.C. 1966.

transformation is currently being considered by theological seminaries.

At the other end of the scale, a five-year bachelor's program is or has recently been offered to some extent in professional fields such as pharmacy, architecture, city planning, library science, and engineering. In some institutions, the B.A. is awarded after four years and the professional baccalaureate after the fifth year; in others, the fifth-year bachelor's degree is the only one granted. Most faculties would probably approve the principle (see Chapter 7) that a fifth-year continuation of the undergraduate program should be recognized by a bachelor's degree, with the master's degree being reserved for work at a graduate level involving an element of independent study and productivity. A few institutions still honor this principle. The trend, however, is to award the master's degree for all academic programs extending to five or six years. The Bachelor of Arts in Library Science thus becomes the Master of Arts in Library Science, and the five-year Bachelor of Architecture program can be upgraded into a six-year Master of Architecture program. These changes are probably desirable.

The bachelor's degree is also awarded by a few institutions on the successful completion of off-campus, adult education, or extension work equivalent in amount and pattern to that required for the baccalaureate earned in residence. For example, the University of Oklahoma offers the Bachelor of Liberal Studies (B.L.S.) degree on this basis (Burkett and Ruggiers, 1965). At Northwestern, students in the evening division may earn the Bachelor of Philosophy or the Bachelor of Science in General Education.

EVOLUTION OF THE B.A. IN THE UNITED STATES From the founding of Harvard in 1636 to the present day, the bachelor's program leading to the bachelor's degree has been four academic years in legnth and has emphasized both general and specialized competence in the liberal arts. Efforts to reduce the time span for the baccalaureate from four to three years, detailed in Chapter 4, have generally been unsuccessful. Any well-prepared student today can complete the baccalaureate in three years by several avenues. He may come into the university with advanced placement and credit, take an unusually heavey load of courses during the academic year, or continue his studies through the summer terms. Few, however, elect to accelerate.

The evolution of the baccalaureate in the United States, therefore, must be viewed in the light of internal changes rather than of modification of its external form. We have already discussed briefly the changes wrought by raising the age of college entrance in the nineteenth century from 15 to 18 and the influence of the development of a strong secondary school system on the raising of our better undergraduate school programs from secondary school to university status. It remains here to detail briefly the major changes in the liberal arts baccalaureate curriculum, bearing in mind that this subject deserves a monograph in its own right. Curriculum is relevant in the present work only as it relates to the general problem of academic degree structures.

At the risk of enormous oversimplification, we may divide the evolution of the American baccalaureate into four stages: (1) the standardized classical curriculum, which prevailed from 1636 to perhaps 1750; (2) the introduction of modest components of science and modern studies from 1750 to the end of the Civil War 1865; (3) the heyday of the free elective system from 1865 to 1910; and (4) dual emphasis on general education and subject-matter specialization from 1910 to the present. Each may be characterized briefly.[2]

During the first century of higher education in America, Greek and Latin only were required for college matriculation. These languages were studied not only for themselves but in order to be able to read and study such works as Aristotle and other Greek philosophers, medieval treatises reconciling Greek philosophical views with the Christian world, polite letters in both Latin and Greek, and basic mathematical texts in Latin. The curriculum was singular and inflexible. It differed from that at Oxford and Cambridge only in placing somewhat more stress on the learning of Hebrew, considered a desideratum for Puritan clergy in New England.

Beginning about 1750 and continuing up to the Civil War, the single-track classical curriculum was attacked with increasing intensity. Repeated efforts were made to incorporate more science, modern languages, and even practical subjects in the college curriculum. Supported by such national figures as Benjamin Franklin and Thomas Jefferson, some progress was made. In 1756, William Smith established at the College of Philadelphia a program in which English was the lingua franca and in which modern English authors and science were stressed equally with Latin, Greek, and philos-

---

[2] The reader is referred to Brubacher and Rudy (1958), Rudy (1960), and Rudolph (1962) for more extensive discussions of this general topic.

ophy. Jefferson's early concepts of curriculum modernization met partial fulfillment with the opening of the University of Virginia in 1825. George Ticknor, fresh from Göttingen, was able to persuade Harvard to permit a limited number of electives in the same year. The movement was delayed by Yale's conservative defense of the classical curriculum in 1828, but was reinvigorated by Ralph Waldo Emerson's Phi Beta Kappa address at Harvard on "The American Scholar" in 1837. "Thoughts on the Present Collegiate System in the United States" by President Francis Wayland of Brown, published in 1842, influenced the public and to a lesser extent the academic community. In 1851 and 1852, Harvard and Yale respectively established separate but inferior status scientific curricula leading to separate degrees. Although the single-track classical curriculum remained overwhelmingly prevalent up to the Civil War, the stage was set for its demise.

The appointment of Charles William Eliot as President of Harvard in 1869 not only lifted that institution to greatness, but resulted in the triumph of the elective system. From then until Eliot's retirement in 1909, Harvard and many followers became increasingly liberal in allowing students to choose their own courses and faculties to teach their own interests. By 1897 the Harvard student's prescribed course of study had been reduced to a year of freshmen rhetoric. The present complexity of course offerings and curricula within the American university had its genesis in this movement.

As with all reforms, the elective system had its excesses and its weaknesses. Never fully accepted across the country, the extreme elective system was increasingly modified from 1910 on, resulting in the gradual development of the modern baccalaureate curriculum in which the faculty specifies that a student obtains a general education from a measured selection of *distribution* courses over the spectrum of liberal arts, as well as a specialized competence through the choice of a *major* or *concentration* in a single subject of subject-matter area.

A number of important innovations in the undergraduate curriculum has influenced the American scene in the twentieth century. Among these were the efforts at the University of Chicago under Robert M. Hutchins, Mortimer T. Adler, and others to lead a return to a common liberal arts core curriculum emphasizing the common classical culture of the Western world, and their longer-lived progeny, the Great Books program at St. John's College in

Annapolis. Chicago also introduced general survey courses, an innovation widely adopted at other colleges and universities. Efforts to individualize collegiate instruction were pioneered by such institutions as Harvard, Swarthmore, Princeton, and Reed. Antioch attained national attention with its work-study program, involving alternate terms of college residence and work experience. Hiram developed an intensive course system in which subjects were taken in series rather than concurrently. Progressive education at the collegiate level was given its freest rein at the now-defunct Black Mountain College and has prospered at a number of other institutions, among which Sarah Lawrence and Bennington were early adherents. Noteworthy, too, has been the extension of the B.A. and B.S. umbrellas to cover a wide variety of combined liberal arts-professional curricula, especially in the state universities.

PRESENT CURRICULUM IN THE LIBERAL ARTS Despite extensive experimentation and the wide range of curricula currently offered in the United States, remarkable agreement exists about the general outlines and principles of the B.A. curriculum in our leading liberal arts colleges, whether within or without complex universities.

A comparison of undergraduate curricula between 1957 and 1967 was undertaken by Dressel and DeLisle (1969) for institutions offering liberal arts programs (one-third, or 371, of all such institutions were requested to supply materials; 322 responded). During this 10-year period, undergraduate curricula changed remarkably little. The main findings with regard to general education or distribution requirements were as follows:

1 Formal requirements in English composition, literature, and speech decreased.

2 Foreign language requirements increased, with two years (or the equivalent) being by far the most common requirement.

3 The use of proficiency tests for meeting requirements in writing, speech, and foreign language increased.

4 Requirements in philosophy and religion were reduced with these subjects more frequently appearing as options in a distribution requirement.

5 The specification of mathematics as a requirement or an option increased.

6 There was some tendency to reduce physical education requirements and to eliminate credits and grades for it.

7   Basic and general requirements remained at approximately 37 percent of the degree requirements and were roughly divided into 17 percent for humanities and 10 percent each for social and natural sciences.

As regards the major concentration areas, little change was found over the 10-year period:

1   The departmental major remained the most common pattern, but there was evidently an increase in the use of a broader theme, area, divisional, or interdepartmental approaches.

2   Major requirements were supplemented by cognate or related course requirements in some 60 percent of the institutions, but there was some decrease in the amount and in the specification of such requirements.

3   There was great variation in the concentration or major requirements although the modal practice remained at 24 to 32 credits or eight courses.

We have attempted to generalize the typical liberal arts curricula from an analysis of the programs of 39 responses from the 42 undergraduate programs having the highest College-Rater composite index in 1967.[3] The modal curriculum in these prestige institutions is similar to that described by Dressel and DeLisle. Most commonly it is stated in terms of eight courses per year for four years, amounting to 32 courses for the B.A. or B.S. degree. During the freshman year, the student usually takes a course in English and a program in physical education. Before the end of his sophomore year, he should meet his foreign language proficiency (second-year college level) by examination or course work, meet distribution requirements of two courses each in humanities, social sciences, and natural sciences, and elect a major. As an upperclassman, the student completes concentration requirements, typically eight courses in a major department, area, or interdepartmental program and four courses in an allied, cognate, or minor field. If his program is humanities oriented, he receives the Bachelor of Arts degree; if science oriented, the Bachelor of Science.

More marked than the trend in curriculum change has been the increased use of some means of individualization within the undergraduate liberal arts program. Dressel and DeLisle summarize the major developments between 1957 and 1967 as follows:

[3] Published by College-Rater, Inc., Allentown, Pa.

1   Almost one-half or more of the institutions provide advanced placement (85 percent), honors programs (66 percent), independent study (58 percent), seminars (51 percent), and study abroad programs (47 percent). This represents at least twice the number of colleges and universities making these provisions ten years ago.

2   Increasing to a lesser degree are comprehensive examinations (40 percent), tutorials (22 percent), senior thesis or project (15 percent), field work experience (13 percent), residence hall programs (11 percent), and community service programs (4 percent). All have doubled in use in the last decade.

3   Course rather than credit units and more flexible grading patterns permitting pass-fail or pass-no credit now appear in about 15 percent of the institutions.

Our own views agree with the conclusions of Dressel and DeLisle that the undergraduate curriculum has changed remarkably little, that independent study programs tend to be utilized by the few rather than for the majority, and that curriculum change is cyclic and subject to short-lived fads. New ideas for the most part are old ideas refurbished and brought back into service. Institutions introduce again what they had and discarded. What passes for innovation at one institution is being discarded at another. All in all, our undergraduate baccalaureate program in the liberal arts is quite stable.

DISTINCTION BETWEEN THE B.A. AND THE B.S.   The custom of two separate liberal arts bachelor's degrees grew up in England where the faculty of arts is separate from the faculty of sciences. In the United States, where these faculties are commonly combined into a single college, the two degrees are still used, but the distinction between them has been blurred to a considerable extent. Indeed, in some instances, there is little logic in the choice of the degree name.

Ideally, American practice should be to award the B.A. without choice to students who concentrate in languages, literatures, other humanities, history, and the arts and similarly to grant the B.S. in the social and natural sciences. Many institutions, particularly the state universities, indeed do exactly this.

Because the B.A. is older and historically the more prestigious degree and because most faculty simply do not feel strongly about the matter, some institutions (e.g., Haverford and Michigan) grant the B.A. more or less automatically while allowing science students an option to request the B.S. instead. Still others grant the B.S. only in combined programs with engineering or applied science (Swarthmore and Princeton). For a residual few (e.g., Brown), the B.A. simply indicates that the student has met the language requirement and the B.S. that he hasn't. This practice, fortunately, has almost disappeared and should because it carries on the old snobbery that a classical education is better than a scientific one and that the B.A. is superior to the B.S.

Among the prestige liberal arts colleges, the B.A. was traditionally the only baccalaureate degree and to a large extent it remains so today, being granted to all successful undergraduate students regardless of field of concentration. A number of new campuses that are primarily liberal arts oriented have continued this practice, one which has the merit of simplicity and clarity.

Since most students are educated today in complex universities where the gamut of curricula available runs from the traditional and classical to the highly applied, it would seem that the maintenance of two baccalaureate degrees, one in arts and the other in science, should continue to be the dominant pattern. No invidious distinctions should be made between them, however. They should represent differing but equal curricula. Only in borderline fields should the student be given his choice. When the concentration is clearly in the arts, that should be the degree. The same with science. While it may be appropriate to have differing distribution requirements for the two degrees, they should be comparable in breadth, difficulty, numbers of courses required, and in general philosophy. The B.S. should never be an easier B.A. or a B.A. without a language.

CHANGES IN THE LIBERAL ARTS BACCALAUREATE Although there is much questioning and reevaluation of undergraduate education today, the force of student dissent and of faculty reaction has largely been directed at the environment and the philosophy of higher education rather than at the formal degree structure involving four years of study leading to the bachelor's degree. A few comments, however, on current developments are relevant to our topic.

In the vanguard of progressive higher education are a group of small liberal arts colleges (Antioch, Bard, Goddard, Hofstra, Loretto Heights, Monteith College of Wayne State, Nasson, New College at Sarasota, Northeastern Illinois State, Sarah Lawrence,

Shimer, and Stephens) who have banded together into a Union for Research and Experimentation in Higher Education.[4] Since 1967, their conferences and joint programs have been concerned with new experimental college ventures, new patterns in liberal arts education, the learning environment, teaching, and "beachhead" operations to permit students to work and learn in real-life problem environments as opposed to the campus. In general, these institutions stress independent study to a greater extent than do conventional liberal arts colleges, their baccalaureate programs are less structured and less formal, and they put less emphasis upon grading and other forms of conventional academic evaluation.

One new institution that will initiate a truly unconventional undergraduate liberal arts curriculum is Hampshire College, under construction at Amherst, Massachusetts. Borrowing more from the English than from the American tradition, Hampshire will do away with the course-credit system, provide tutors rather than lecturers, and vest evaluation in a separate director of examinations. Students must pass a foreign language examination, pass comprehensive examinations successively in three divisions (I, basic; II, intermediate; III, advanced), and submit an acceptable intensive independent study or project. While a four-year period will be the modal length of study, the student may meet these requirements much sooner or much later with or without attending any seminars or courses. Flexibility is stressed but the basic four-year baccalaureate program remains.

One innovation directly related to degree structure is the recent decision of the University of Michigan to offer a Bachelor of General Studies (B.G.S.) degree to students who choose to freely elect their own courses rather than to follow the faculty-directed distribution and concentration requirements in literature, science, and the arts. Adopted as a direct result of student efforts to eliminate the language requirement, the B.G.S. program requires that 60 of the 120 semester hours elected be in upper-division courses and that no more than 20 hours be elected in a single subject. In essence, the program is a return to the free elective system of Harvard at the turn of the century.

Efforts at Chicago to create a collegiate institution offering the baccalaureate at the conclusion of the general education phase and proposals of Ward, Kaysen, and Woodring to reintroduce this con-

[4] Headquarters at Antioch College, Yellow Springs, Ohio.

cept with broader choices of curriculum have been detailed in Chapter 4 although they are equally relevant here. We may add that Woodring (1968) describes the ideal three-year collegiate program as consisting of three years of liberal education, terminating in the B.A. degree for all college students. Included would be the humanities, fine arts, natural and behavioral sciences, and mathematics. Perhaps a period of major concentration could be taken in one of these broad areas but there would be no major in a single discipline during the undergraduate period. The college would not offer vocational training, this responsibility being delegated to separate vocational schools. This new liberal B.A. program would be offered in state colleges, cluster colleges within universities, the independent and church-related institutions now called "liberal arts colleges," and some of the stronger junior colleges. Under Woodring's plan, all professional training would be subsequent to the B.A. and be recognized with the master's degree.

In looking to the future of the liberal arts college, Schmidt (in Brickman and Lehrer, 1962) envisages the continuation of the conventional four-year B.A. program but with evolutionary changes in the institutions that offer it. He suggests that most liberal arts colleges will become predominantly lower-division (i.e., freshman and sophomore) institutions offering general study programs; that larger universities will maintain a traditional school of liberal arts, declining in size and linked more closely with the graduate school; and that a handful of distinguished colleges will continue the liberal tradition, spurning the popular trend, maintaining rigorous intellectual standards, and restricting themselves to a highly selected student body.

A corollary of such proposals, and indeed of the junior college movement as well, is that there is a place for a senior or upper-division college, taking in students at the end of two years general study in a junior college or similar institution and offering the baccalaureate after two years of advanced study. A number of such institutions have been established and their current status has been summarized (Altman, 1969). Except where part of a multi-campus system such as Concordia Senior College in Fort Wayne, Indiana, and Capitol Campus of Penn State, these institutions simply have not attracted the requisite numbers of qualified students. Florida Atlantic University is attempting to meet this problem by admitting a limited number of highly qualified high school graduates directly into the junior year, while the University of

Michigan is extending its programs at its Flint and Dearborn campuses to four years. The upper-division college movement is now practically defunct.

RECOMMEN-
DATIONS Our survey of the liberal arts baccalaureate indicates that the four-year program, balanced between distribution and concentration offerings and catering to students who enter college at the age of 18 after 12 years of schooling, is firmly entrenched and is unlikely to be materially changed in the near future.

In this academic degree structure all students admitted initially to the B.A. should complete their baccalaureate in not more than the equivalent of four academic years and perhaps more rapidly. The 16-course or 120-semester-hour or 180-quarter-hour requirement should be the maximum rather than the standard requirement for the baccalaureate. There is no reason why the student should not be recommended for the degree with fewer formal credits as soon as he has met the levels of academic attainment set for the general education (distribution), specialization (concentration), and other curriculum standards. Such a relaxation in the duration of the baccalaureate program would seem to have general merit.

Should, as we have recommended in the previous chapter, the associate's degree or certificate be required for admission to the bachelor's program, the same principles would apply, but two years (8 course, 60 semester hours, or 90 quarter hours) would be the maximum rather than the standard requirement for the baccalaureate.

The three-year baccalaureate followed by a two-year master's program is much more logical than the 4–1 pattern of today. If students can be brought into these programs after 11 rather than 12 years of schooling, so much the better. We should not be sanguine, however, about the implementation of these proposals. The more feasible solution is to encourage the advanced student to begin his graduate program while still an undergraduate. Graduate schools could well be far more lenient than they are in granting advanced standing for graduate work taken by the undergraduate. In fact, there seems no valid reason why the student who enters college with advanced standing, who continues to accelerate throughout his undergraduate years, and who wishes to maintain undergraduate status for the full four-year period could not earn the master's and bachelor's degree simultaneously at the end of that period.

As to nomenclature, the use of a single degree designation Bachelor of Arts seems best for the liberal arts college. For the universities, however, and wherever two parallel but equal tracks are desirable, one in the arts and one in the sciences, the two degrees Bachelor of Arts and Bachelor of Science should be offered.

The Bachelor of General Studies is an appropriate name for an alternative free-elective or cafeteria-style curriculum for those students who do not wish the certification implied by following faculty decisions on appropriate liberal arts curriculum requirements. If such an alternative is made available, it should be clearly identified for what it is.

Although we have not discussed the point, it seems entirely justifiable to offer a bachelor's degree in continuing education. As with the free-elective residential curriculum, it should have a separate name, generally accepted by the academic community, that clearly identifies the nature of the educational experience. Bachelor of Liberal Studies is not a bad choice.

7. The Master's Degree

Although the master's degree dates back to the founding of the first universities, it has undergone more vicissitudes than the bachelor's or the doctor's. Gradually downgraded to the point of becoming a formality in England, it was revived as a degree in course and as a first professional degree in the United States and, more recently, in western Europe. Problems exist, however, in lack of uniformity of standards, in the multiplicity of forms of the degree, and in the fact that the holder of the bachelor's degree may proceed directly to the doctorate without picking up a master's degree en route.

EVOLUTION OF THE MASTER'S DEGREE The word *master* is derived from the Latin word *magister* meaning teacher. The Master of Arts degree originated at the University of Paris in the twelfth century as a formal designation of a licensed teacher in the faculty of arts. At the University of Paris in the twelfth century the student after two years of study in the arts, provided that he was at least 14, could if he so desired become a bachelor or apprentice teacher. After an additional five to six years he could undergo a formal public examination, receive a license from the chancellor, and be initiated into the guild of masters. The Master of Arts degree, therefore, was the highest degree offered by the faculty of arts although the student holding this license could study toward the doctorate in the other medieval faculties of medicine, canon law, or theology.

Gradually, the magic number of seven years became associated with the master's degree and, after the English baccalaureate became a four-year degree, the master's degree was increasingly awarded more or less automatically to anyone in good standing three years after the award of the baccalaureate. The English practice was carried on into the United States with the founding of Harvard College. During the seventeenth century, many students at Harvard spent from one to three years studying on campus in the interval between the award of their baccalaureate and their master's degree, but as time went on the Master of Arts came more and more simply to signify that the student was more or less engaged in literary or professional pursuits and that he had paid to the college a fee prescribed by its regulations. This is still the practice with the M.A. at Oxford and Cambridge. On the Continent, however, the master's degree gradually fell into more or less complete disuse.

During the nineteenth century, several efforts were made to restore the master's degree to an earned status (Rudolph, 1962). The University of Virginia offered the M.A. to students as an earned degree in 1831, but probably more at the baccalaureate than at the modern master's level. Harvard in 1831, the University of the City of New York, in 1835, and the University of North Carolina in 1856 made abortive efforts to provide for formal postbaccalaureate study.

The University of Michigan is credited by Eells (1963) with having been the first major university to provide for the rehabilitated master's degree. In December, 1858, the regents of the university resolved that the Master of Arts and Master of Science be conferred upon holders of the bachelor's degree (after a minimum period of at least one year) provided that they pursued at least two courses each semester, that they passed an examination before the faculty in at least three of the studies so attended, and that they presented a thesis to the faculty on one of the subjects chosen for examination. The first earned master's degrees were awarded by the university in 1859 with an M.A. to James C. Watson and an M.S. to Devolson Wood. The University of Georgia followed in 1868, Harvard in 1869, and by 1896 the earned one-year master's degree had effectively supplanted the three-year degree of the old type without residence or examination requirements.

The development of the master's degree in the United States from its inception to the nineteen thirties has been detailed by John (1935), who includes a summary of requirements for higher degrees in 1899, institution by institution.

In the United States at the present time the master's degree is generally recognized as the first postbaccalaureate degree both in the liberal arts and in professional fields. Almost universally the period of study is from one to two years. Programs involving less than one academic year of study do not qualify for the master's certification. Programs that require three years of postbaccalaureate study generally are recognized by the award of an appropriate doctor's degree.

In 1963-64, some 328 different master's degree titles were reported to the U.S. Office of Education (Chase and Breznay, 1965). They all fall, however, into two general categories: the liberal arts master's degree and the professional master's degree. The liberal arts master's degree may be identified by the undifferentiated titles *Master of Arts* and *Master of Science.* In contrast, the professional master's degree may be recognized by the modified use of these generic terms (e.g., Master of Arts in Library Science) or by separate professional designation (e.g., Master of Business Administration).

Analysis of the number and types of master's degrees is complicated by varying usage of the several degree names by different institutions. The problem is particularly acute in the field of education where many students take the M.A. or M.S. and many others take professional titled degrees. From the 1963-64 data of Chase and Breznay (1965), we can only surmise that a large percentage of the 31,292 Master of Arts and the 24,336 Master of Science degrees were taken by teachers studying in advanced education programs. In addition, however, this group is clearly identified with the 15,146 Master of Education degrees awarded by 193 institutions, the 5,653 Master of Science in Education from 77 institutions, the 2,485 Master of Arts in Education from 34 institutions, and the 1,083 Master of Arts in Teaching from 38 institutions.

In short, we cannot obtain viable information on the number of master's degrees awarded in a given field by reference to the degree titles. We must go back to U.S. Office of Education data based upon statistics provided by the institutions themselves. Referring to Table 2, we find that 140,722 master's degrees were awarded in 1965-1966, of which 36 percent were in education, 30 percent in the arts and sciences, 10 percent in engineering, and 9 percent in business administration. Among the minor professional fields, social work and library science each contributed 3 percent of the total.

While nomenclature for the master's degree presents similar problems to that for the baccalaureate, it is even more complex and chaotic. Yet the same trends are discernible and the same recommendations may be made.

The basic principle has been well stated by the Council of Graduate Schools (CGS) in the United States (1966) that the M.A. or the M.S. without designation be universally used for scholarly research and teaching-oriented programs; that the Master of Education, the Master of Business Administration, the Master of Music, etc., be used for the professionally-oriented programs; and that the number of names used for the master's degree should be kept as small as possible. We should note that CGS does not recommend continued use of the doubly modified title such as *Master of Science in Education.*

For our recommendations, we refer you back to Chapter 2.

THE MASTER'S DEGREE IN THE LIBERAL ARTS The Master of Arts and Master of Science degrees are offered in the liberal arts by colleges of arts and sciences and by many schools of education in recognition of the completion of one academic year of work beyond the baccalaureate. There are few generally accepted program requirements for such a degree: usually a minimum of 24 to 30 semester hours of academic credit are required (equivalent to 36 to 45 quarter hours); a major portion of this work must be taken in the student's field of specialization; a cognate or minor requirement is usually included; a specified proportion of the academic work must be in graduate-level courses; and all hours elected must carry graduate credit. A limited number of hours of graduate credit may be transferred from another institution and a limited number of hours may be taken in extension courses or as a part-time student. Most institutions require that at least one full term be spent on campus as a full-time student. There is no consistency in practice as to whether or not a master's thesis or a foreign language is required. These requirements vary widely from campus to campus and from department to department within most campuses.

The liberal arts master's degree serves two broad functions. First, it represents the successful completion of the first step in a general liberal arts graduate curriculum. As such it may be taken or ignored by students admitted to a graduate department in the expectation that they will continue on toward the doctorate. In such institutions, and this includes most prestige universities, students are admitted directly into the doctoral program upon the completion of the baccalaureate. The better students and others who are sure of their capacity are expected by faculty and students alike to ignore the master's degree and work solely for the doctorate. The unsure and the ultracautious apply for the master's en route. Those who are not permitted to continue to the doctorate or who are counseled against doing so are frequently given the opportunity of taking the master's degree as their terminal recognition. As a result, the master's degree in liberal arts subjects in prestige universities has taken on the characteristics of a consolation prize. It is not surprising, therefore, that the better the graduate school, the lower the repute of the master's degree. Weaker universities frequently offer stronger master's programs. It is a curious fact that the faculties on many campuses underrate the importance of the master's degree. At Michigan, for example, many of the faculty think that they are primarily concerned with the Ph.D. program even though their departments produce several times as many master's as doctor's year after year.

The second general use of the liberal arts master's degree is for the certification of subject-matter competence by secondary school teachers. In fact, the master's degree is becoming the basic professional degree for teaching. Such a use is obviously a more affirmative concept than that referred to in the previous paragraph, and it is therefore not surprising that the M.A. and M.S. degrees earned in this context generally carry greater prestige than those earned in the former. In fact, they often may well be better degrees.

Partly because those in the second category are teachers to begin with or have deliberately chosen teaching in the secondary school as a career, and partly because those in the first category frequently end up in secondary school teaching despite their original career aspirations, the liberal arts master's degree basically has become a degree preparing for careers in secondary school teaching. The degree is therefore, as might be expected, most commonly awarded in education and those subject-matter fields where the subject is taught in secondary schools. In most states, teachers must continue their education at the postbaccalaureate level in order to obtain permanent certification and improvement in rank. Obviously teachers required to take courses for these purposes prefer those which count toward the master's degree. As a result graduate schools are under heavy pressure to lower admission standards to accommodate all baccalaureate holders who are active teachers and to qualify all courses offered to this population as carrying graduate credit applicable toward the master's degree. These factors, coupled with the second-class status of the master's degree at prestige institutions, have resulted in a general lowering of the prestige of the master's degree.

Many efforts have been made to revitalize or rehabilitate the
M.A. and M.S. degree. A few recent examples should be discussed
briefly.

Committees of the American Association of University Professors
(AAUP) in 1932 and of the Association of American Universities
(AAU) in 1935 and 1936 undertook to develop recommendations
for the standardization of the master's degree. The 1935 AAU
committee under the chairmanship of W. J. Robbins noted that the
master's degree may be a research degree, a professional degree,
a teacher's degree, or a cultural degree. It should culminate five
years of study in institutions of higher education where the fifth
year is at a graduate level. In contrast, a fifth year of undergraduate
work should be recognized by the awarding of a second baccalaureate. The master's degree should require one full academic year
of residence during which a unified program with a definite objective should be followed. Freshman-sophomore courses should
not carry credit toward the master's degree. Course credit but not
residence credit could be transferred. A thesis should be required
but it could be research, expository, critical, or creative in character.

The 1936 AAU committee was concerned with the general problem of graduate work for teachers in secondary schools and recommended that master's programs designed for this group should
involve greater care in admission, that the programs should not be
highly specialized, but rather should have more unity of purpose.
This report recognized that postbaccalaureate study for all secondary school teachers was desirable, that it should involve the subject-matter department, and that the preparation of teachers is the
function of the university as a whole and should not be delegated
to the school of education or to any other subunit.

In a study published in 1939, Stansbury sought the constructive
criticism of secondary school teachers who had completed their
master's work. His conclusions were that since the master's degree could be conceived as being primarily for secondary school
teachers, a lenient policy of admission to graduate study should be
adopted but the degree program should be strengthened through
expert guidance and more adequate curricula. Stansbury estimated
that 75 percent of the liberal arts master's degrees at that time were
earned by public school teachers. His survey of their evaluation of
their master's experience is as valid today as it was in 1935-36
when it was undertaken.

A decade after its previous effort, the AAU (1945) again devoted a major committee report to the problem of the master's program. This committee under the chairmanship of R. G. D. Richardson, attempted to formulate an ideal for the M.A. and the M.S. and for some of the professional master's degrees. The main criticisms dealt both with defects in admission and administrative procedures and with poor methods of instruction. Under the first category, admissions procedures were found to be less uniform for the master's than for the baccalaureate or the doctorate. Many M.A. students were simply not of graduate caliber, and much M.A. work was found to be undergraduate in its character. Under the second category, the master's instruction was found to involve too often a continuation of undergraduate course procedures with too much emphasis being placed upon the accumulation of facts, unnecessary duplication of courses, and insufficient subject-matter content in courses designed for secondary school teachers. The 1945 AAU committee recommended that different types of master's programs be identified by separate degree designations. The M.A. and the M.S. should be primarily research degrees. The M.A.T. and the M.Ed. should be teaching degrees, the former identifying competence in a subject-matter field and the latter specialization in administration. Technical subjects should be identified by the M.A. or the M.S. degree with the addition of a professional modifier. In general the master's degree should require one year of residence, should be completed within an overall time span of five to seven years after the initiation of study, and should involve a comprehensive examination, a thesis or an essay, and a language requirement.

A little more than a decade later (1957-1958), the issue was again before the Association of Graduate Schools (AGS) when the Committee on Policies in Graduate Education suggested that the master's degree be revitalized and oriented toward secondary school teachers. The committee argued than an affirmative M.A. was preferable to a negative A.B.D. (all but dissertation). It proposed (1958) the establishment of a graduate entrance examination board to administer essay examinations exclusively with the hope of selecting students' master's programs more effectively than could be done by objective testing. In a follow-up article, Elder (1959) proposed that master's programs ought to be entities in themselves, designed *de novo,* each having its own pattern and each its own beginning and end. In other words, it should be offered as a separate program from the doctorate and not as a mark either of partial progress toward the doctorate or as a consolation prize to doctoral students who hadn't made the grade. "In this connection, we might just as well say openly—I point a finger at some areas in my Cantabrigian back yard—that universities should either improve their weak or easy or consolatory master's programs or should stop awarding that degree in those fields. Gresham's law[1] works too surely." Elder proposed that the revitalized master's degree should require at least a year and a half of study in which the student in his first year would concentrate on his subject and on methods of research. In the first half of the second year, he should take one more seminar, do some teaching in a college, and write a master's essay (not a thesis). The essay should show something of what he has learned but it should not be pretentious enough to claim originality.

In 1966 the Committee on Evaluation and Accreditation of the Council of Graduate Schools in the United States (CGS) adopted a general statement on the master's degree, available in pamphlet form (Council of Graduate Schools in the United States, 1966). This statement outlines desirable conditions that should be met by institutions offering the master's program and summarizes present thinking with regard to the program itself. With regard to the liberal arts master's degrees CGS recommends that the master's degree should only be offered when there are at least four or five professors in the subject-matter field of proven scholarly ability; that there should be associated strength in closely related fields; that the faculty should be suitably housed, provided with logistic support, the opportunity for research and scholarship, and should not be overloaded with course teaching. The master's program itself should consist of a coherent sequence of lectures, seminars, discussions, and independent studies or investigations designed to help the student acquire an introduction to the mastery of knowledge, creative scholarship, and research in his field. At least one full academic year of study should be required over and beyond any remedial courses designed to remove deficiences in preparation for entrance to the master's program. No credit should be given for courses which are designed to provide for merely the refreshing or broadening of the bachelor's knowledge in his field without

---

[1] When two coins are equal in debt-paying power but unequal in intrinsic value, the one having the least intrinsic value will remain in circulation and the other will be hoarded.

substantial advancement. As contrasted with earlier statements by graduate deans, the 1966 CGS statement minimizes the importance of the master's thesis but points out that a comprehensive rigorous examination over the field is usually a part of quality programs.

Relatively little formal attention has been given by national committees or associations to the design of master's programs in individual subject-matter fields. The Committee on the Undergraduate Program in Mathematics of the Mathematical Association of America, however, did publish in 1967 a statement on the desirable design of the first graduate component for a prospective college teacher, a component for which the master's degree would be suitable recognition. This program would involve first the completion of a strong mathematics major if it has not been completed by the time the student begins graduate work; a full year of work in at least two of the fields of modern algebraic theory, in analysis, or geometry from a topological point of view; and at least one semester of teaching a class in undergraduate mathematics under the close supervision of an experienced teacher. The committee has prepared a rather detailed program description. In place of a master's thesis, a comprehensive examination is recommended. Foreign languages are not recommended for the master's degree in mathematics. While the M.A. program is considered an essential part of the preparation of a college mathematics teacher, an advanced graduate component involving at least a second year of graduate study is considered advisable to prepare a prospective college mathematics teacher as discussed in Chapter 9.

The Carmichael Reform

The suggestion of the AGS dean's committee of 1957-1958 that the master's degree be rehabilitated and specifically designed to train college teachers was taken up by Oliver C. Carmichael in 1959 with the result that pilot programs were established by the Fund for the Advancement of Education (Ford Foundation) in 1960 to see whether or not it would be feasible to establish a three-year program beginning with students in the junior year and leading to the master's degree. As Carmichael summarized his plan in 1961, it was designed to provide a master's degree which would serve as a qualification for college teaching in junior college or the first two years of four-year colleges. The plan presupposes that membership in the program will be selected from the upper 15 to 20 percent of the undergraduate study body selected not later than the beginning of the third undergraduate year. Those chosen would be enrolled as "pregraduates" just as those planning to study medicine would enter as premedical students and would constitute a kind of honors group which would move more rapidly into graduate courses, independent reading assignments, the independent preparation of papers, and the passing of the Ph.D. foreign language requirements while still an undergraduate. As a result of the special tutorial attention given to a small group of superior students with a consequent opportunity for individual reading, study, and writing, these students should be able to obtain a limited amount of teaching experience during their senior undergraduate or postbaccalaureate year of study, prepare a master's thesis, and still graduate at the end of the fifth year. Carmichael proposed that the degree be titled *Master of Philosophy* with the abbreviation M.Phil.

None of the institutions experimenting with this reform adopted the suggestion of the Master of Philosophy title but rather awarded the Master of Arts instead. At the time that support from the fund was terminated, the general conclusion seemed to be that the program had been successful in attracting high-grade liberal arts students into graduate school but that it had not persuaded them to cease their graduate training at the master's level in order to seek a career in underclass college teaching. Rather the better students continued on toward the doctorate in the conventional mold.

The Toronto Master of Philosophy

Perhaps the best example of the revitalized master's degree is the Master of Philosophy program (Phil.M.) as offered by the University of Toronto and the University of Waterloo. In contrast with the Master of Philosophy program at Yale, which is discussed in the following chapter, the Canadian Master of Philosophy is a special program for a regularly admitted group of students who aspire to a two-year general course of graduate study qualifying them to teach at the collegiate level.

At the University of Toronto, the course of study leading to the Master of Philosophy requires full-time residence for a period of two years beyond the honors baccalaureate in the same discipline and consists chiefly of courses and seminars. In addition, the candidates write a major essay or research paper which reflects individual independent scholarship although it does not necessarily represent an original contribution to knowledge. The Toronto School of Graduate Studies has established standards for admission for the Phil.M. that exceed those for the Ph.D. in order to minimize any implication that the Phil.M. is a second-class program for less competent students. The program was initiated in 1964-65 with 29 students enrolled primarily in the language departments. In the following year, 23 new candidates were enrolled and by the autumn of 1966, eight candidates had received the new degree. Of the first group of degree recipients, most were employed immediately by Canadian universities and colleges (including the University of Toronto itself) while two decided to proceed on to the Ph.D. A Phil.M. graduate who proceeds on to the Ph.D. is not subject to additional residence requirements, although he may require more time to complete his studies than a student who has concentrated solely on obtaining the Ph.D.

The Toronto Master of Philosophy, therefore, is a two-year upgraded master's program offering a more general programming of liberal arts courses to a separately admitted group of students. It differs from the Candidate of Philosophy approach in the United States in that the C.Phil. normally requires three rather than two years, is offered to students who are admitted as regular Ph.D. applicants, and represents the completion of the general studies phase of the doctorate rather than of a separate core program of studies.

Present Status of the M.A. and the M.S. Current views on the functions and future of the master's degree were summarized in a panel discussion at the 1963 meeting of the Council of Graduate Schools. Among the multiple functions of the master's program are (1) the provision of an introduction to graduate study, (2) a remedial period to cover deficiencies in undergraduate education, and (3) a terminal professional program.

The problem of the master's degree is well summarized by Snell (1965), who argued for increased financial support of the master's as well as of the Ph.D. programs. Those engaged in mass production of the master's degree should vigorously review their standards. "Even if the prestige of the master's degree cannot be bolstered, it is important to prevent its decline." Snell felt that little was to be gained by asking Ph.D. students to earn the master's degree unless a thesis or equivalent research and writing are required. Too many master's degrees are being awarded in education and too few in subject-matter fields. Admission to master's programs should be limited to students who have achieved undergraduate records with at least B grades unless especially high scores on Graduate Record Examinations or other evidence of unusual ability warrants their admission. Improved guidance and program planning is needed especially early in the student's graduate study. Snell concluded that the master's degree is not on the way out, that the statistical evidence of burgeoning expansion makes this obvious, and that there is clear evidence as to a growing need for vigorous master's programs in American universities.

Despite the many efforts at reform, the fact remains that the master's degree today is remarkably similar to what it was at the beginning of the century. It still is awarded in recognition of at least one year's work past the baccalaureate, but the degree itself signifies very little as to the program elected, the caliber of the courses taken, or the performance of the student at the graduate level. As Berelson (1960) puts it, "The very diversity of the master's degree troubles those people who want a degree to mean one thing only or at most a very few." If, as Berelson points out, true graduate work requires orientation to research and the advancement of knowledge as well as independent work in the form of the thesis and comprehensive examination, then it is fair to say that much master's work today is not graduate in character but more nearly on the order of a fifth year of undergraduate work. With the demands of diversity and the stress of numbers, the degree has been weakened, at least in prestige. Most of Berelson's consultants acknowledge that the master's degree has become easier to get at their institution as compared to 20 years ago. This comment may be taken as relating primarily to the liberal arts M.A. and M.S. rather than to the professional master's degrees discussed below. Berelson questions whether the master's degree can indeed be revitalized on the historical grounds that this cannot be achieved simply by setting up requirements or standards:

The prospects of making the Master's a highly respected, research-oriented, 1 1/2- or 2-year degree for college teachers on a national scale are, I think, not bright. There is too much going against it: the historical decline, the lowered prestige, the diversity of meaning, the numbers of claimants relative to the numbers of faculty available for sponsorship and guidance, the competitive disadvantage relative to the doctorate, the coolness of the better colleges, the reluctance of the better students, the poorer career prospects, the low return on investment. I conclude that this clock cannot be turned back.

Whether this gloomy prognostication will hold or whether the master's degree in the liberal arts can truly be strengthened may be evaluated in some measure from the success over the next few years of Toronto's effort to establish a strong two-year program separate from the doctoral program and Yale's attempt to assign the Master of Philosophy title to mark the successful completion of the general studies phase of the doctorate (see the next chapter).

We should note that, although nominally a one-year program, the master's is in fact closer to a two-year program for the average student. In their study of attrition of graduate students, Tucker, Gottlieb, and Pease (1964) found that the mean number of years of enrollment at the master's level was 1.8 years for students who eventually received the Ph.D. and 1.9 years for students who didn't. In a statistical study of doctoral recipients from 1958 to 1966 (National Academy of Sciences, 1967), the median number of years from graduate school entry to the master's degree was found to be 2 years. Remarkably little variation was found from field to field in either of these studies. Although these data are derived from studies of doctoral student populations (master's students have been little studied in themselves), they do seem to indicate clearly that in fact if not in requirement, the M.A. and the M.S. are two-year degrees in the United States today.

PROFESSIONAL MASTER'S DEGREE In general, the master's degree is better standardized in individual professional fields than it is in the liberal arts. The result is that the master's degree is often held in higher repute as a professional than as a liberal arts degree.

At the same time, it is important to recognize that variations in the articulation between baccalaureate and graduate study create variations in professional master's programs. Sometimes these are covered by a single degree title; sometimes by two or more. Furthermore a nomenclatural practice is not always consistent as between different institutions in the same professional field.

The major patterns of undergraduate-graduate articulation involving the professional master's degree include:

1 An undergraduate program in a profession followed by a master's program in the same profession. In this instance, the baccalaureate is the first professional degree.

2 An undergraduate program in the liberal arts followed by a master's program in a profession. In this case the master's is the first professional degree.

3 An undergraduate program in a profession followed by a master's program designed to remedy the student's undergraduate deficiencies in basic science or the arts.

4 A professional field requiring five or six years of study from university matriculation to the first professional degree, which may be either at the bachelor's or the master's level.

In general, the principles governing the professional master's degrees are similar to those discussed in connection with the liberal arts master's program. Time spans are apt to be longer, however, with 1 1/2- to 2-year requirements being common. Programs tend to be more rigorously constructed and frequently more rigorously administered. Professional organizations frequently take the lead in revitalizing and formalizing professional master's programs. These and related developments may be illustrated by brief discussions of professional master's programs in business administration, fine arts, engineering, and education.

Business Administration The Master of Business Administration (M.B.A.) is granted both to students whose undergraduate study was in that field and who work an additional year for the master's and to students who come into business from a liberal arts background and take an integrated two-year program leading to the first professional degree. The master's program in this field is subject to program accreditation by the American Association of Collegiate Schools of Business (Council of Graduate Schools in the United States, 1966). An acceptable M.B.A. program is one to which superior students are admitted, most courses are taught by full-time faculty, and with few exceptions the faculty members hold the appropriate doctoral degrees. Physical facilities must be satisfactory. To be accredited, the school and its programs shall have been in operation for a period of time. Students completing degree programs in business must either as undergraduates or as graduate students complete the equivalent of the undergraduate core in the fields of economics, accounting, statistics, business law, business finance, marketing, and management. At the M.B.A. level the program beyond the core shall be broad in nature and aimed at general competence in overall management. At least one year of advanced work is required in classes reserved exclusively for graduate students.

Fine Arts The present status of the Master of Fine Arts program was surveyed nationally by the Midwest College Art Conference (1965), and recommendations were made to establish acceptable nationwide standards on the basis of returns from 43 institutions offering the degree. The M.F.A., rather than the Ph.D., is accepted by the College Art Association as the terminal degree for graduate work in the studio area of the fine arts. The master's program is well established and normally requires at least two full academic years of graduate-level work. Students entering the master's program should have a bachelor's degree with a major in art as well as adequate exposure to general studies as an undergraduate. The emphasis in the graduate program is upon the studio practice of some aspect of art, with the intent of educating students for professional careers as painters, sculptors, printmakers, designers, ceramists, and photographers. In contrast, the M.A. degree is considered appropriate for students in art history. Departments offering the M.F.A. degree should have active professional artists of high repute on the teaching staff. Other institutional and curriculum standards are detailed by a committee which reported to the conference. These include the requirement that the M.F.A. student should pass a comprehensive examination and produce a thesis which should be an original work of art or group of such works.

Engineering A major recent effort to revise the professional degree is to be found in the report of the Committee on Goals of Engineering Education (American Society for Engineering Education, 1968) under the chairmanship of E. A. Walker. In the field of engineering, students coming into graduate school after undergraduate training in engineering follow a professional master's program in engineering (Master of Engineering and related titles). At the same time, many engineering departments can appropriately offer a parallel Master of Science program for students who come in with a bachelor's degree in physics, mathematics, or other related natural sciences.

Engineering is a case where the first professional degree is now offered at the bachelor's level but where the trend is toward moving it to the master's level. While students can now be graduated at the bachelor's level and be qualified for certain varieties of industrial employment, the Walker committee expects that before long only the full five years will constitute a fully recognized engineering curriculum suitable for commencing a professional career. Thus, for some students the master's program is part of a basic professional program commencing at the freshman level and extending over five years, while for others it will be a self-contained graduate program. In no case, however, is it argued that the degree be awarded merely for a fifth year of undergraduate courses. The master's degree, in short, should be a graduate degree but not a research degree. In the matter of the master's thesis, the report of the Committee on Goals of Engineering Education distinguishes between schools which have a large doctoral program and those which primarily operate at the master's level. In the former case, both the students and the faculty are thought to be better served if supervised research experience is emphasized at the doctor's rather than at the master's level. In the latter case, however, a master's thesis performs a vital role in providing an opportunity for creative self-learning experience for the student who may not go on elsewhere for the doctorate. At the present time, the master's thesis is no longer common in engineering, being required mostly in the smaller schools.

Education We have already pointed out that 36 percent of all master's degrees are in the field of education, and that in addition, many if not most of the recipients of the Master of Arts and Master of Science are or become teachers. The titles of the professional master's degrees in education are many. According to Chase and Breznay (1965), the most common are *Master of Education, Master of Science in Teaching, Master of Arts in Education,* and *Master of Arts in Teaching.* Also used at from four to six institutions are the titles *Master of Teaching, Master of Science for Teachers, Master of Science in Teaching,* and *Master of Arts for Teachers.*

We have not made any exhaustive study of the one-year master's program in education as this is a topic requiring careful and thoughtful study by scholars in the field itself. Undoubtedly, there are significant differences or at least nuances which differentiate this plethora of degrees. If there are, it is certain that few outside the profession appreciate them. Confessing only a partial understanding of the practices and problems, therefore, we make bold to suggest some sort of degree nomenclature for the one-year master's program along the following lines:

Master of Arts or Master of Science: For students who follow up an undergraduate program in education with a graduate program in a subject-matter field.

Master of Education: For students who follow a professionally-oriented graduate program in the field of education.

Master of Arts in Teaching: For students who graduate in liberal arts and wish to qualify as a teacher within a fifth year of study.

Our understanding is that the above suggestions more or less conform with present practice. If the profession could get together and agree upon three or so standard master's degrees along the lines of the above pattern, a great deal of confusion could be avoided. All the other names, of course, should be dropped.

Within the last decade, attention has shifted from efforts to revitalize the liberal arts master's degrees to establishing parallel programs for college teacher preparation. As Blegen (1959) put it:

> I regard it as absurd to suppose that the multiform and multipurpose Master's degree can, in fact, or should, be replaced by some new and rehabilitated Master's degree, but I would place alongside the many existing Master's degrees a two-year program for college-teacher preparation. I do not propose a watered-down Doctor's degree, but a Master's degree representing solid subject-matter mastery plus orientation in the problems of American colleges and of effective teaching. I am not concerned about the precise phrasing of the Master's degree, though it might be desirable to differentiate it in some way from the usual Master's degree.

At the present time, the problem of graduate programs designed to prepare college teachers is of great concern. Some of the degree programs suggested or under trial are at the master's level. One such is the Master of Arts in College Teaching recently introduced at the University of Tennessee. This and related programs are discussed in Chapter 9.

Higher Master's Degree Whereas the master's degree is commonly thought to be an intermediate degree between the bachelor's and the doctor's degree, the term *master* is sometimes used to designate a second-level professional degree even though the first-level degree may be the doctors's. Thus, the Doctor of Medicine who takes additional course work during his residency to train himself for a research career may frequently earn the Master of Science degree. He may thus qualify himself as an academician in a clinical field and therefore as being perhaps more eligible for employment on a medical school faculty. Similarly, whether the first professional degree in law is known as the Bachelor of Laws or Juris Doctor, the second professional degree is at the master's level, Master of Laws.

The problems with the professional master's degree seem largely to arise from nomenclature rather than from substance. Too many names for master's degrees exist, and there is too little consistency in their use from institution to institution around the country. Assuming that it would be possible to standardize and to reduce the number of names for master's degrees, however, the professional master's seems to be in generally good shape. A certain amount of confusion is bound to exist in those professional fields where the first professional degree is being moved from the bachelor's to the master's level but this is a product of evolving professional standards and should bother no one. Similarly there seems no reason why the same master's title cannot be used for a one-year program for students continuing on in the same profession from the baccalaureate and a two-year program for those coming into the profession after the baccalaureate in another area as long as both classes of students reach the same level of professional competence at the time of completion of the master's program.

RECOMMEN-
DATIONS

Looking at the master's degree as a whole, it is our belief that the fatal flaw in our present usage is that the master's degree may be bypassed en route to the doctorate, and that as a result, the master's degree is somehow relegated to second-class or consolation-prize status. It is the first graduate degree and represents a significantly higher stage of accomplishment than the baccalaureate. It should be highly respectable. It can be made so, however, only if it is required of everyone in accordance with the general hypothesis we have outlined in Chapter 3. Such a requirement may not do much for those who successfully continue on to the doctorate. Properly conceived, however, taking the master's degree en route will not slow them down and it will give them insurance. The same requirement, however, can accomplish a great deal for the much larger number of students who begin graduate work with the doctorate in mind but who never reach it. They will have attained a respectable stage from which they can enter the world of employment.

Upon completion of the baccalaureate, therefore, all students should be admitted only as candidates for the master's degree. No students would be admitted at this time directly to the doctoral program. Only by such a change in our present policies can the principle of progressive, noninvidious steps be put into practice. As a result the master's degree would become a required and necessary stepping stone en route to the doctorate. The fact that all students would be admitted only as candidates for the master's and must earn this degree means that the master's degree would always mark successful forward progress. It would, therefore, provide an appropriate stopping place for those who choose not to go further. It is only the fact that many graduate schools admit students fresh out of the baccalaureate into doctoral programs that gives the connotation of consolation prize to the master's degree. We suggest that this practice must change to make the Master of Arts and Master of Science degrees fully respectable. Efforts to beef up the master's degree by requiring an extra period of study or a more carefully planned academic program may be desirable in themselves. Such efforts may not create a really respectable degree, however, if the students are not selected as rigorously as those who are chosen at the baccalaureate level to continue on directly to the doctorate.

Actually, the requirement of taking the master's degree en route to the doctor's would not affect the majority of present-day doctoral students who already do so voluntarily. Recent data published by the National Academy of Sciences (1967) indicate that only 20 percent of doctorate recipients from 1958 to 1966 failed to elect the master's degree. The percentage of those who did not varied from a low of 4 percent in education to 6 percent in business administration, 13 percent in the arts and humanities, 20 percent in social sciences, 22 percent in biological sciences, 31 percent in physical sciences and engineering, and a high of 47 percent in religion and theology. Of those who did take the master's degree en route, 81 percent took it in the same field as that in which they eventually took their doctorate.

As with the baccalaureate, the master's program should have a finite maximum time duration, tempered by incentives for early completion of an accelerated program. Probably the maximum duration for the student passing through M.A. or M.S. programs en route to a doctorate should be one academic year of work. At the other extreme, students able to complete all the requirements for the master's degree while still enrolled as an undergraduate should be awarded the bachelor's and master's degrees simultaneously.

Other master's programs, such as the aforementioned Master of Philosophy and appropriate professional masters may well require two years. Programs that require more than two years, however, should be recognized through the awarding of a higher degree.

In order to hasten the movement of the superior student into doctoral study, the opportunity should exist for students to move more quickly from the baccalaureate through the M.A. to the advanced graduate studies phase. Perhaps the successful passing of doctoral qualifying exams, commonly given by many departments in many institutions in the first year of graduate study, should also qualify the student for the master's degree, permitting him to move after one semester or one or two quarters into the doctoral program. The master's program would thus be equated with the qualifying stage of doctoral studies and become an integral part of the continuum of liberal arts study. The requirement for a master's thesis should not be universal. Students could be encouraged, though, to elect courses in which major effort is placed on the preparation of a substantial term paper, a paper which could well be called a thesis under appropriate conditions.

In our proposed degree structure, the student meeting the requirements for the master's degree would have the choice of ending his academic training at that point, moving into a professional doctor's program, or continuing on with a doctoral program in the liberal arts.

8. *Intermediate Graduate Degrees in the Liberal Arts*

By intermediate graduate degrees we mean academic degrees for programs that extend beyond the master's level but which do not reach the doctor's level. Such programs are usually two to three years in length and differ from the Ph.D. in that they are designed to qualify an individual as highly knowledgeable in a given field rather than as capable of carrying out independent research and scholarly work.

THE TWO PHASES OF THE AMERICAN PH.D. The European doctorate in the liberal arts and sciences has long been based almost entirely upon a major thesis or dissertation. In America, however, as the Doctor of Philosophy program has evolved over the years it has come to embody additional requirements which add up to the demonstration of general scholarly competence in the individual's chosen field. These requirements most often involve required residence on the university campus, demonstration of competence in one or more foreign languages, graduate-level course work in the chosen field of specialization, graduate course work in one or more cognate or minor fields, sometimes the passing of general qualifying examinations, and almost invariably the passing of comprehensive examinations in the individual's chosen field of specialization. Only after the doctoral student completes these general requirements is he usually "admitted to candidacy" and thereby formally authorized to undertake the second phase, that of writing the doctoral dissertation.

DEVELOPMENT OF INTEREST As this differentiation of the American Ph.D. program into two parts has proceeded, the possibility has developed for recognizing the completion of the first or general studies phase with a certificate or degree. Much earlier, though, recognition was conferred through popular usage with the appellation "A.B.D."—all but dissertation. The letters are generally used in mild reprobation to designate individuals who are away from the campus, who are on a full-time job, who are delayed in the completion of the dissertation, and who may very well never get around to completing their doctorate. As Berleson (1960) summarizes the dilemma of the A.B.D. holder:

Almost all the liberal arts colleges, all but 3-4%, have some ABD's on the faculty. The college presidents reported an average of six or seven an institution. Taking account of the sampling returns, I estimate that in the entire system there are upwards of 10,000 ABD's with the serious intention of completing their dissertation and getting the degree.

The situation is uncomfortable and undesirable to all concerned. The uncompleted dissertation hangs over the candidate like a black cloud, interfering with his career, his domestic life, even his peace of mind. The employing institution wants him to finish and often uses salary or promotion as pressure for completion, so that another Ph.D. can be added to the rolls; too often the situation is a source of continuous tension between the young faculty member and his employing department or administration. The doctoral institution has the problem of keeping track of the candidate and the worry of another potential case of attrition so near the end of the line, the department feels it must pass an inferior product for neatness' sake, and the major professor is faced with another case of supervision at long distance and in bits and pieces.

Actually, there is nothing invidious in the formal recognition of those who have completed the general studies phase of their doctorate as long as this designation marks the successful completion of doctoral studies to date rather than failure to complete the following dissertation stage. To be acceptable, the degree or certificate should connote "passing the comprehensive" rather than "all but dissertation." Recognizing this, a number of individuals in recent years have proposed, and a surprising number of institutions have experimented with, degrees and certificates affirming the successful completion of the general studies phase of the doctorate. The names proposed differ but the various concepts are very similar. Most attention has been centered around the granting of degrees or certificates designated as Doctor of Arts, Master of Philosophy, Candidate in Philosophy, and even the Doctor of Philosophy itself. The very multiplicity of suggestions is an indication of the lack of general acceptability of any one. Other titles proposed include *specialist, licentiate, scholar, diplomate,* and *director.*

The earliest proposal to recognize the passing-the-comprehensive stage with a degree or certificate that we have found was made by Dean George B. Pegram of Columbia in his annual report for 1938:[1]

If the attainment by the student of a stage of knowledge and understanding of his chosen subjects equivalent, except for the dissertation, to that desired for the recipient of the Ph.D. degree were more clearly defined and attested by a certificate or even a degree, it might well be that boards of education, industrial and other employers, and the public generally would come to attach proper importance to the qualifications of such students. It is obvious that a man may be a scholar of understanding and may become a teacher of power and influence or may succeed well in one of many scholarly occupations without ever having done the special work of research for his dissertation that by the best practice distinguished the attainment of a Ph.D.

Current interest in the intermediate degree in liberal arts en route to the Ph.D. stems largely from 1965-1966. In the former year, Dean Moody E. Prior of Northwestern University discussed the possibility of an intermediate degree (Walters, 1965) as follows:

It is common to say that research and good teaching go together, but everyone knows that the two are not invariably found together in that relationship like a binary star, and it might be better to say, and truer, that continuous study in the most interesting materials available to one's field is essential to good teaching. It may therefore be possible to question seriously and honestly, whether for some graduate students and for some careers in teaching, especially in colleges and junior colleges where the advancement of learning is not an essential responsibility of the faculty, the time which went into the dissertation were not better spent in gaining breadth, in studying auxiliary and cognate areas, and in expanding one's horizons. In a well-planned course of study for such students, seminars would provide an initiation into the experience of research and meaningful organization of results. A comprehensive examination would terminate the program, and could also serve the secondary purpose of qualifying those with the requisite ability and motivation who underwent a change of mind about their career to proceed to the Ph.D. by fulfilling the dissertation requirement. Such a program would meet the objection that no teacher at the college level should lack some firsthand experience of what research means in his discipline, as well as the further objection that an intermediate degree would create a category of second-class academic citizens who would be forever excluded from a university career. It would,

[1] Quoted in *School and Society,* 49:321-322 (1939).

above all, discourage from a demanding and rigorous academic exercise those who do not have the taste or the requisite talents for it, but who do have the other qualifications for careers for which this exercise is not an absolutely essential preparation. One thinks of all the lost souls who wander today in an academic limbo because, though they have successfully completed a serious and demanding course of study, they have no respectable academic symbol of identification because their teaching position neither permits the time nor provides an incentive to meet the dissertation requirement for the Ph.D.

Dean Pegram's and Dean Prior's proposals are echoed in later suggestions for the creation of the Doctor of Arts, Master of Philosophy, and Candidate in Philosophy degrees and certificates.

At the level of the subject-matter disciplines, interest in intermediate graduate degrees has developed from time to time, particularly in those areas where more teaching positions at the college level have opened up than can be filled by the production of Ph.D.'s. Mathematics and physics are good examples of areas where the demand for college teachers is high and the doctoral thesis requirements are exacting.

In the field of mathematics, it has long been recognized that the research training provided by the traditional Ph.D. program is not necessary for the preparation of teachers of general undergraduate courses in mathematics (Mathematical Association of America, 1935). Indeed, maintaining the fiction that such a degree is required may dissuade able teachers from entering the profession even though, in 1964-65, barely one-quarter of the new full-time mathematics teachers employed by four-year colleges had Ph.D.'s. The Committee on the Undergraduate Program in Mathematics of the Mathematical Association of America has been active in drafting a general undergraduate curriculum in mathematics and in outlining the training for a college faculty to teach the courses in this curriculum. In 1967, it specified a strong master's program which would provide for careers teaching mathematics in the lower-division courses whether in two-year or four-year institutions. To prepare teachers to handle all of the courses in their four-year undergraduate program, the committee recommends a second graduate component bringing the student up to the approximate level of competence measured by Yale's Master of Philosophy or Michigan's and California's Candidate in Philosophy. Specifically called for are (1) a year course in one of the three fields (algebra, analysis, topology-geometry) in addition to master's work in these areas, (2) a second year of graduate study in at least one of these fields as well as additional graduate courses in mathematics, (3) a graduate research seminar, (4) a seminar or reading course in elementary mathematics from an advanced viewpoint, (5) a comprehensive examination, and (6) a lecture project designed to test the student's ability to prepare and deliver a seminar talk.

In physics, the Physics Survey Committee of the National Academy of Sciences and the National Research Council (1966) recommended serious consideration of the establishment of an intermediate graduate degree in the following terms:

Our technology requires a vast army of professionals to keep it in motion. Industries that are involved in research, development, and even production of modern products have increasing needs for scientists who have much greater exposure to many areas of modern physics, such as quantum mechanics, than can possibly be realized in an undergraduate program. Many of these industrial jobs may require some exposure to the techniques and results of modern physics, while not demanding the training as a fully independent investigator that is the primary aim of the research experience provided in the Ph.D. program. The junior colleges and some four-year colleges, faced with shortages of physics teachers, could also benefit from the availability of such people.

In some sciences, this intermediate level of training may be provided by the established master's degree program. However, the physics master's degree in many universities has become a consolation prize for students unable to qualify for doctoral candidacy. A few universities have strong master's programs in physics; they should protect their standards and encourage expanded participation in them. Despite such efforts, the coinage of the master's degee may already have been so debased that serious consideration should be given to the establishment of an intermediate degree comparable to the present Ph.D. in terms of course requirements but less demanding in the requirement for the completion of truly independent and original research. For college teaching, for example, the research experience might well consist of the development of new demonstration experiments or original curriculum materials rather than original research per se. For industrial work it might consist of participation as a junior member of a research team in a continuing project for six months to a year, sufficient to acquire familiarity with a particular research technique.

Unless students completing these programs can be given recognition, status, and prestige commensurate with their accomplishments, many who lack a genuine interest in research careers will still try to push on to the Ph.D. as a status symbol or a passport to lucrative employment, and may actually be lost to some types of employment, including college teaching, and certain applied or operational activities in which they could make far more effective contributions. Prospective employers should accord the necessary recognition to such programs, and not insist on the Ph.D. as a status symbol when another type of training would actually be more appropriate to their requirements.

The proposal to recognize the completion of the general studies phase of the doctorate inevitably becomes confounded with many proposals to create special degrees at approximately the same level designed to prepare individuals for college teaching. While recognizing that the two concepts are interrelated and that in fact the same degree title could well be used in both instances, the present section is confined to proposals to recognize formally the successful completion only of doctoral studies up to the dissertation stage. Parallel proposals involving such professional components as teaching internships and exposure to professional education courses are considered in the following chapter.

DOCTOR OF ARTS The title *Doctor of Arts* (D.A.) has been around for some time, but until recently the degree has been purely honorary in the United States (Eells and Haswell, 1960). Because of its obvious parallel with the Bachelor of Arts and the Master of Arts, however, it has recently come into prominence—first as a proposed designation to reward the completion of the general studies of the doctorate up to the dissertation, and more recently as a title of a degree program recognizing the completion in the liberal arts of an expository rather than a research dissertation.

In this first sense, the proposal owes its impetus to Fredson Bowers (1965), professor of English at the University of Virginia, who suggested that the Doctor of Arts (D.A.) or Doctor of Liberal Arts (D.L.A.)—the latter suggestion to avoid confusion with district attorney—be granted upon satisfactory completion of "a program that would intermesh at an early stage, for economy, with Ph.D. training but would cut off a year or two earlier with the omission of the dissertation, at an intermediate point between the present M.A. and the research Ph.D." Professor Bowers conceived that the Doctor of Arts holder "could always add the Ph.D., in the British manner, by writing a dissertation and passing the special examination that accompanies it."

In 1966, the Select Committee on Education of the University of

California at Berkeley, under the chairmanship of Prof. Charles Muscatine of the department of English, picked up Bowers' idea and recommended that "the graduate council at Berkeley should frame necessary legislation creating a new degree of Doctor of Arts, to require preparation equivalent to that normally required for advancement to candidacy for the Ph.D., but without requiring a dissertation." The Muscatine committee did, however, modify Professor Bowers' concept to suggest that each department would require "a learned paper," possibly the candidate's best seminar paper suitably edited as if for publication, in lieu of the dissertation.

The University of California, however, elected to use the degree name *Candidate in Philosophy* rather than the title *Doctor of Arts,* and as such the degree is currently offered on the Berkeley and Los Angeles campuses. As of the time of writing, no university has adopted the *Doctor of Arts* concept in its original predissertation form, although, as discussed later, Carnegie-Mellon University has introduced it in the form requiring an expository thesis.

MASTER OF PHILOSOPHY The title *Master of Philosophy* (M.Phil.) is not a new one. As discussed elsewhere it has been used for a number of years at English and more recently at Canadian universities to identify an upgraded master's program. It has also been used earlier in the United States. Eells and Haswell (1960) indicated that at their time of writing, three United States institutions offered the Master of Philosophy degree. We have not identified these but assume that the title is used by them more or less synonymously with that of Master of Arts.

In 1966 the graduate faculty at Yale effected a major revision of its degrees between the bachelor's and the Ph.D. First, Yale eliminated the M.A. and the M.S. degrees except for a few nondepartmental terminal programs. Second, it authorized the granting of a certificate of study to a student who had successfully completed a year or more of work without qualifying for any degree. Third, it established a Master of Philosophy degree to be awarded at departmental option to students who had completed all requirements for the Ph.D. except the dissertation. Yale's graduate dean John Perry Miller (1966) was well aware that there was a danger that the new degree would become a convenient consolation prize for students who were not competent to complete the Ph.D. To counteract the fact that "examining committees face the temptation of passing a student so he could receive his Master of Philosophy degree with the hope that informal advice would prevent him from going on or that eventually he will fall off the vine." Yale established the principle that any student recommended for the Master of Philosophy degree may proceed toward the Ph.D., and would have first claim on a place in the department's quota and upon financial aid, at least for a limited period of time. If, however, he does not make satisfactory progress within the conventional six-year time limits for the Ph.D. degree, his candidacy may be terminated. In opting for the Master of Philosophy degree, Yale considered and rejected the Doctor of Arts proposal on the grounds that "the doctoral degree is appropriately reserved for programs with a strong research component." Similarly, Yale considered the Candidate of Philosophy as a possible alternative to the Master of Philosophy, but questioned, "Is it quite as elegant?"

In 1967 Rutgers University also adopted the *Master of Philosophy* concept. There, it is offered as an intermediate degree in 27 out of the 53 departments offering the doctorate to provide recognition that a prospective doctoral candidate has successfully and expeditiously completed a major phase of his graduate studies and has achieved a comprehensive mastery of his general field of concentration. Recipients of the degree are automatically eligible to proceed further toward the Ph.D. if, within four years after receiving the M.Phil., they wish to do so. The M.Phil. degree requires a minimum of two years full-time graduate study, most of which must be spent in actual course work. All requirements for the Master of Philosophy must be met within four years of first registration at Rutgers. This time-limit feature is intended as an incentive to more rapid progress. Students who don't make it within four years can always earn the Ph.D. as a consolation prize!

At the University of Kansas, the M.Phil. is offered in history, requiring an additional year of work past the M.A. and a teaching internship for those who have not already had teaching experience beyond the secondary level. The program is supervised by the history department and does not require courses in professional education. A reading knowledge of one foreign language, the successful passing of a comprehensive examination, and a three-credit-hour research paper, however, are degree requirements.

The University of Southern Mississippi is offering the M.Phil. degree to prepare junior college teachers in subject-matter fields. A minimum of 46 quarter hours of work beyond the master's degree or 92 beyond the bachelor's is required. Curriculum standards call for the meeting of proficiency standards in a foreign language, computer science, or statistics; one-quarter of full-time residence on the Hattiesburg campus; the passing of qualifying and comprehensive examinations; and the submission of a thesis of considerable scope. Since the work done for the M.Phil. will be applicable to the Ph.D., it can be awarded only by departments authorized to grant the Ph.D. Successful students may continue on to the Ph.D. by taking additional course work, spending an additional year in full-time campus residence, and meeting Ph.D. language, comprehensive examination, and thesis requirements.

While the title *Master of Philosophy* has considerable merit, its use implies an effort to upgrade the master's degree as well as to establish a new degree at the all-but-dissertation level. The title, therefore, seems most suitable for institutions which are concentrating solely upon the doctorate and are therefore in a position to eliminate the M.A. and the M.S. degrees. Since this is not the case in most graduate schools, the Master of Philosophy degree may well have relatively little general acceptance.

CANDIDATE IN PHILOSOPHY At the same time that the Doctor of Arts and Master of Philosophy titles were being considered by other institutions, the graduate deans of the "Big Ten" were considering the same concept under the name *Candidate in Philosophy.* The word *candidate* is from the Latin word meaning clothed in white, as in the case of Roman office seekers. In the United States it has been used both in the general sense of identifying applicants for a degree and in the specific sense of denoting doctoral students who had been formally qualified to prepare a dissertation and therefore had been "admitted to candidacy" (Spurr, 1967).

In Europe, however, the same word has for many years been an accepted graduate degree title. In the Soviet Union, the degree Candidate of Sciences is normally awarded to the general graduate student at the completion of his formal studies at the university, while the degree Doctor of Sciences is awarded in recognition of special scholarly attainment, usually many years later. Other Eastern European countries—Bulgaria, Czechoslovakia, and Rumania—follow the same *aspirantura* system. Finland, Sweden, Norway, and Denmark all offer the candidate's degree, either in philosophy, science, or in a designated field of specialization.

The award of the Candidate in Philosophy certificate was suggested by Dean Robert H. Baker of Northwestern University and introduced by the University of Michigan in May, 1966. The graduate deans of the CIC universities (Big Ten plus Chicago) attempted to standardize the concept with a statement issued in December, 1966, which included the following:

A Candidate's Certificate, to be called "Candidate in Philosophy," is proposed for the purpose of recognizing formally the successful attainment of that stage in the doctoral program marked by the passing of a comprehensive examination and the completion of essentially all requirements up to the doctoral dissertation. The certificate is intended to mark an intermediate point in the advance toward the doctorate at a level widely recognized in American graduate schools.

This recognition would designate not those who are unsuccessful, but rather all those who have successfully completed this stage and who are considered to be qualified to prepare a dissertation regardless of whether or not they may actually do so. It affirms accomplishment to date. It regulates neither the duration of time nor the conditions under which a dissertation may subsequently be prepared. Its award does not confer with its candidacy for an indeterminate period at the awarding graduate school. Neither does the certificate lapse since it is a statement of prior achievement, not of status in a program.

Since the term "Candidate in Philosophy" implies an intermediate status, it would be awarded only in those departments or fields authorized to confer the doctorate.

The concept of such recognition of intermediate accomplishment en route to the doctorate in no way conflicts with the development of terminal intermediate degrees designed to meet the needs of other students who aspire to career goals for which the Ph.D. would not be the appropriate academic degree.

As of the end of 1968, the issuance of the candidate's certificate has been authorized by the University of Minnesota, Northwestern University, Indiana University, the University of Michigan, and the University of Wisconsin among the CIC institutions, and by the University of Rochester, the University of Washington, the University of Virginia, and the University of Hawaii among others.

The faculties of the University of California found the title *Candidate in Philosophy* more acceptable than the Doctor of Arts proposed by Bowers and the Muscatine committee. The C.Phil. is offered as a degree at UC Berkeley and UCLA. The concept of the candidate's certificate is applicable to other doctorates than the Ph.D. At a number of institutions, the Candidate in Education certificate is given at the appropriate stage to Doctor of Education candidates. Similarly, candidate's certificates are available in musical arts and business administration.

At the time of writing the Candidate in Philosophy, whether granted as a certificate or a degree, is the most widely adopted designation for the successful completion of the general studies stage of the doctorate. It is also the only such title that is not used in more than one sense among current major American, British, and Canadian universities.

DOCTOR OF PHILOSOPHY Many opponents of the concept of an intermediate liberal arts degree between the Master of Arts and the Doctor of Philosophy have no objection to recognizing the successful completion of the general studies stage of the doctorate up to the doctoral dissertation, but they do have real difficulty in finding any acceptable title for such recognition. On one hand any designation including the word *doctor* has all the connotations of a second-class doctor's degree and is thought to suffer in comparison with the Doctor of Philosophy as well as possibly damaging the current status of the latter degree. On the other hand, any title not including the word *doctor* is claimed to be unsalable in view of the claim that community and other junior colleges, liberal arts colleges, and regional state universities under the influence of accrediting pressures attach undue emphasis to the number of doctors on their faculty. Some critics, then, question the acceptability of such titles as *Master of Philosophy* and *Candidate in Philosophy.*

One possible solution to this dilemma, if indeed it be one, is to downgrade the Doctor of Philosophy itself to recognize the satisfactory completion of this earlier stage. This concept has been articulated by Jacques Barzun (1968) who first suggests that the best solution would be to give every native-born American a Ph.D. at birth, but then considers the problem of the A.B.D. and decides that since only a Ph.D. is thought to be good enough for a college or a university teacher, the only way we can save the talent that we are now throwing down the drain is to "award the Ph.D. immediately after the orals, provided that the candidate can show 'technique'—a passable M.A. essay or senior thesis. For that is all the streamlined Ph.D. of today will test in any case."

Downgrading the Ph.D. is certainly a possible answer to the critics who believe that college teachers must have a doctorate and that any other liberal arts doctorate but the Ph.D. is second class. It is doubtful, however, such a radical proposal could be sold to the graduate faculties of our leading universities. If it were adopted it would create a vacuum at the independent research level which could be filled by a second or research Ph.D. or by a higher doctorate of another title in the European tradition. The higher doctorate is explored in Chapter 11.

**PRINCIPLES
GOVERNING
INTERMEDIATE
DEGREES** As discussions on the intermediate degree have progressed, general agreement has been reached on several basic principles governing its development and codification.

First, the degree should be intermediate rather than terminal. It should be awarded to students on the main track from a liberal arts baccalaureate to a philosophical doctorate. As such, it should mark the attainment of progress substantially beyond the M.A. or M.S., but substantially short of the Ph.D.

Second, the degree should be philosophical rather than professional. The new intermediate degree should not entail separate admissions standards, independent selection of students, or distinctive graduation requirements. By maintaining the new degree in the mainstream of philosophical education, the dangers in offering two separate courses for graduate study would be avoided. If there were alternate paths, one would inevitably become more desired and preferred, while the other was relegated to students who either were forced or who had chosen to set their sights on a lower goal. The concept of separate but equal has not worked in other aspects of education; there is no reason to expect that it would work here. From a practical standpoint, the existence of two tracks would result in substantial misclassification of students at the outset and serious problems of transferability as the paths continued to diverge. The intermediate degree, then, should be awarded to the population of students who have a common set of aspirations at the initiation of graduate study. The fact that some will cease their formal education at a point in midcourse while others will continue on to the doctorate is entirely appropriate and not derogatory in any sense.

Third, the degree should be awarded at the level of attainment marked by the completion of all doctoral requirements but the dissertation. This level is normally identified by the passing of a comprehensive or preliminary examination and by formal admission to candidacy. While it is recognized that diversity in marking this stage does exist among leading American institutions, the stage itself is clearly recognized everywhere, and there is at least as much uniformity in its current definition as there is in the requirements of our universities for the master's or the doctor's degree.

Fourth—and this is critical—the degree should be a mark of affirmation and not one of negation. The successful intermediate degree receipient should be considered as one who has met and passed a level of achievement and not one who has failed by not going further. The great majority of those who reach this level will go on to prepare a dissertation and gain the Ph.D. in due course —whether in one year or five. Others will begin but never submit a dissertation. Still another group may be persuaded, either by their own or others' judgments, not to attempt a thesis. Still more, although capable of writing a dissertation, will find that they have met their academic objectives at this stage, that they are not interested in the type of detailed and extended scholarship required by the doctoral dissertation, and that they can better pursue their scholarly goals in other ways. Students in all these groups will have passed the hurdles thus far, however, and should have the right to attempt a thesis if they so wish. For the intermediate degree should not be a consolation prize; it should be a formal recognition of the completion of an advanced stage in graduate study.

Fifth, the intermediate degree should have a new title that will assume, with time, an appropriate status. With more than 300 master's degrees titles currently being used, it hardly seems plausible to expect the world of higher education—much less the general public—to attach higher prestige to yet another. However modified, it will be considered a master's degree. Perhaps more critically, there is real reason for doubting that our customers (the graduate students themselves) or their clients (the institutions that will hire them) will settle for a master's degree of any name to designate a status so far along the path toward the doctorate. Conversely, although valid arguments can be made for using the doctor's title for an intermediate graduate degree, it seems to be inevitable that any such doctorate would be relegated to second-class status, even accepting the remote possibility that it could be sold to the faculties of our major universities.

Sixth, the possibility exists of recognizing the fact that the intermediate stage of graduate study between the master's and the doctor's is currently not as well established as the others by giving certificates at these stages rather than degrees. On this basis many of the institutions offering the Candidate in Philosophy for the completion of the general studies phase of the doctorate have elected to recognize the stage with a certificate rather than a degree. Decisions to this effect had certain practical implications. In the first place, the concept of a certificate frequently proved to be more acceptable to faculties generally sympathetic to the problem of recognizing the candidacy stage but not fully convinced that such recognition should be at the full and formal degree level. Even more importantly, however, the granting of the certificate by the faculty has usually been on the basis that all students reaching that stage would automatically receive the certificate, whereas in those institutions which chose to mark the completion of this stage by a degree, the awarding of the degree has most often been optional, department by department and student by student. At such institutions as Michigan, Northwestern, Indiana, Minnesota, Wisconsin, and Washington, the Candidate in Philosophy certificate is awarded to all students upon admission to candidacy. This practice meets the present recommendation that the candidacy stage be one through which all students pass. On the other hand, where this stage has been recognized by the formal granting of a degree as with the Master of Philosophy degree at Yale or the Candidate in Philosophy degree at the University of California, the candidacy stage becomes an optional stage much as the master's stage (M.A. and M.S.) and thus carries with it the same intrinsic weaknesses that are associated with the liberal arts master's degrees.

EFFECT ON THE PH.D. The establishment of an intermediate degree permits the tightening of departmental requirements for the Ph.D. through the mechanism of providing an alternate degree qualifying graduate students for teaching careers. Under our present system, faculties are apt to be a little generous with marginal doctoral students, knowing full well that the reject left with a B.A. or M.A. will have limited career activities in postsecondary teaching. Should students first qualify for the intermediate degree, however, they would be qualified for junior college or other underclass teaching assignments. Many will be satisfied with this achievement; others will continue the quest for the higher degree. On their side, the departmental faculties can set and enforce quality standards, knowing they need concern themselves only with the best who have reached the previous high level of attainment.

Will the intermediate degree distract students from the end goal of the doctorate? The answer is clearly yes for those students who are only marginally qualified for the Ph.D. and whose attainment of the degree is more influenced by compassion and the need for college teachers than by the enforcement of the highest academic standards. More than compensating for this loss in numbers, however, will be the gain from those too fainthearted or too poorly financed at the start to embark upon a Ph.D. program of four to eight years' duration, but who would be willing to set out for a port only two to three years in the future.

PRESENT STATUS Institutions of higher education in the United States offering Candidate in Philosophy, Master of Philosophy, Doctor of Arts, and related degrees are listed in Table 5 together with information on the date of initiation of the award, its general characteristics, and the number of certificates or degrees awarded through 1968. We may conclude from these data that, in marked contrast to earlier movements in which many of the same arguments and recommendations were put forth with no result, the present attempt at innovation appears to have prospered. Perhaps it is an appreciation of the fact that the graduate deans and faculties have at last joined the ranks of the activists, but the general response from faculties, graduate students, and even the national press has been most gratifying. Major discussions of the intermediate degree concept took place in the Association of Graduate Schools in 1966 and Council of Graduate Schools meetings in the fall of 1966 and 1967. Other panel discussions were held by the Midwest Modern Language Association and the American Institute of Biological Sciences in 1967. It may well be that the year 1966 will in the future be accepted as having clearly dated the initiation of the third major philosophical graduate degree in American education.

NOMENCLA-TURE Although the concept of a graduate degree in the liberal arts intermediate between the master's and the doctor's has achieved considerable acceptance, no such broad agreement has been reached as to its name.

If we accept the fifth of the general principles suggested above to the effect that any degree between the master's and the doctor's should have a name other than master or doctor, we rule out as an intermediate graduate degree the titles *Master of Philosophy* and

TABLE 5 *Intermediate graduate degrees in the liberal arts*

Institution	Award	Degree (D) or certificate (C)	Awarded to all (A) or individual basis (I)
University of Toronto	Master of Philosophy	D	I
University of Waterloo	Master of Philosophy	D	I
University of Michigan	Candidate in Philosophy*	C	A
Yale	Master of Philosophy	D	I
Northwestern	Candidate in Philosophy	C	A
Indiana University	Candidate in Philosophy	C	A
University of Minnesota	Candidate in Philosophy	C	A
University of Rochester	Candidate	C	A
Rutgers	Master of Philosophy	D	I
University of Virginia	Certificate of Candidacy	C	I
UCLA	Candidate in Philosophy	D	I
UC Berkeley	Candidate in Philosophy	D	I
University of Wisconsin	Certificate of Philosophy	C	A
University of Washington	Candidate in Philosophy†	C	A
University of Hawaii	Certificate of Progress	C	I

*Also Candidate in Education, Candidate in Musical Arts.
†Also Candidate in Business Administration, Education, and Musical Arts.

Doctor of Arts. Both titles, however, continue to have a completely valid use to identify degrees at the named level. The Toronto Master of Philosophy degree defines an upgraded and completely justifiable academic program at the master's level. Similarly, the Carnegie-Mellon Doctor of Arts defines an alternative program to the Ph.D. at the doctor's level in the field of mathematics. These usages are to be commended and do not fall under the above caveat.

Any name other than master or doctor will be unfamiliar and unacceptable at first. Furthermore, its etymology and previous connotations will conjure up inferences that may color its interpretation. Nonetheless, the best course is to agree upon a single name to identify the intermediate graduate degree stage with the hope that in time it will take on the meaning given it by the American university world. This has happened to the associate's degree and should occur with the intermediate degree.

Among the names in current usage for the intermediate graduate

Date authorized	Date first granted	Number through 1968
Nov. 1963	June 1965	46
Dec. 1964	Oct. 1966	1
May 1966	May 1966	1,877
May 1966	June 1967	330
Dec. 1966	Feb. 1968	375
April 1967	Jan. 1968	500
May 1967	Jan. 1968	1,870
May 1967	Mar. 1968	478
Jan. 1967	May 1968	4
June 1967	June 1967	25
Feb. 1968	June 1968	40
Feb. 1968	Sept. 1968	56
Apr. 1968	Sept. 1968	850
May 1968	retroactive to July 1967	346
Aug. 1968	Dec. 1968	8

degree or comparable academic programs are *specialist, candidate, diplomate, scholar, director,* and *licentiate.*

The Specialist in Education degree is well established in the field of education to recognize a year of graduate study beyond the master's degree (Chapter 9). At the present time, there is a tendency to offer similar programs in subject-matter fields under the titles *Specialist in Arts* and *Specialist in Sciences,* particularly among the state colleges and universities that have developed out of teachers colleges. The usage of the specialist title in the liberal arts will undoubtedly continue to spread. Because of the high degree of association of the title with professional education and the former teachers colleges, however, it is doubtful that the title will become predominant in the major complex universities or the universities which have evolved from liberal arts colleges. Furthermore, the intermediate graduate degree in the liberal arts may be said more properly to prepare generalists than specialists.

The term *candidate* has ready identification with the act of admission to candidacy for the doctorate and, indeed, equates in general terms to that stage of progress in graduate studies. In addition, it is used in northern and eastern Europe to recognize more or less comparable achievement. For these reasons, *candidate* has been the preferred choice of the majority of American universities that have embarked in recent years on the formal recognition of intermediate graduate status. Its acceptance is far from complete, however. Substantial opposition to the term arises from two chief sources. First, the common English meaning of the word refers to an applicant for office and therefore its use to identify prior accomplishment rather than aspiration seems inappropriate. Second, a distinction must be made between a *candidate* who has completed the first phase of his doctoral studies and who is permanently certified as to this fact and a doctoral student who has been *admitted to candidacy* and therefore has the right over a specified time period to submit a dissertation. We have previously made the point that it is desirable to clearly separate the recognition of prior accomplishment in one stage of higher education from admission to the next higher stage. In this connection, the dual use of *candidate* is confusing and we regretfully concede that, if a better word can be found, it should be adopted.

For a number of years, Michigan State has offered a Diploma for Advanced Study in the arts and sciences parallel to its specialist program in education, but has had few takers. In 1969, the University of Miami in Florida is initiating a Diplomate in College Teaching which is discussed in the following chapter. Peyton C. Teague of the University of South Carolina has suggested the generic *scholar* (Scholar in Philosophy, Scholar in the Arts, and Scholar in the Sciences). The title *laureate* would be parallel to the Italian *laurea* at very much the same academic level and has been occasionally used in the past in the United States. A remote possibility is the *director* degree used in the areas of health, physical education, and recreation for programs which extend beyond the master's degree but not as far as the doctorate. All of these titles have merit, but there has been no trend toward their acceptance.

Having become convinced after three years trial that the candidate's title has serious defects and is therefore not likely to gain full acceptance, we suggest the European *licentiate* as the most viable alternative. Etymologically, *license* covers the granting of formal permission by authority to practice a profession, such as teaching. In France, the *license* is the first earned University degree. In Germany, the *lizentiat* has had a long history as the higher degree in theology, and has recently been introduced by the University of Konstanz as a general degree at essentially the same levels as the American intermediate graduate degree. These practices have migrated to the United States to a limited extent. Eells and Haswell (1960) list as current degrees the licentiate in canon law, dramatic art, philosophy, sacred theology, and theology. In addition, the licentiate has in the past been awarded in the United States in arts, sciences, and some score of additional designations.

The title *licentiate*, therefore, has ample historical precedent and parallel usage in the university world. Its root implies the license to teach and this is a desirable implication. It is neither master nor doctor, but can easily and acceptably be categorized as above the master's and below the doctor's.

RECOMMEN-
DATIONS

The general studies phase of the doctorate should be formally separated from the individual effort or dissertation phase by the universal award of a degree or certificate.

The first phase of the doctorate should require at least one academic year of formal study in residence beyond the master's degree and should involve the completion of all academic requirements normally associated with doctoral study except for the dissertation. Included should be the completion of additional course work past the master's, the meeting of foreign language requirements, the acquisition of competence in whatever research methodologies and tools are relevant to the student's field of scholarship, and finally the satisfactory completion of a formal set of comprehensive examinations.

All students continuing their courses of higher education past the master's degree should apply for and be admitted to this intermediate graduate level. Once they have met the requirements, they should all be given the appropriate degrees or certificates regardless of their future plans. At that time, those who desire to continue on to the doctorate should separately apply for and be admitted to this higher level.

As with the other stages in the overall degree structure, there would be a great deal of merit in utilizing the intermediate graduate stage both to accelerate qualified students and to prevent the unnecessary drag-out of time spent by the average student. It would be well to consider placing a two-year standard maximum time on the completion of the intermediate program dated from the granting of the master's degree. Basically this would involve granting the degree to all students who have maintained a B average in a specified program consisting of advanced graduate courses, seminars, independent reading, and research effort past the baccalaureate. If such a limit can be successfully established, then much of the prolongation of study associated with the doctor's degree can be eliminated. Earlier completion should be encouraged with students being given their degree or certificate recognition as soon as they pass the comprehensive examinations and meet the other requirements qualifying them to concentrate upon their individual study.

The appropriate name for this intermediate graduate stage will only become apparent over a period of time as various alternatives are tried. Since the stage is higher than the master's but lower than the doctor's, neither of these terms should be used. Such proscription, however, does not mitigate against the use of Master of Philosophy to identify an upgraded Master of Arts program or of Doctor of Arts to denote an alternative to the Doctor of Philosophy in which the ability to work independently as a scholar in areas other than research is demonstrated.

Of the various names suggested, *candidate* has been the most widely adopted. It has disadvantages, however, in that the term suggests future aspirations rather than past accomplishments and that its use to identify the successful completion of an intermediate graduate program is easily confused with the concept of candidacy for the doctorate over a limited period of time. We suggest, therefore, the title *licentiate* as being more satisfactory, and recommend *Licentiate in Philosophy* (L.Phil.) as the generic degree title between *master* and *doctor*. *Diplomate* or *laureate* would also be acceptable.

9. Other Intermediate Graduate Degrees

Intermediate graduate degrees evolved first in the professional fields. Various professional engineer (Eng.) degrees have been awarded in limited numbers. In recent years, the Specialist in Education (Ed.S.) degree has achieved widespread usage. Related to these professional degrees in engineering and education are recent intermediate graduate degrees designed specially for the preparation of college teachers.

PROFESSIONAL ENGINEER One professional intermediate graduate degree of general interest is that of engineer, usually modified by the name of a field of concentration such as Chemical Engineer or Civil Engineer. Its general status has been recently summarized in the report of the Goals Committee (American Society for Engineering Education, 1968). The degree typically involves two years of graduate work beyond the bachelor's degree, and usually involves a thesis. In some cases the program lies along the same path as the master's and doctor's programs; in others the candidate for the engineer's degree follows a separate path. In 1966, 229 such degrees were awarded, primarily by MIT (126), with other major producers at Stanford (41), Columbia (36), Michigan (10), Cal Tech (8) and U.S. Naval Postgraduate School (6).

After reviewing the evidence, The Goals Committee concluded that an intermediate graduate degree provides the opportunity for an advanced program to meet special professional objectives. Since the existence of a tradition and an adequate number of graduates each year gives the engineer's degree an established role, the committee recommended that engineering schools explore and utilize more fully the opportunities provided by this degree.

In a recent evaluation of the engineer's degree at the University of Michigan, a faculty committee concluded that considerable variation exists in departmental standards. Some departments have given the engineer's degree as a consolation prize for a failed Ph.D., whereas most departments have treated it as an honest six-year degree oriented toward design. One department has discouraged students by making the engineer's degree virtually as demanding in time and effort as the Ph.D.

COLLEGE TEACHERS

The preparation of teachers is one objective of virtually all graduate degree programs. We have already seen that teaching, particularly in secondary schools, is the usual career for those whose terminal degree is Master of Arts or Master of Science. In the last chapter, we discussed at length the development of intermediate graduate programs in the liberal arts which produce graduates who are most likely to take employment as teachers of undergraduate courses. In the following chapter, we shall see that college and university teaching is the major goal of Ph.D. recipients in all but a few fields where governmental and industrial service draw a large share of the graduates. In a very real sense, therefore, all of the graduate degree programs in the liberal arts are teacher-training programs in fact if not in design. The master's degree qualifies the student to become a secondary school teacher; the intermediate graduate degree certifies him for advancement, either within the school system or to the undergraduate college system.

In addition, however, there is a growing interest in graduate degree programs which are specifically designed to train college teachers. In addition to providing graduate-level instruction in a subject-matter area, these college teacher-training programs are characterized by a component of professional education courses and a required internship in college teaching. Much overlap exists. Many students in conventional master's, intermediate, and doctor's programs do in fact include these components.

Development of Interest

Interest in special graduate programs for college teachers dates back to the beginning of the present century in the United States. Mezes (1920) cites Horne (1908), Pitkin (1909), and Wolfe (1916) as having previously proposed separate training courses for college teachers. In his own essay, he suggested that the model for a special Ph.D. program for college teachers should consist of two parts supervised apprenticeship, two parts a broad course of study and investigation in a subject-matter area, and one part pedagogical study and investigation. The three components and the mix suggested have not changed materially in the 50 years since this article was written.

In the middle twenties, a committee of the North Central Association investigated the professional training of college teachers (Haggerty, 1927). It found that administrators did not at that time consider professional training in education when recruiting faculty, graduate schools in the American Association of Universities did not in general make provision for professional training in education in their graduate programs, but despite this indifference, the instructors recognized that professional education courses would have been useful in their own training. The committee concluded that the improvement of college education would be retarded at that time by a rule requiring undergraduate college teachers to have had professional courses in education.

Coming to more recent times, the Fund for the Advancement of Education asked a "Committee of Fifteen" to evaluate several fund-supported experiments related to the improvement of education. In its report (Strothmann, 1955), this committee addressed itself specifically to the question of a professional degree for teachers. Admitting that the Ph.D. degree as such is not a teaching degree, they were unable to agree upon an alternative. While some suggested a new teaching doctorate under such a name as *Doctor of Humane Letters,* others believing that Gresham's law would inevitably work, argued that such a teaching degree could not live in harmony with the older research degree. The committee did agree, though, that graduate schools were not paying sufficient attention to providing effective training for college and high school teachers.

In a report on graduate study at Columbia, Rosenhaupt (1958) discussed the possibility of a new teaching degree beyond the master's level which would be less specialized than the doctor's degree and which would not require a long dissertation. Such a teaching degree would take a minimum of two and a maximum of four years. He concluded, however, that it would be highly improbable that any degree other than the doctorate would ever be fully accepted by the academic community.

A more positive note was struck by McGrath (1959) who argued forcefully that graduate schools should provide programs for intending college teachers which should be broader and less research oriented than the conventional Ph.D. He thought that future college teachers should be required to attend a seminar for at least one academic year to gain an understanding of the whole enterprise of higher education and the place of their own work in it and that they should serve an apprenticeship in a college classroom under the supervision of an accomplished teacher before assuming sole responsibility for instruction.

The arguments against separate training programs and careers for undergraduate teachers are presented most perceptively and persuasively by Jencks and Riesman (1968). To them, the whole spirit of proposals for a separate teacher's degree is self-defeating in that no real progress can be made as long as teaching is seen as a soft option for those who cannot make it in the hard option of research. They suggest that the better solution is an internship and residency program in college teaching which would come after the completion of the doctorate, thus drawing upon the success of the medical profession in attracting their better students into practice as well as into research.

The whole philosophy and state of the art in the preparation of college and university teachers is ably summarized in a recent article by Heiss (1968). In a survey of attitudes of teaching assistants conducted at Berkeley, some three-quarters reported that their assignment had increased their interest in teaching, but only 60 percent felt that they had been given enough guidance. Miss Heiss also reported that approximately one-third of the current Ph.D. programs now require some teaching experience. In a study currently under way at Berkeley, some 35 percent of 1,600 respondents in 12 academic fields at 10 outstanding universities felt that a teaching degree should be introduced in their field. A larger number (44 percent), however, were opposed. Among her recommendations, Miss Heiss suggested that in any plan for reform in the preparation of college teachers, the proponents must resist the temptation to transfer the responsibility to "teach for teaching" over to the school of education. Programs for teaching will only be successful if they involve full institutional commitment, the involvement of top faculty, and adequate financial aid to the students. If these criteria can be met, serious consideration should be given to the development of a new degree for college teaching. Any such program should involve teaching internships which are designed to further the training of the teacher.

Demand for College Teachers   Much of the ebb and flow of interest in special programs for the training of college teachers depends upon the current job market for the year's crop of graduates and upon whether the discussant is a bull or a bear on the future growth of higher education. It is not our function to evaluate various efforts that have been made to forecast the demand for college teachers over the years to come (Cartter, 1966). In any event, a great many college teachers will be needed. What is more critical, however, is the question of whether or not our present degree programs are as well suited as they could be to prepare these teachers in whatever number is needed. On the basis of program concept and suitability alone, we have ample justification for reexamining our existing graduate degree programs and for suggesting and experimenting with new advanced programs for the training of college teachers. We assume also that accrediting agencies will properly evaluate and take into consideration new teacher-training programs. It is hoped that they will also deemphasize the Ph.D. where it is inappropriate training for the task at hand.

TWO-YEAR COLLEGE TEACHERS
It is implicit in our discussion of college teaching that we are primarily concerned with those who will teach undergraduate courses and not with the combined graduate teacher-research scholar who is produced by the conventional Ph.D. program. The need for college teachers is greatest in the introductory, survey, and general courses in any given subject-matter area. These courses make up the bulk of the lower-division program in all four-year colleges and are increasingly a major part of the academic program for transfer students in our community and junior colleges. In this sense, any program training individuals to become undergraduate-course teachers will produce graduates equally employable in four-year and two-year colleges. Two-year colleges, however, do differ from four-year colleges in their basic philosophy, in their total range of offerings, and in their competitive position. It is well to consider the special needs of two-year colleges for teachers before discussing the specific program proposals for their training.

The importance of the problem of training and supplying teachers for junior colleges is illustrated by the fact that three recent panel discussions have been devoted to it by the Council of Graduate Schools (1964, 1966, 1967). In these, it was pointed out that most two-year college teachers move up after teaching at the secondary school level, and that a large percentage are continuing or attempting to continue their graduate study. Nearly one-half have the bachelor's degree with the others equally divided having had more or less formal education.

The problem facing these teachers is bluntly presented by Garrison (Council of Graduate Schools in the United States, 1966) in the following words:

Take the mint-new product of a graduate program in English—whether he has achieved an M.A. (either earned or by consolation), an M.A.T., an M.Phil., a Candidate Degree, a Doctor of Liberal Arts, or whatever euphemistic label sanctifies an A.B.D. Take, for that matter, the successful Ph.D. Inevitably in his early years of teaching, he will have to instruct English Composition. English Comp is almost universally a freshman experience, whether in junior colleges or in four-year institutions. But the typical graduate school product in English will be about as well equipped to teach this course as a rabbit is to bite a lion to death. It would be the rare graduate program that would have prepared him for the realities of his first job; for students who hate to read; for students who wouldn't know a run-on sentence from a three-gaited horse; for students whose language habits have long since been distorted by the verbal barbarities of the rock 'n' roll disk jocky, the TV commercial, the peer group jargon; yet for students who, if they realistically saw the need to write clearly, would eagerly learn to do so—or try to learn.

Suggestions for the appropriate type of graduate training for prospective two-year college teachers follow similar patterns. At the 1964 CGS meeting, Feliz described a 1½- to 2-year program leading to the master's degree designed to round out a broad competence in the student's subject-matter area. In addition, the student would have a psychology course which deals with late adolescence, assessment, and learning, with emphasis on the junior college setting. The third semester would involve student teaching in a community college and accompanying seminar in the graduate school.

The American Association of Junior Colleges (Gleazer, 1964) encouraged the establishment of special programs for the preparation of two-year college teachers in both academic and occupational fields, emphasizing certain desirable common elements, namely, (1) students should be recruited from diverse sources, (2) the program should involve the maximum participation of nearby junior colleges, (3) teaching internships in junior colleges should be an integral part of the program, (4) the program should be flexible, (5) it should have a university-wide rather than a single school base, (6) the program content should be designed to develop teaching competence in two related subject-matter fields, and (7) the program content should be related to the nature of the junior and community colleges, student characteristics, and guidance services. Gleazer envisaged that such programs should be at the master's level for prospective teachers of academic subjects and at the bachelor's level supported by relevant industrial or other experience for technology instructors.

At the 1966 CGS meeting, Macmillan argued for an enriched Master of Arts in Teaching degree to prepare students for careers as two-year college teachers of academic subjects. Such a degree would follow a program emphasizing subject-matter competence at the graduate level and would require two full years of study. Included would be a formal exposure to courses in the psychology and philosophy of the teaching and learning processes as well as a carefully planned teaching internship. Ideally, the program should be open-ended in that the qualified degree recipient might continue on for his doctorate.

Garrison (1967) reported on a survey of junior colleges and junior college teacher attitudes. The most general criticism he met with from teachers was that the graduate courses they had had were too often slanted toward the need of the prospective Ph.D. in content and in treatment rather than toward the need of the undergraduate college instructor. There was general agreement that a Ph.D. was not necessary for junior college teaching. Rather, new teachers in the liberal arts should have a solid baccalaureate in a subject-matter field followed by a broadly based master's degree of at least one academic year and a summer or, even better, a 16-month to 2-year Master of Arts or Master of Arts in Teaching program to permit the mastery of two closely linked subject areas such as sociology and anthropology or history and political science. As with the others cited, Garrison recommended the inclusion in such programs of a modicum of supervised teaching experience and a brief exposure to the history of education and education psychology. Many of his respondents spoke of their need for a good course in adolescent psychology dealing frankly and directly with the kinds of problems commonly met on the junior college campuses.

While the above examples demonstrate that there is general agreement on the desirability and general characteristics of a two-year course for the training of junior college teachers, related questions of status have yet to be resolved. As was brought out at a conference on preparing two-year college teachers for the 1970s sponsored by the American Association of Junior Colleges in 1968, the junior colleges and the junior college teachers themselves are doubtful that a two-year graduate program would give them the status or preparation of four-year college faculty members. Their response, incorporated in a set of guidelines published by the National Faculty Association of Community and Junior Colleges (1968), was to propose a two-year program leading to the degree of Candidate in College Teaching (C.C.T.) which could be converted into the degree of Doctor of Arts in College Teaching (D.A.C.T.) after one academic year of full-time teaching followed by a postteaching evaluation seminar, an evaluation of the candidate's written log and terminal report, and an oral doctoral examination. The case for this type of Doctor of Arts (D.A.) program is summarized by Wortham (1967).

A program designed specifically to train junior college teachers has been offered by Appalachian State Teachers College at the master's level since 1957. It is a 54-quarter-hour course (alternatively, 45 plus thesis) and emphasizes a professional education approach (Council of Graduate Schools in the United States, 1966).

ADVANCED DEGREES FOR COLLEGE TEACHERS One common thread running through all the discussions of the preparation of teachers for two-year colleges is that such preparation is in many ways similar to that needed for teachers of undergraduate courses in four-year colleges. True, the basic concepts and breadth of programs of the two-year college differ from that of the baccalaureate-granting institution, but the individual qualified to teach in one is qualified to teach the same academic subjects in the other. Furthermore, there are both practical and status advantages in being able to switch. For these reasons, we suggest that it is more appropriate to deal with the general problem of programs for the preparation of undergraduate teachers rather than programs specifically designed for teachers who seek employment in either two-year or four-year institutions.

We have already defined three general levels of graduate degrees in the liberal arts relating to programs that do not necessarily have components of professional education built in as requirements. These are (1) the master's program as the initial liberal arts graduate program extending a minimum of one year (Master of Arts, Master of Science) and a maximum of two years (Master of Philosophy); (2) the intermediate graduate program extending at least two years and completing the general studies phase of graduate education, leading to such degrees as Candidate in Philosophy or Licentiate in Philosophy; and (3) the doctor's program in which, in addition to the studies at the intermediate level, a dissertation or similar demonstration of completed individual effort is required. Many of the graduates of all of these liberal arts levels do in fact go into college teaching; students with the master's degree going most frequently into two-year colleges, those with intermediate degrees being qualified for general undergraduate teaching, and those with the doctorate aspiring to university teaching posts.

Against this background, we may set a parallel classification of graduate programs specifically aimed at producing teachers. In contrast to the liberal arts degree above, these teaching degrees are characterized by the requirement of at least a modicum of exposure to professional education subjects as the history of education, philosophy of education, and educational psychology. More importantly, such teaching degrees require a supervised teaching internship with concurrent or subsequent constructive criticism or evaluation.

At the first, or master's, level the appropriate teaching degree title is *Master of Arts in Teaching* (M.A.T.). Basically a one-year program, it prepares secondary school rather than college teachers. It is generally agreed that a two-year program is the minimum for the training of college teachers.

At the second, or intermediate, degree level the program for the training of college teachers requires at least one year of graduate education beyond the master's degree or two year's past the baccalaureate. Among clearly identified professional teaching degrees under development or evolution in this area are the specialist (in education, arts, or sciences), various diplomas including the Diplomate in College Teaching, the proposed Candidate in College Teaching, and possibly the licentiate. The title *doctor* should never be used to identify either a program that can be completed in two years or one that does not include a major period of independent creative effort.

The third, or doctor's, level is identified in the realm of the teaching degree primarily with the *Doctor of Arts* or *Doctor of Arts in College Teaching* concepts. The Doctor of Philosophy and Doctor of Education degrees also may be broadened to include academic programs designed to prepare teachers rather than research scholars. In any event, a minimum of three academic years of fulltime study is required and a dissertation or similar exhibit of independent individual work must be submitted.

Omitting the first level as not qualifying the college teacher, we will discuss the intermediate teaching degrees in the remainder of this chapter, referring the reader to the previous chapter for the intermediate liberal arts degree and to the following chapter for all types of doctoral programs.

The last few years have seen a considerable development in intermediate degree programs specifically designed to prepare undergraduate teachers. Among those actually being offered are Specialist in Education (Ed.S.) and related two-year graduate programs at a large number of institutions, Master of Arts in College Teaching (M.A.C.T.) at the University of Tennessee, and the Diplomate in Collegiate Teaching (D.C.T.) at the University of Miami (Florida).

Specialist Many schools of education offer a two-year program extending one year past the master's degree for the further education of teachers and school administrators. Such a program may or may not lead to a degree. Its purposes vary widely. One function of this program, however, is to train college teachers.

The development and current status of two-year intermediate graduate degrees in education representing two years of graduate work have been summarized by Boylan (1964) and Koenker (1967) and discussed by two National Conferences on the Intermediate Graduate Degree (the first in 1967).

According to Boylan's inquiry, the two-year certificate has been given by Teachers College, Columbia University since 1936, but the first two-year degree in education was a Master of Education program introduced by the University of Denver in 1947. The first Specialist in Education degree was awarded by Colorado State College in 1952. The University of Kansas became the first university to offer the same degree in 1954. By 1967, Koenker estimated that 116 institutions were offering programs in this general area.

The chief purpose of these programs is to prepare students for administrative, guidance, supervisory, and other specialized positions for the public schools. The concept of the intermediate degree has become broadened in recent years, however, to include the training of college teachers. In 1957, 24 institutions stated this latter purpose as being met.

The two-year graduate program is generally open to qualified students with the master's degree and is predominantly terminal in character. Qualified students, however, may generally apply for admission to the doctoral program after completion of the intermediate program.

In 1964, institutions were about equally divided in whether they offered degree or nondegree certificate programs (Boylan, 1964). Table 6 summarizes the titles and the numbers graduated from the principal institutions involved. Of the 38 degree-granting institutions responding in 1964, 29 used the title *specialist,* 4 used *master,* and 3 *diploma.* Of the similar group of 39 certificate-granting institutions, the term *certificate* was used in 1964 by 17, *specialist* by 15, and *diploma* by 5.

As institutions consider the use of the title *specialist* to identify

TABLE 6 *Principal two-year graduate programs in teacher education*

Institution	Year started	Title	Total two-year awards
Degree programs			
University of Tulsa	1952	Professional Diploma	39
University of Bridgeport	1955	Professional Diploma	300
New Mexico State University	1956	Specialist in Education	45
University of Florida	1958	Specialist in Education	70
Indiana University	1959	Specialist in Education	47
Kansas State Teachers College at Emporia	1959	Specialist in Education	38
California Los Angeles State College	1961	Master of Science in Counseling	47
University of Michigan	1961	Specialist in Education	37
George Peabody College		Specialist in Education	57
Certificate programs			
Teachers College, Columbia University	1936	Professional Diploma	3,422
Harvard University	1950	Certificate of Advanced Study	249
New York University	1951	Specialist in Education	447
University of Virginia	1952	Certificate for Advanced Study	100
University of Connecticut	1954	Diploma in Professional Education	391
University of Minnesota	1954	Specialist in Education	39
University of Colorado	1955	Professional Certificate	75
American University	1958	Professional Certificate	30
University of North Carolina	1961	Certificate for Advanced Study	93
University of Georgia		Specialist in Education	192

SOURCE: Adopted from Boylan, 1964.

intermediate graduate programs for teachers of subject-matter fields in addition to similar programs for educational administrators and specialists, the suggestion has been made that the titles *Specialist in Arts* and *Specialist in Science* be used to identify the new category (Putnam, 1967). Western Michigan University has recently initiated these degrees for students with subject-matter specializations.

In 1969, the American Association of State Colleges and Universities and the National Conference on the Intermediate Degree jointly sponsored a position statement on the specialist's degree. A minimum of two academic yeárs of graduate study beyond the bachelor's degree is called for to strengthen an individual's area of specialization in such subjects as English, educational administration, mathematics, and guidance. Admissions should be selective. Provision should be made for seminars, independent study courses, field and research projects, and a supervised internship or practicum. The specialist degree is not to be thought of as a research degree, but the student should become well acquainted with research in his field of specialization and should develop an understanding of research methodology.

Master of Arts in College Teaching

In contrast with the specialist's degree which arose from the practice of adding an additional year's study to the conventional master's programs, a number of intermediate graduate programs have been developed *de novo* with the explicit objective of training undergraduate college teachers. The Master of Arts in College Teaching (M.A.C.T.) program initiated in 1966 at the University of Tennessee is such a program (Reese, 1967). Basically a 2-year program, it can be completed in 1½ years. The degree is offered in conventional subject-matter areas. The standard requirements are 57 quarter hours in subject-matter fields, 3 quarter hours devoted to a seminar in college teaching, and either six quarters of part-time service as a teaching assistant or one quarter of full-time teaching experience. Thus, the M.A.C.T. program meets many of the recommendations for the training of junior college teachers detailed above.

Diplomate in Collegiate Teaching

A D.C.T. program will be initiated in the fall of 1969 at the University of Miami (Florida) as a two-year program to prepare the undergraduate teacher. Since the training is designed to produce the generalist, the term *specialist* is inappropriate. Sixty semester credits are required, of which at least forty must be in the academic disciplines. Professional education courses will deal with the nature of the college student, the nature of collegiate instruction, American community college program, and an internship in community college teaching. Miami-Dade Junior College and other nearby institutions are cooperating in the program. Similar in nature to the Tennessee M.A.C.T. program, the Miami D.C.T. is unequivocally a two-year program and involves the active participation of junior colleges in the teaching internship.

RECOMMEN-DATIONS A great similarity exists between the various proposals and actual intermediate degree programs designed to prepare graduate students for careers as undergraduate teachers. Such programs should require at least two academic years and should be normally completed by well-qualified students within this time span. Not more than three years of full-time effort should be required. Basically, the degrees should be under the control of the subject-matter departments. The curriculum should be largely concentrated in either one broad subject-matter area or in two closely related disciplines. Breadth rather than depth should be emphasized as the prospective teacher will be primarily concerned with introductory, general education, and survey courses. A modicum of exposure to courses in higher education, philosophy of higher education, and educational psychology, especially with regard to the college-age adolescent, is desirable. Finally, a supervised internship is a must, and it should be accompanied or followed by a seminar involving collation of experiences, constructive criticism, and evaluation.

As with the intermediate graduate degrees in the liberal arts, there is little general agreement as yet on the nomenclature of intermediate graduate degrees designed for teacher preparation. At least three general approaches are competing for favor.

The accepted name in teachers colleges and in those state universities with a strong school of education tradition is *specialist.* It is to be expected that subject-matter programs in these institutions may lead to the Specialist in Arts and Specialist in Science degrees. We do not recommend that this happen, however, for two reasons. First, the typical undergraduate teacher-training degree in a subject-matter field is generalist rather than specialist in nature, making the latter title a misnomer. Second, the title *specialist* has evolved as a degree in professional education, and thus has taken on a strong school-of-education flavor. It is not to be expected that subject-matter departments in colleges of arts and sciences will adopt it readily.

The second trend is to regard the two-year teacher-training program in the subject-matter fields as an upgraded master's program and to adopt the Toronto-Waterloo version of the Master of Philosophy (M.Phil.), albeit with the addition of special teacher-training components. We see nothing wrong with this approach except that this type of master's program is inevitably confused with the Yale-Rutgers A.B.D. type of M.Phil. program. We tend to agree with Berelson and other authorities cited in Chapter 8, however, that the upgraded master's degree will not have sufficient status to survive and prosper. We shall not be unhappy if it does, but we don't predict that it will.

The third alternative, then, is to settle on a new name to identify the intermediate degree level between the master's and doctor's. This is our recommendation. Referring to the discussion in the previous chapter on nomenclature, the most likely terms at the moment seem to be *licentiate, diplomate,* and *candidate.* We recommend them in that order. Whichever is used, though, we recommend that the subject-matter orientation of the intermediate degree for colleges teachers be emphasized by the modifiers philosophy, arts, or science. We recommend the generic Licentiate in Philosophy (L.Phil.) as the best single solution to the generic intermediate degree offered by subject-matter faculties in the arts and sciences, whether as a straight liberal arts degree or as a degree specifically designed to prepare undergraduate teachers.

10. *The Doctor of Philosophy Degree*

In the United States, most of the criticism and proposals for reform of the doctor's degree center around the Doctor of Philosophy. This degree dominates not only the liberal arts but also most professional fields outside the classical learned professions of theology, medicine, and law. Our concern here, therefore, is primarily with the Ph.D. In the following chapter, we shall deal with other doctorates, such as Doctor of Education, Doctor of Arts, and the professional doctorates.

EVOLUTION OF THE PH.D. We have already seen that the concept of the Ph.D. was introduced into the United States early in the nineteenth century by Americans who studied in Germany and returned to teaching posts in our major Eastern universities. The degree itself was first granted in this country at Yale in 1861 to Eugene Schuyler, James Morris Whiton, and Arthur Williams Wright, all of whom had previously earned their baccalaureate from the same institution (Rosenberg, 1961). Whiton studied in the Yale department of philosophy and the arts from 1859 to 1861, continuing his Latin, Greek, and German without an instructor but passing examinations in each. In addition, he studied Sanskrit two hours weekly for two years with Prof. William D. Whitney and turned in a six-page handwritten thesis in Latin, an essay on the proverb *Brevis vita, ars longa.* Whiton's dissertation still exists (Rosenberg, 1966). Wright's is missing but had the title "Having Given the Velocity and Direction of Motion of a Meteor on Entering the Atmosphere of the Earth, to Determine its Orbit about the Sun, Taking into Account the Attractions of Both These Bodies." Schuyler apparently submitted a study entitled "Wedgewood on English Philology" which was printed the following year in *Bibliotheca Sacra* as a review article of 24 pages (Rosenberg, 1962).

The 1860 decision of Yale to offer the doctorate was specifically designed "to enable us to retain in this country many young men, and especially students of science, who now resort to German Universities for advantages of study no greater than we are able to afford." The requirements were at least two years of study on campus past the bachelor's degree, a satisfactory final examination, and a thesis giving evidence of high attainment.

The Ph.D. in the United States, however, derived its major impetus from the founding of Johns Hopkins in 1876 followed by Clark University and Catholic University in 1889 and the University of Chicago in 1890. In that latter year, Harvard established its graduate school, an action soon followed by such state universities as Michigan, Wisconsin, Nebraska, and Kansas (Rudolph, 1962). By the turn of the century, the Ph.D. had become the desiderata for appointment to major university faculties. It still, however, was a short-term degree, requiring two years of postgraduate study at the better universities and grading into dubiously honorary degrees at the poorer ones.

The development of the Ph.D. at Johns Hopkins in its early years (Hawkins, 1960) greatly influenced practices at other institutions. Standards established were high in 1876, but the degree was a two-year one and the thesis requirement lenient by present-day standards. The required period between the bachelor's and doctor's was lengthened from two to three years in 1881. A graduate academic council was created to control the program in 1883. The requirement for subordinate studies was increased from one to two years in 1884. The format of the thesis was outlined, the use of the typewriter recommended, and the requirement of a copy for the library was initiated in 1885. In 1887 the French and German reading examinations were added, an official adviser was required, and two outside examiners were appointed to read the thesis.

Students played an important part in the development of standards for the Ph.D. through affiliated graduate clubs on the different university campuses (John, 1935). The first club was founded at Harvard in 1889. The first joint meeting of affiliated clubs was held by Harvard, Cornell, and Johns Hopkins students in 1893. The Federation of Graduate Clubs, organized in 1896, held annual conventions for a number of years. At its 1896 convention, it recommended that the minimum requirements for the Doctor of Philosophy degree should be (1) the previous attainment of a bachelor's degree or equivalent, (2) the completion of at least two years of resident graduate study, one year of which should be on the campus of the institution conferring the degree, (3) an adequate examination, and (4) a thesis embodying the results of original research, bearing the written acceptance of the professor or department in charge.

John's 1935 survey of doctoral requirements for 1899, however, indicates that while 7 universities (Brown, Bryn Mawr, George Washington, Minnesota, Missouri, Vanderbilt, and Yale) required 2 years of residence, Chicago required 1½ and the other 13 institutions listed (including California, Columbia, Cornell, Harvard, Johns Hopkins, Stanford, Michigan, Pennsylvania, Princeton, and Wisconsin) required only 1.

Efforts to standardize the Ph.D. at the institutional level derived strength from the activities of the Association of American Universities beginning in 1900 and the National Association of State Universities dating from 1905 (John, 1935). By 1908, a committee of the latter association had recommended that the period of postgraduate study for the degree be at least three years, one of which should be in residence at the degree-granting institution. The AAU followed suit in 1916 so that the concept of a three-year rather than a two-year doctorate was generally accepted prior to World War I.

The evolution of the Ph.D. in the twentieth century has been marked by a greater standardization of quality, the elimination of the Ph.D. as an honorary degree, the extension of the Ph.D. to applied fields and indeed to virtually all subject matters taught in the university, and the prolongation of the Ph.D. period to the present four to five years of enrollment and seven to eight years of total elapsed time.

By 1935, our present Ph.D. practices had fully evolved. A survey of requirements at different institutions by John indicates that while the basic thrust of the program has changed remarkably little, the trend has been to substitute the requirement that the dissertation be microfilmed rather than being printed, to add flexibility to or even to drop the foreign language requirement, to add more course work at the graduate level, and to put increased emphasis upon early "qualifying" examinations.

CURRENT STATUS OF THE PH.D. The present status of the Doctor of Philosophy program has been thoroughly dissected and objectively analyzed by Berelson (1960) and ably characterized by Prior (in Walters, 1965). There is no need to paraphrase their treatments of the subject here.

As we have already seen (Chapter 8), the total period of graduate study leading to the Ph.D. in the United States has become gradually subdivided into three more or less formal stages. The first is the master's stage although only 80 percent of American Ph.D.'s actually take this degree in passing through to the doctorate. The second is the intermediate stage involving the completion of all requirements up to the dissertation and leading to admission to candidacy and increasingly to the award of an intermediate graduate certificate or degree. The third is the dissertation stage leading to the Ph.D. itself. The trend is toward the formalization of these stages. Dibden[1] has suggested that they be termed *preliminary, intermediate,* and *candidate.* We suggest that the first stage should be termed the master's stage and be made identical to that degree level.

The Ph.D. program normally requires at least as much course work as the master's program in the same field, usually at least one and frequently as much as two additional years of formal study. During this portion of the doctor's program, the student must spend at least one academic year in residence, meet foreign language or research tool (such as mathematics or statistics) requirements, frequently pass a set of qualifying examinations early in the period for doctoral study, and almost invariably pass a set of comprehensive examinations before being admitted to candidacy. As a candidate, the student must prepare a doctoral dissertation theoretically embodying the results of original research but practically compensating for lack of originality by length. He must also go through a formal defense of his dissertation, an exercise which may or may not be public and may or may not constitute a real examination by the faculty examining committee. Since these practices were summarized by Berelson in 1960, the chief change has been the movement at major graduate schools away from an across-the-board requirement of a reading knowledge of French or German to departmental requirements. The result has been that many departments have opted for one language in greater depth, while others—primarily in the social sciences, business administration, education, and some fields of engineering—have eliminated completely any foreign language requirements. Since the former requirements were often only nominal, the actual effect of this movement has been to strengthen and make more relevant the language requirement in many disciplines.

[1] Unpublished memorandum, 1965.

Present concepts of the doctoral program are summarized in a statement first published jointly by the Council of Graduate Schools and Association of Graduate Schools in 1964. The following excerpt is representative:

A doctoral program consists of lectures, seminars, discussions, independent study, and research designed to assist a student to acquire as well as to contribute to knowledge in his field. During his first year or two of study, a doctoral student may take a number of formal lecture courses and seminars to advance his knowledge of his field, of its scholarly tools (foreign languages, mathematics, etc.) and of its relationship to other disciplines. Frequently, he begins his research shortly after entering the program. After satisfactory completion of his formal advanced study and examinations, he may be "admitted to candidacy" for the doctoral degree and may then devote nearly all of his time to completing his research and compiling the results in his dissertation. The final doctoral examination consists mainly of a defense by the candidate of his research and dissertation.

Doctoral programs are primarily concentrated in the large complex universities. Indeed, one concept of a university in the United States is that of an institution which offers Ph.D. programs. So much status is associated with the designation *university* that enormous pressures build up for a college to offer the doctorate so that higher-grade faculty and students can be attracted. These pressures are particularly strong in the state colleges that have evolved from teacher-training colleges and in new state institutions that are currently being developed as regional four-year institutions of higher education. They also exist within the established and prestigious liberal arts colleges (Bowdoin, 1967). Such institutions as Wesleyan and Vassar have recently initiated Ph.D. programs or are in the act of so doing. The Council of Graduate Schools (1965) has a general statement outlining the minimum standards for new doctoral programs and formal steps in consideration of a new doctoral program.

THE DRAG-OUT PROBLEM The 1964 CGS-AGS statement on the Ph.D. recommends that although there has never been a definite time limit for the earning of a doctorate, the course of study should involve not more than three or four years of full-time study and research beyond the baccalaureate.

The facts are otherwise. From selected statistical studies of doctoral programs in the United States (Tucker, Gottlieb, and Pease,

1964; Wilson, 1965; National Academy of Sciences, 1967) we obtain a generally consistent picture of the time spans involved in graduate studies. Similar data have been obtained from studies of the doctoral students at individual universities such as Columbia (Rosenhaupt, 1958), Michigan (Bretsch, 1965), and Harvard (Doermann, 1968). English is one academic discipline that has been studied thoroughly in respect to the actual nature of its doctoral programs (Allen, 1968). In this work, we shall attempt to provide an insight as to the major findings rather than present many data from these statistical studies.

The 1967 National Academy of Sciences data are the most representative but are restricted in their interpretive value due to the limitations inherent in the basic data and the consequent statistical analysis. The complexity of the program of the Ph.D. drag-out is often better presented in the less comprehensive studies, particularly by the discussions of Berelson (1960), Wilson (1965), and Allen (1968). In evaluating time-span data, analysis should extend beyond the computation of the *median,* i.e., the time span or age at which one-half the cohort of graduate students has reached a specific point in their progress. The distribution curves are usually highly skewed with the *mode* (the time span or age which occurs oftenest) being near the minimum time period and being several years less than the median. For instance, for 17,865 individuals who received their doctorate in 1966 (National Academy of Sciences, 1967), the median total time span from the bachelor's to the doctor's degree was 8.2 years, while for the modal group, 2,275 in all, it was 5 years. Furthermore, 1,650 completed their graduate studies in 4 years, a fact that would not readily have been surmised from the median figure. Similarly, the median time span from the master's to the doctor's was 5.2 years contrasted with the mode of 3 years. The high median values result from the long drag-out of from 8 to 24 years for one-half the Ph.D. population while the other half has in fact gone through more or less expeditiously.

General Time-span Patterns With this caveat in mind, we may run through the most characteristic patterns for the conventional arts and sciences as a whole.

First, the *median* pattern is determined by the time span at which one-half the successful Ph.D. students will have completed each stage. The median student will have completed his bachelor's degree after four years at the average age of 22. He will then work or undergo military training for two years, beginning graduate school at 24.[2] His master's degree will require two full years despite the nominal one-year requirement so that he will be 26 when he passes this gate. It will take him six additional years to obtain the doctorate. A little more than three of the six will be required for admission to candidacy and a little less than three for the completion of the dissertation. Thus, he will receive his Ph.D. at the median age of 32. During the 10 years of graduate study, he will be enrolled for a total of 5 years and he will be working either within or without the university for an additional 5. In other words, the median doctoral program can be characterized as a half-time program extending over a decade, with the other half-time devoted to teaching, research, and nonacademic employment in various patterns.

The largest single group, however, will move through much faster. The *modal* group member will complete his baccalaureate at 22, will enter graduate school at 24, and receive his master's at 26 as does the median group. From then on, however, he will accelerate substantially, being admitted to candidacy in a little less than two years and requiring only a little more than one to complete his dissertation. Thus, he will receive his Ph.D. at 29 rather than 32.

The highly intelligent, well-balanced, and strongly motivated student can, of course, complete his doctorate more quickly. The numbers are much fewer than are fondly imagined by the faculty. The fastest common pattern is for such students to begin college at 17 rather than 18, complete their baccalaureate in three years at 20, begin graduate school at 22 after work or military service, and earn their doctor's degree in four years without taking the master's en route. They would thus be 26 when awarded the Ph.D.

Obviously, students could easily move directly from their baccalaureate into graduate study and often do. We hold the view, however, that even the ablest students will usually take one to two years off from studies sometime in their university experience, and we program this hiatus between the baccalaureate and the initiation of graduate study.

[2] National data are inconsistent at this point. While Wilson found a median lapse of 1.6 years from the baccalaureate to graduate school entry, the National Academy of Sciences gives only 0.3 years. However, the latter study also gives a total time span for graduate study of 8.2 years which, when subtracted from the median age of 31.8 at which the doctorate is earned, yields an approximate figure of 23.6 years for beginning the graduate study. We may thus infer a two-year hiatus for the NAS study as well.

TABLE 7 *Time-span of doctoral study by academic fields*

Field	Number Ph.D.'s 1958-1967	Median total, years	Time-span enrolled, years*	Median age at end, years†	First postdoctoral activity, percent‡		
					Post-doctoral study	R&D	Teaching
Chemistry	12,814	5.5	4.8	28.0	32	48	16
Mathematics	4,890	6.1	5.1	28.6	7	31	56
Physics-astronomy	7,929	6.4	5.6	28.8	23	55	18
Engineering	14,239	7.0	5.1	29.8	6	53	29
Biological science	14,733	7.1	5.4	30.3	34	34	27
Earth science	2,995	7.5	5.4	30.5	11	44	30
Psychology	9,273	7.0	5.4	30.9	12	23	29
Philosophy	1,471	7.8	5.4	31.2	2	4	90
Agriculture and forestry	4,738	7.9	5.1	31.4	9	57	23
Classics	585	8.3	5.8	31.6	4	4	87
Health science	2,338	8.7	5.6	32.0	20	41	23
Economics and statistics	4,707	8.0	5.0	32.1	2	30	56
Political science	3,129	8.7	5.4	32.5	3	11	70
History	4,657	9.0	5.7	32.6	2	3	88
Anthropology and archaeology	898	9.5	5.6	32.7	7	21	67
English	5,051	9.7	5.8	32.9	1	1	95
Sociology	2,094	9.4	5.8	33.4	3	24	67
Business administration	2,294	9.8	5.3	33.4	1	9	76
Speech and drama	1,818	10.3	5.3	33.6	2	4	78
Modern languages	3,117	9.5	5.7	33.8	2	6	89
Religion and theology	1,621	11.6	7.3	34.1	1	2	74
Fine arts and music	1,516	11.9	6.0	35.0	2	2	86
Education	21,856	13.7	6.7	38.0	1	6	48
ALL FIELDS	131,194	8.2	5.4	31.6	11	28	44

*For 1963-1967 doctorates.

†For 1958-1967 doctorates.

‡For 1963-1967 doctorates. In addition, 30 percent of psychology and 14 percent of religion and theology Ph.D.'s went into professional practice, while 9 percent of political science and 34 percent of education Ph.D.'s went into administration.

SOURCE: National Research Council, *Report on Doctoral Programs,* Washington D.C., 1968, 154 pp.

We should note that, despite the usual characterization of the Ph.D. as a three-year degree, less than 2 percent actually earn it within three years of the bachelor's degree and less than 12 percent do so within four years.

Although financial support is one factor contributing to the drag-out of the doctor's program, it is by no means the limiting one. The three-year fellowship granted under Title IV of the National Defense Education Act (NDEA) and the traineeships made available by the National Science Foundation have been only moderately successful in improving either the drag-out or dropout of doctoral students. For students who have received Woodrow Wilson Dissertation Fellowships, the modal period for dissertation completion has been four years. It is too soon to appraise the success of the Ford Foundation's four-year program in the social sciences and humanities. This program has the merit, however, of using financial incentives as a device to influence both faculty and students to conform to a four-year pattern.

Time-span Patterns in Various Fields Considerable variation exists between the various disciplines within the conventional arts and sciences and the professional fields in which the Ph.D. is awarded. General time-lapse characteristics for 24 general fields recognized in the National Research Council statistics are summarized in Table 7, while Table 8 (National Acad-

TABLE 8
Age at doctorate

Field	First quartile*	Second quartile†	Third quartile‡
Physical sciences and engineering	27	29	32
Biological sciences	28	31	35
Social sciences	29	32	37
Arts and humanities	30	34	38
Business administration	30	34	39
Religion and theology	32	35	39
Education	34	38	44
ALL FIELDS	28	32	37

*One-quarter of all successful Ph.D. recipients received the doctorate at this age or younger.
†One-half received the doctorate at this age or younger.
‡Three-fourths received the doctorate at this age or younger.
SOURCE: National Academy of Sciences (1967) analysis of data from the National Research Council. Data are for 1966 doctoral recipients.

emy of Sciences, 1967) indicates the spread in ages for the first, second, and third quartiles by broad divisions of learning.

From the data summarized in Table 7, it is apparent that the time pattern for the doctorate is quite different for the natural sciences, the social sciences and humanities, and some of the professions. Only in the physical sciences, mathematics, and engineering can the Ph.D. student expect to graduate before he is 30 years old. He will spend nearly as much time at the university as any other Ph.D. student, but he will work outside the university less and thus will graduate earlier. In chemistry, physics, biological sciences, and the health sciences, he will be very apt to take on a postdoctoral fellowship or traineeship before seeking permanent employment. In the natural sciences as a whole, he is more apt to move into research and development with governmental agencies or industry rather than immediately into the academic world.

In the social sciences and humanities, the time span of enrollment for the doctorate is a year longer than it is for the natural sciences. Employment opportunities both within and without the university in the social sciences and humanities tend to be in teaching rather than in research with the result that it takes eight to nine years total time in these areas rather than the six or seven required for the natural sciences. Teaching is the usual first postdoctoral activity in the social sciences and the predominant one in the humanities.

Finally, the professions tend to attract doctoral students well along in their careers, who work long and part-time for the doctorate so as to qualify themselves as academics as well as professionals. Education is by far the longest drawn-out program. A third of the education Ph.D.'s go into administration upon graduation.

Psychology is a special case, being in part a social science, in part a natural science, and in part a profession. Psychology Ph.D's are processed quickly and tend to distribute themselves on graduation between ample opportunities for postdoctoral study, research, teaching, and professional practice.

That the data for the median student are generally indicative of trends for the broader group is demonstrated in Table 8 which gives the average age by divisions at which the first, second, and third quartiles of students completed their Ph.D. Again, the early completion pattern in the physical sciences and engineering contrasts sharply with the long drag-out pattern in education.

In attempting to get at the causes of these patterns, Wilson

(1965) found in his studies of Southern universities that Ph.D.'s were most slowed down in the social sciences and the humanities by discontinuity of attendance and the necessity of writing the dissertation off-campus, factors largely attributable to financial problems. Confirmatory evidence is provided by Allen (1968) in the field of English where finances, problems of completing the dissertation, and military service were reported as the major delaying factors.

THE DROPOUT PROBLEM
Many fail to finish their Ph.D. programs. The problem of attrition has been relatively less studied than the problem of attenuation because data are more readily available on those who succeed and whose records are complete than they are on those who drop out and disappear from view. Nevertheless, limited information is available.

Tucker, Gottlieb, and Pease (1964) studied attrition for all students enrolled between 1950 and 1953 in work beyond the master's degree or its equivalent in the traditional arts and science fields at 24 selected universities. Those who had not completed their Ph.D. ten years later (1962) were considered dropouts. Attrition was found to average 38 percent, ranging from 23 percent for prestige private institutions to 54 percent for smaller and less highly rated universities. These figures must be interpreted remembering that the sample includes only those students who have successfully completed their master's or its equivalent, but that it also includes those in this category who were not planning on earning a doctorate or who subsequently transferred to other graduate schools. The authors estimated 31 percent to be a more reasonable overall attrition percentage for the period between the master's and the doctor's. Of those who dropped out, about one-fifth had reached the dissertation stage and therefore would have earned intermediate degrees had they been available. The overall attrition of 38 percent varied, being highest in the humanities (50 percent), followed by the social sciences (41 percent) and the natural sciences (29 percent). Dropouts do not fall by the wayside for want of trying. On the average, they spend a longer period of years after the baccalaureate reaching candidacy status (11 years) than do successful candidates completing their dissertation (9 years).

Tucker, Gottlieb, and Pease concluded that the major reason for dropping out of Ph.D. programs was lack of motivation. They felt that most of the dropouts had gone as far in their doctoral programs as was consistent with their levels of ability and that most of them seemed to be engaged in work consistent with their education and motivation.

In a study of the first 1,096 students appointed to NDEA Title IV fellowships in 1959 and 1960, Arlt (1963) found that three years later 341 had resigned and only 102 had completed their doctorate. Of the students who had received NDEA Title IV fellowships at the University of Michigan from 1959-60 through 1964-65, only 51 percent had completed their doctorate by 1968-69 and most of the rest can probably be considered dropouts. Apparently, not even financial support over a three-year period can greatly influence the rate of attrition.

Institutional practices coupled with financial support, however, can. Telling data are supplied by Mooney (1967) who studied attrition among Woodrow Wilson Fellows appointed from 1958 to 1960. In this study, attrition is defined as failure to complete the doctorate by 1966 after six, seven, or eight years as the case may be. Of all the Woodrow Wilson scholars, 35 percent had earned the Ph.D., another 3 percent had acquired a professional degree, and an additional 43 percent a master's degree. While 42 percent of the men had completed their doctorate, only 16 percent of the women had done so, a figure independent of the women's marital status. Among the men, the success ratio was highest at Princeton (63 percent) and other smaller but distinguished graduate schools and lowest at Michigan (32 percent), Columbia (33 percent), and other large graduate schools. The success ratio is greatest in the natural sciences (65 percent of the males), followed by the social sciences (34 percent) and the humanities (31 percent) in the usual order. Within individual fields, chemistry (85 percent of the males) and psychology (67 percent) were the surest subjects, while religion (4 percent), musicology (6 percent), and fine arts (9 percent) were the least.

Summarizing the dropout picture, we may conclude that from one-third to two-thirds of the population of prospective doctoral students will in fact earn their Ph.D. within an 8 to 10 year time span. The percentage of success will be highest (70 to 80 percent) for males studying physical science or psychology at a small distinguished graduate school and very low for women studying humanities and the arts at a large but less distinguished university (5 to 15 percent).

Even accepting the conclusions of the Tucker study (1964) that students go about as far as they can go and that they end up in appropriate employment niches, the fact remains that few apparently end up with a degree that affirmatively marks the stage they have reached. In short, they are considered by all as dropouts rather than as individuals who have successfully moved a long way up the ladder of higher education and have affirmatively reached an appropriate level. The recommendations in the present report that the master's and intermediate graduate degrees be required en route to the doctorate and that students be admitted to only one stage of graduate study at a time are directed toward the solution of this ill-named attrition problem.

CRITIQUE OF THE PH.D.

Much has been written about the Ph.D., mostly in criticism but occasionally in defense. Some of it is worth quoting. More of it is repetitious. A brief review, however, is appropriate.

The fear of the Ph.D. octopus hearkens back to William James (1917) who, in 1903, decried the practice of universities restricting professorial appointments to Ph.D. holders. His proposals for reform were that graduate schools should "give the doctorate as a matter of course, just as they give the bachelor's degree, for a due amount of time spent in patient labor in a special department of learning, whether the man be a brilliantly gifted individual or not"; that universities should look for faculty of substance rather than for those with doctoral titles; and that highly qualified students should set the example of refusing to take a higher degree in order to freely follow their more immediate intellectual aims. James undoubtedly influenced A. Lawrence Lowell who used his influence and his personal fortune to establish the Society of Fellows at Harvard in 1932 to provide a prestigious alternative to the Ph.D. (Brinton, 1959). The society has prospered but virtually all the junior fellows now elect to take the Ph.D. anyway.

Many years and many writers later, we find Jacques Barzun (1945, 1968) arguing that the American doctorate is a costly and time-consuming ordeal and that many students find the dissertation step beyond their strength financially, socially, and emotionally. He regretfully concluded that "as long as college catalogues are printed with degrees following names, and people believe that all Ph.D.'s are created equal, these letters will exercise a baneful influence on American higher education." His facetious solution is to give everybody a Ph.D. at birth. More seriously, he suggests giving doctoral students their degree immediately after the orals with a passable essay or thesis. Later, the student could submit his published writings for a second Ph.D. with honors.

Particularly cogent is the discussion of graduate school reform by Jencks and Riesman (1968) which emphasizes the increasing professionalism of the academic community and lays much of the blame for it on the control of the Ph.D. program by the academic department. The authors call for more mobility and anarchy in graduate studies to "marginally reduce the pervasive influence of the academic guilds and enhance the position of men working on applied rather than pure problems."

The verbosity of the critics notwithstanding, many faculties find nothing wrong with the Ph.D. programs in their particular school. For instance, the 1969 Harvard Committee on the Future of the Graduate School concluded that:

To the gratification of the Committee, and somewhat to its surprise, it encountered *no sentiment whatever* in favor of any of these possible changes in the present Harvard system, and we are therefore happy to reaffirm our own strong beliefs on these issues, as follows. A single faculty teaching both undergraduate and graduate students is the glory of the Harvard system. We prefer a decentralized Graduate School where the departments make binding recommendations upon the Dean. We do not wish to institute a "teaching degree," and we regard the dichotomy—so often encountered—between "teaching" and "research" as a false one.

The status and problems of the American Ph.D. today are ably described by Hollis (1945), Berelson, (1960), and Prior (in Walters, 1965). Most of the criticism and many of the suggestions for reform center on relatively few issues: (1) that the Ph.D. program should be shortened to four years of total graduate study for the average student; (2) that the Ph.D. program should be more structured and possibly more rigorous; (3) that the dissertation should be shorter and more flexible; (4) that the Ph.D. program should be broadened to better serve to prepare college and university faculty who will be primarily teachers rather than scholars; and (5) that, failing these reforms, alternative doctoral programs should be set up to qualify college teachers. Each of these topics will be treated separately below.

THE FOUR-YEAR PH.D. Many have argued that the American doctorate takes too long to earn, possibly in terms of years enrolled and certainly in terms of overall elapsed time from graduate school admission. Our current concern with the problem comes from the time-span studies discussed earlier in the chapter and from the statement of the AGS Committee on Policies in Graduate Education in 1957 denouncing the uncertainties in the time span of American doctoral studies and recommending that "the whole program should take no more than three years of residence. In the first two years a man should take what courses he needs, and should have all the freedom from prescribed courses for his own individual work that his previous training will allow. At the end of his second year he should take his general examinations. At the end of his third year, he should have completed his thesis."

In a detailed analysis of the Ph.D. program in the field of English where long-drawn-out doctorates are the rule, Allen (1968) made his prime recommendation, that the Ph.D. in English be regarded as a four-year degree. This recommendation was unanimously concurred in by the members of the advisory committee of the Ph.D. study of the Modern Language Examination. It will be interesting to see the extent to which it is followed by our major graduate departments in this subject-matter discipline.

The call for a shortened time of doctoral study has been echoed by many others (Council of Graduate Schools in the United States, 1962). Princeton, under the leadership of Sir Hugh Taylor, is one institution that has made a determined effort to achieve it on a school-wide basis. Its success has been considerable in that Princeton has achieved probably the shortest drag-out time and lowest dropout record of any major graduate school. Internal resistance from both faculty and graduate students is great, however, and the gains are slowly being nibbled away by attrition. Cornell, too, has achieved considerable publicity with its six-year Ph.D. program, supported by the Ford Foundation and offering the promise of the A.B. degree in three, the M.A. in four, and the Ph.D. in six years from university matriculation. Under faculty pressures, however, it has been transmuted into a three-year accelerated undergraduate program with the promise that its graduates, like any others, can complete the Ph.D. in three years according to the catalog if they are good enough. More promising is the effort of the Ford Foundation, through the investment of more than $40 million, to influence 10 major universities to develop viable four-year doctoral programs in the social sciences and humanities. The results of this massive trial are not as yet in, but the prospects are brighter than they turned out to be for the earlier NDEA Title IV program where fellowships were given to the students without pressures being put on the departments to provide actual programs matched to their catalog statements.

Although most graduate deans now espouse the concept of the four-year normal time span for the doctorate, many of the faculty and graduate students themselves do not. As Sinnott (1959) puts it: "The day is long past when a four-year college course can give a person the training needed for a scholarly or professional career. In the case of a doctor or a lawyer or a college professor, at least five years' work beyond the bachelor's degree is necessary before a man is really on his feet, and it often may be two or three years longer." Jencks and Riesman (1968) buttress this latter position by pointing out that when all the extraneous effort is taken out of the present doctoral program, "the typical doctoral candidate spends the equivalent of between three and four full-time years working on his degree." This hardly seems excessive. "Doctoral study may well be dragged out too long in some individual cases, but the reason is not that the requirements are too burdensome but that individual students choose, for financial, personal, or intellectual reasons, to mix their doctoral work with other things."

Nonetheless, we conclude that the four-year doctorate is a worthy objective and that it should be vigorously sought. We agree with Berelson (1960) that it is better for all concerned if the work is done speedily, consecutively, and in residence.

THE STRUCTURED PH.D. Most of those who argue for a shortened and regularized period of time for the Ph.D. realize that a major reason for the present prolongation of this period is the general lack of clearly defined and carefully spelled out requirements and of a specific timetable for the average high-grade graduate student to meet these requirements. As is recognized in the present four-year Ford Foundation program, students can be expected to finish in four years only if the faculty has structured a four-year doctoral program and exerts pressure to have it followed. Berelson (1960) puts it well in recommending that the program for doctoral training be tightened, by which he means that it be clearer, more compact, more specific and that it include more supervision and direction by the faculty.

The AGS 1957 committee report joins its recommendation for a three-year program with corollary recommendations for tighter admissions policies, for examinations in the first year of graduate study of one language and the writing of connected English prose, for individual counseling beginning before initial registration, and for required exposure to seminars during the first two years of doctoral study.

Structuring does not imply uniformity. As Heard (1963) points out, Ph.D. study cannot be converted to the kind of lockstep system that has been used in training for medicine and law. Nevertheless, with better identification and counseling of students before and after they enter graduate school, with clarified and better organized statements of departmental expectations of doctoral students, and with the provision of financial support for students while working on the dissertation, graduate departments should be able to put through the majority of their students in four years if they put their collective mind to it. This is what we mean by the structured Ph.D.

A structured Ph.D. program may well be a stronger Ph.D. program. As Sinnott (1959) points out, the ideal Ph.D. program should have all three dimensions of length, breadth, and depth in proper balance. In a series of suggestions for the restoration of scholarship in graduate study, Spivey (1958) couples his recommendation of a three- to four-year doctor's program with higher admission standards, more attention by the faculty, more work but fewer courses, full-time residence, and emphasis on research and writing as being central to the doctorate.

The best set of basic requirements we have run across for structuring the Ph.D. are those of Wilson (1965) who recommends that graduate departments should (1) develop distinct patterns of expectations regarding the understandings, knowledge, skills, and competencies expected of successful candidates; (2) specify the amounts, types, and combinations of curricular, teaching, research, and clinical experience which are thought to be central to the development of the desired attributes; (3) incorporate these elements into a programmatic model; and (4) develop and implement a basic strategy for translating programmatically projected expectations into actual patterns of student progress.

Perhaps not all these desiderata can be achieved. Nonetheless, as Princeton has shown, a structured and tightly controlled four-year doctoral program may well substantially reduce the drop out and drag-out situation while maintaining high academic quality.

THE SHORTER DISSERTATION   If the shorter Ph.D. is to be more generally achieved, it follows not only that the program should be more clearly defined and structured but also that the dissertation requirements should not be excessive. We have moved a long way in the reverse direction from the first six-page doctoral dissertation at Yale in 1861 to the modern Ph.D. dissertations in English, of which 53 percent are 151 to 300 pages in length, 32 percent are 301 to 500 pages, and 6 percent are over 500 pages long (Allen, 1968).

Many have called for briefer dissertations. The AGC 1957 committee suggested that the thesis should be a modest *specimen eruditionis,* evidencing the use of techniques of research, ability to organize findings, and competence in verbal presentation. The subject should be small, compact, and of interest and use. The thesis should show original but not necessarily creative work. Berelson suggests a median of 100 pages and an upper limit of 250. Allen points out that most dissertations in English have only a few worthwhile points to make and that a short study is all that should be asked of the student. Clearly, the faculty should not only accept shorter dissertations but they should insist on having them.

At the same time, a broader choice of dissertation topics may well be appropriate in many fields. Tronsgard (1963) pointed out that standards of acceptability have changed over the years. Status studies, descriptive studies, and case studies are not deemed scholarly nowadays. Furthermore, historical, philosophical, and conceptional analyses, although scholarly, are often considered to have little relevance to existing practices. If the dissertation is to cease being a roadblock, Tronsgard argues that more conceptual theses and position papers should be accepted, that students should be allowed to work on empirical dissertations as a team rather than as individuals, and that graduate schools should provide staff whose primary responsibility is to help on dissertations. The conclusion seems to be obvious that emphasis on shorter dissertations and the judicious acceptance of broader variety of dissertations should reduce the time required for the doctorate without a commensurate decrease in standards.

We should point out that the doctoral dissertation may not be in itself the logical component of all Ph.D. programs. Alternative devices and broader definitions of theses can be used to provide training for individual research at the doctoral level. Harvey Brooks[3] has suggested a four-year doctoral program:

. . . with the first two years devoted primarily to course and laboratory work and the last two years devoted to a varied research experience, cul-

[3] Personal communication, April 9, 1969.

minating in a thesis or report but not necessarily requiring an original production as at present. In other words, the Ph.D. would be awarded after satisfactory performance in a research environment for a certain length of time. The recipients of the Ph.D. would then compete for a smaller number of post-doctoral positions of two to three years duration in which the individual would be expected to produce one or more truly original pieces of research and to become launched on a research career. It would be expected that virtually all individuals going into research-oriented university faculty positions would have at least two years of post-doctoral research experience. There might be as a result a considerable increase in the population of post-doctorals, at least in the leading departments and especially in fields which do not now have very much post-doctoral study. The post-doctorals could well act as partial mentors for the Ph.D. candidates who might in fact move into two or three research groups during the course of their research experience. The purpose of the research experience of the Ph.D. would thus be to provide more variety in exposure to various research techniques and concepts with less depth of specialization. The Ph.D. without subsequent post-doctoral experience would be regarded primarily as preparation for college teaching and most kinds of industrial research. It would be expected that all graduate students at this level would go through the same Ph.D. experience, even if they later embarked on post-doctoral work. However, it is possible in practice that the very brightest students who were clearly headed for long-term research careers might specialize somewhat more even in their Ph.D. experience than the other students who expected to terminate with the Ph.D.

A similar view was expressed in a recent address by John Bardeen[4] with regard to graduate training in physics. He argued that physics faculties should not require a long thesis but should be satisfied with something simpler so that most students would finish in three to four years. To meet the needs of those Ph.D.'s in physics who are going on to careers in basic research and graduate education, an expanded program of postdoctoral research should be introduced as a recognized part of the educational system.

THE PH.D. AS A DEGREE PROGRAM FOR COLLEGE TEACHERS

At the core of the never-ending dispute on the merits of the Ph.D. program is the argument as to whether the Ph.D. is a degree that exists primarily to train research scholars in the traditional arts or sciences or whether it should also encompass the preparation of college teachers and advanced professionals in general.

[4] Albert A. Michelson, Edward W. Morley Award Address, Case Western Reserve University, October 3, 1968.

The purist argues for the former. As Prior (in Walters, 1965) points out, the Ph.D. program possesses a clear logic and propriety when it is centered on the production of the learned scholar "with emphasis on depth of knowledge and on the cultivation of those tools and habits of mind which enable a man to go beyond what he has learned and to exercise independence in the understanding of his chosen branch of knowledge and in advancing it." If these structures limit the Ph.D. program, many current Ph.D. programs are probably misnamed. Hollis (1945) reminds us that "almost every graduate faculty in the nation has an able and articulate contingent who follow the lead of Abraham Flexner and Norman Foerster in declaring that the Ph.D. degree should not be given for work in home economics, library science, physical education, speech, and a score of other fields that are semiprofessional or even more narrowly vocational in nature."

The pragmatists, however, have clearly won. The Ph.D., like it or not, is a degree which prepares for careers as teachers and as professionals as well as for scholarship. It is given in virtually all fields of learning within our universities and clearly will continue to be so offered. The Ph.D. is a teaching degree and a professional degree. It is and it will be many things to many people. Our graduate schools have the responsibility for designing it so as to serve these various objectives.

Much has been written on the research Ph.D. and the teaching doctorate but little need be repeated here. Carmichael (1961) exemplifies the separatist approach in arguing for parallel but equal Doctor of Philosophy programs, one abbreviated Ph.D. for research and one abbreviated D.Phil. for careers as teachers. The arguments for a doctoral program minimizing the research dissertation frequently rely upon statistical evidence that most Ph.D.'s publish little after they have exhausted the mine of their dissertation. For instance, Jernegan (1927) estimated that only one-quarter of history Ph.D.'s are consistent producers. The fact that an individual may not repeat an experience, though, does not imply that the experience was not good for him.

Most faculty and administrators, therefore, would probably agree with Schmitt (1965) that teaching and research must go together, although in different mixtures and patterns for different individuals. As Jencks and Riesman (1968) point out, the teaching-research dilemma is a false one, the real problem being to marry the two enterprises.

The American Ph.D. program is broad enough to build into it the necessary elements to make it suitable for the preparation of teachers and professionals as well as of research scholars. To a considerable extent, we are already doing this. Many departments are now requiring supervised teaching experience for all their doctoral students and this is all to the good. If formal courses in education are thought desirable, the department has the option of requiring students to take them. A department has the right to broaden the concept of the dissertation to include expository as well as research treatments of a topic, as Dartmouth has done in the field of mathematics. An English department can accept dissertations whose merits lie in the evidence of the creativity they contain as well as in the more conventional trappings of scholarship.

In short, there is no reason why the Ph.D. cannot be offered as a three- to four-year program suitable for turning out research workers, teachers, and professionals. The only question is whether the faculties of the individual departments will face up to the multivariate careers of the products of their doctoral programs and build in the necessary flexibility. Parallel doctoral programs with other names are created only to circumvent the nostalgic purists.

RECOMMEN-DATIONS The Doctor of Philosophy degree has evolved in the United States until today it identifies the generic program at the highest level of formal training for a career in scholarly research, teaching, and related professional fields. We see much to commend the use of the single degree title to encompass closely related programs for students who are not certain of their career goals and who may end up in quite different activities than they earlier envisaged. As Hollis (1945) has concluded, there is no need for a single pattern of competence at a given degree level. Instead, there should be a number of identifiable patterns with the educational content determined in each instance by the relevant social and occupation needs. Only the one title, *Doctor of Philosophy,* is needed. The name of the degree should not be expected in itself to reveal the exact nature and quality of the work done by the individual. Only a detailed study of his transcript, his dissertation, and the faculty's recommendations can really show how well the new Ph.D. has performed and how well he can be expected to perform in a particular employment situation. A personal interview will add a great deal to this appraisal.

In short, the Ph.D. is a good degree and is appropriately broad in scope. It is, however, insufficiently categorized in the majority of academic departments with regard to what is expected of the student in terms of performance and time. The four-year norm for the total period of graduate study is much to be desired. The four-year program should lead to a stronger rather than a weaker degree if it is properly conceived and properly administered. Specifically, the faculty should be more closely involved in the Ph.D. program of the given student from beginning to end. They should insist on shorter dissertations and should encourage a greater breadth in the topics and treatments of the dissertations. There seems no reason why the dissertation experience should consist of one massive study presented in one massive manuscript. A variety of experiences and of presentations might well provide more valuable educational training.

The requirement of supervised internships in college teaching is to be encouraged in most Ph.D. fields, but such experience should be designed to benefit the doctoral student and not serve as a means of providing cheap instruction for the undergraduate.

Although we recommend the above reforms, we are not so sanguine as to think that they will be soon or widely adopted. Failing reform of the Ph.D., the next best solution is to create alternative doctoral programs that can accomplish what the Ph.D. could but does not do. We consider such alternative liberal arts doctorates in the following chapter along with parallel professional doctorates.

11. *Other Doctor's Degrees*

In addition to the Doctor of Philosophy, a number of other doctor's degrees have been tried or proposed in the liberal arts. Although Eells and Haswell (1960) list several hundred doctoral degrees that are or have been used in the United States, the great majority are honorary, spurious, or are no longer in use and may be disregarded in the present study. A few, however, are relevant to the problem of academic degree structures. Particular attention should be paid to the Doctor of Education and to doctorates designed to recognize creativity rather than research. Currently, too, there is wide interest in programs for the preparation of college teachers leading to such degrees as Doctor of Arts (D.A.). Finally, although our study is centered on degree structures in the liberal arts, a few comments on professional doctor's degrees are in order.

DOCTORATES IN THE CREATIVE ARTS Doctoral degrees have been established in the field of music to recognize the highest levels of performance or of composition. The name of the most common of these degrees is *Doctor of Musical Arts* (D.Mus.A.). The Doctor of Music degree is predominantly honorary. Music faculties that award the doctorate in performance or composition have by and large been diligent in establishing and maintaining standards at levels that place the Doctor of Musical Arts degree on a par with the Doctor of Philosophy in musicology. At most institutions, the advanced work in performance or composition is done on campus. At Yale, however, the student completes his residence with the Master of Music program and later submits his accomplishments in either performance or composition for the doctoral degree. Effort is very largely individual, and Yale holds the view that it can frequently be done better off campus than on.

Proposals have been made from time to time to recognize creative writing in a similar fashion. The State University of Iowa has

granted the Ph.D. for creative writing in lieu of a research dissertation since 1930 or 1931, but currently admits relatively few applicants to this program because the academic requirements take up
more of the writers' time than they are willing to devote to it. This
broadening of the concept of the philosophy degree has never caught
on elsewhere. Gates noted (1929, quoted in Atkinson, 1945) that
some such title as *Doctor of Creative Writing* would be more suitable for recognizing distinguished plays or novels than the Ph.D.
A similar concept is at least one of the undercurrents in the interest
of English faculty in the Doctor of Arts degree. The one specific
proposal that has come to our attention, however, is the 1969 report
of an ad hoc committee on new graduate programs in the humanities at Yale which recommends the Doctor of Literary Arts (D.L.A.)
degree for students who complete the regular Ph.D. program up to
the dissertation (i.e., who qualify for the M.Phil.) and who have
achieved public recognition as creative writers by virtue of their
published work after a period of not less than two years. The degree is intended to recognize "work of serious artistic merit comparable in quality and substance to the Ph.D. dissertation and
. . . establish the young scholar-writer as a person qualified to
teach literature, either on its academic or creative side, at the college
and university level. While poetry, fiction, and drama are the forms
principally had in view, the proposal would not exclude biography,
history, criticism, translation from foreign languages, and other
forms of expository or interpretive writing which, while not qualifying as original research, present their materials in a literary form
of more than usual interest."

We see nothing wrong with, and much to commend, high-quality
doctorates in the creative arts such as the established Doctor of
Musical Arts and the suggested Doctor of Literary Arts degrees.
The concepts on which they are based could well be applied to other
fields of creativity.

DOCTOR OF EDUCATION The degree Doctor of Education (Ed.D.) was established by Harvard University in 1920 as a professional degree administered by
the School of Education, rather than by the graduate school. In
the half century following, the Doctor of Education degree has been
adopted by perhaps a hundred institutions (Eells, 1963) with considerable variation in pattern.

Basically, the Ed.D. is a parallel degree to the Ph.D., has similar
requirements, and is grouped with the Ph.D. in graduate school

statistics. It has usually been set up by schools of education as a means of avoiding the too literal application of the essentially alien standards imposed by the dominant graduate faculty from the older and more traditional disciplines (Hollis, 1945). Whether correctly or not, students and faculty alike regard the Ed.D. as an inferior Ph.D. and will opt for the latter if given the choice, settling for the former only when that is the only possible doctoral award.

The reasons for establishing the alternate doctorate in education are various. For one, a Doctor of Education program administered by the school of education allows the admission of students considered as competent and promising by the faculty in education but whose academic qualifications are such that they cannot be admitted by the graduate school controlling the Ph.D. program. This is the case at Teachers College, Columbia University, where Ed.D. applicants can be admitted directly by the college instead of through the Graduate School of Columbia University as is the case for Ph.D. students.

A second reason for the two tracks is as a means of circumventing the foreign language requirement of the graduate school. In a study of the doctorate in education by the American Association of Colleges for Teacher Education cited by Eells (1963), most institutions giving this degree had no language requirement in contrast to the parallel Ph.D. programs on the same campus.

The third common function of the Ed.D. is to provide for a wider range of independent projects than is possible under the traditional Ph.D. requirement of a dissertation based upon original research. In the AACTE study, a number of universities reported that they accepted, in lieu of the dissertation for the Ed.D., a field study or some other extensive terminal project.

The fourth use of the Ed.D. is to provide a doctorate in a subject-matter field for students who successfully pass the comprehensive examinations for the Ph.D. but who submit an expository dissertation on some aspect of teaching that subject rather than a research dissertation on the subject itself. For example, at the University of Michigan, where students working in the School of Education normally elect the Ph.D., the Ed.D. is more commonly taken by students in English, mathematics, and music who take a few hours of professional education courses and write a pedagogical thesis.

A fifth objective that can be accomplished with the Ed.D. degree is the reduction of the time required to earn the doctorate. Occasionally, this shows up in the formal degree requirements. The

University of Toronto, for example, is phasing out its Doctor of Education program which had a one-year residence requirement in favor of the Doctor of Philosophy with a two-year residence requirement. The real saving of time in the Ed.D. program, however, lies in the fact that a student coming back to graduate school from employment in a public school system can often meet the Ed.D. requirements more quickly than he can meet superficially equivalent requirements for the Ph.D.[1]

All of the above reasons contribute to making the Ed.D. a second-class Ph.D. and to the generally low status that the Doctor of Education degree has in the academic world. All, in effect, do set lower standards and provide an easier out.

Nonetheless, we should not forget that education is a valid field of study in its own right and that it is one of the most important professions in our country. While there seems to be little justification for the Ed.D. as a second-class Ph.D., there is every justification for a truly professional Doctor of Education program as challenging and as difficult in its own way as the Doctor of Philosophy. Schools of education are beginning to move on this affirmative note to salvage the degree. For instance, at Teachers College, Columbia, a deliberate effort is being made to design the Ed.D. for administrators and practitioners and to accept quality dissertations based upon an evaluation or assessment of educational experience, the demonstrated ability to effectively utilize the results of research such as by an analysis or survey of research, or theory building from comparative studies or case histories.

Our recommendations are simple. We condemn any practice of granting the Ed.D. as a second-class Ph.D. on similar but lower standards. We argue strongly, however, for a purely professional Ed.D. program, clearly oriented to the profession of education rather than to subject-matter fields and administered in every respect as rigorously as the parallel Ph.D. in the academic disciplines.

DOCTORAL PROGRAMS FOR COLLEGE TEACHERS Most Doctors of Philosophy and Doctors of Education do indeed pursue careers as college teachers. Since these traditional degrees are primarily research oriented, however, they have come under heavy attack over the last 20 years on the grounds that they do not appropriately and efficiently train teachers as opposed to university faculty (McGrath, 1959; Carmichael, 1961).

[1] Education faculties will accept the student's previous course work and experience as counting against an Ed.D. to a greater extent than will faculties supervising Ph.D. programs.

As we have already pointed out in our chapter on the Ph.D., the two alternatives in providing doctoral programs for college teachers are, first, to broaden the concept and structure of the Ph.D. and, second, to create new parallel degrees specifically designed to attract and train individuals who wish to make a career of teaching undergraduates rather than those who are willing to teach undergraduates in order to work as a scholar on a university campus. In effect, the choice is political. If the graduate faculty can be persuaded to broaden its concept of what constitutes research, the Ph.D. can be successfully broadened. If not, a new degree must be created and the graduate school is faced with the alternate problem of invidious distinction in turning out two different kinds of doctorates. We prefer the former solution but fear we shall have to settle for the latter.

The teaching doctorate is at least a three-year program in contrast to the intermediate degree program for the training of college teachers (Chapter 9) which is from two to three years in length. The teaching doctorate can have the same general requirements as the Ph.D. up to the passing of the comprehensive examination and the admission to candidacy. It would be quite appropriate to grant the same certificate or degree at this point to all students without regard to whether they will opt for a research dissertation leading to the Ph.D. or an expository thesis leading to the teaching doctorate. Ideally, in order to avoid the development of invidious comparisons, any requirements for the teaching doctorate such as a supervised teaching internship and an exposure to courses dealing with the problems of college teaching should be added on to the requirements for the Ph.D. rather than being substituted for Ph.D. requirements that might be considered more difficult or time-consuming. In any event, virtually all proposals for new doctorates training college teachers call for the two inputs of supervised teaching and a modicum of professional courses in higher education.

Nomenclature is a problem. Possibly the most ingeneous suggestion is that of Carmichael (1961) mentioned in the previous chapter that the title *Doctor of Philosophy* be used for both programs of study, with that involving the research dissertation being abbreviated Ph.D. and that with the expository dissertation being termed D.Phil. Another noteworthy suggestion is that of Barzun (1968) that the Doctor of Philosophy be granted on passing the comprehensive examination and that a second Doctor of Philosophy with honors be awarded if and when the candidate ever writes an acceptable dissertation. Both suggestions attempt to solve the nomenclatural problem by making the invidious distinction in the foot-note rather than in the text. The distinction is there just the same and will be recognized as such.

This objection is at least partially met by the proposal of Ralph W. Gerard[2] to reserve the title *Doctor of Philosophy* for doctoral programs which involve demonstrations both of mastery in research (through the dissertation) and in teaching. Separate doctoral titles would be assigned to recognize programs which lack either component. Gerard suggests *Doctor of Arts* for the teaching degree and *Doctor of Science* for the research degree. He goes on to say that "if competence in teaching as well as in research is expected of the Ph.D., such competence should be tested if the requirement is to be taken seriously. . . . The student might be required to conduct an actual class before examiners (somewhat corresponding to the completion of a successful research thesis), might be given an oral examination on teaching problems (something like the thesis oral), or might be subjected to any other evaluation procedure deemed appropriate."

We prefer solutions which face the issue and present new names in the hope that sooner or later they will become respectable and perhaps even legitimate. These fall into two categories: the first is one in which multiple doctorates are created to designate the teaching doctorate and the second is the proposal that the teaching degree be known as Doctor of Arts. Although the concepts are much the same, we shall treat the two separately.

MULTIPLE DOCTORATES One notable attempt to create a parallel doctorate for the preparation of college teachers was that of Syracuse University, whose Maxwell Graduate School of Citizenship and Public Affairs offered the Doctor of Social Sciences degree from 1945 to 1969. During this period, some 170 degrees were awarded. Generally successful in its earlier years, it became the largest interdisciplinary program in the graduate school. The degree title has been discontinued, however, and has been replaced by the Ph.D. Furthermore, holders of the Doctor of Social Science can now trade in their degree for the Doctor of Philosophy if they so wish.

A more general solution has recently been proposed by Fred F. Harcleroad[3] who suggests that the Doctor of Philosophy degree be

[2] Personal communication, May 2, 1969.

[3] 24th Annual National Conference on Higher Education, Chicago, Illinois, March 3, 1959.

restricted to its original function as a research degree and that students who are primarily interested in applying their knowledge through teaching or public service should take the appropriate divisional degree from among the Doctor of Science, Doctor of Social Science, Doctor of Fine Arts, and Doctor of Humanities.

Still another solution is to give the doctor's degree in each discipline; for example, Doctor of Mathematics, Doctor of Physics.

We are totally unenthusiastic about these suggestions because on principle we are opposed to the multiplication of degree titles. Furthermore, all of the titles suggested by Harcleroad are established honorary degree titles, and in our view are thus disqualified for use as earned degrees.

DOCTOR OF ARTS

We now come to the proposal that the degree Doctor of Arts (D.A.) be awarded in lieu of the Doctor of Philosophy for a doctoral program of at least three years in length which emphasizes in its recruitment and requirements the preparation for a career as college teachers and which accepts an expository thesis in lieu of the conventional research dissertation.

As far as we can determine, current interest in this proposal has developed from the concern in the field of mathematics that the rigors of the research dissertation in that field preclude many excellent and needed teachers from obtaining the doctorate and thus from finding satisfactory permanent employment in our colleges and universities. A committee of the Mathematical Association of America addressed itself to this problem in 1935 and recommended that two types of doctorates be offered: first, the conventional research doctorate and, second, a teaching doctorate. This latter program would be characterized by additional course work in mathematics and related fields with emphasis on breadth of training, one or more expository papers giving evidence of the candidate's ability to learn independently and to present known mathematical results in good written form, and a major thesis which need not demonstrate research ability but rather a mastery of some field of mathematics and expository ability of a high order. The 1935 committee recommended that either the Ph.D. be given for both types of programs or, alternatively, that the title *Doctor of Mathematics* be given for the second.

The concept was revived with a joint committee of the American Mathematical Society and the Mathematical Association of America which recommended (Moise, 1961) that the teaching doctorate be established and suggested the name *Doctor of Arts.* Both sponsoring organizations approved the report in principle, while the Association's board of governors approved a motion that the preferred name for the new degree be *Doctor of Arts.* According to Moise the distinguishing feature of this new doctorate would be that "the creative dissertation [would] be replaced by a scholarly dissertation which could be historical, critical, or philosophical in nature. Here the idea of historical dissertations is intended by all means to include studies of recent mathematical developments. Whatever the thesis topic may be, the course-work should be adequate to enable the student to read current research literature."

As of 1969, Dartmouth will accept an expository dissertation for the Ph.D. in mathematics, while Carnegie-Mellon University offers the Doctor of Arts program in mathematics on a basis which is identical in all respects to the Ph.D. except for the dissertation. Other mathematics departments blow hot and cold on the concept as the job market for their graduates fluctuates.

The other academic area that has long been interested in the Doctor of Arts degree is English. The reasons here are somewhat different from those in mathematics, being primarily that many potential teachers in English are simply uninterested in the dry and pedantic nature of the task of writing the conventional research dissertation. Humanists have long argued that the very concept of the Ph.D. is anathema to many of those who should be occupying university chairs.

One proposal is that of Fredson Bowers (see Chapter 8), that the Doctor of Arts be granted as an intermediate degree on passing the comprehensive examination. Another is that of Yale's faculty (discussed above), that a Doctor of Literary Arts be awarded in recognition of distinguished published creative effort. As far as we can ascertain, the only institution currently giving the Doctor of Arts in English is Carnegie-Mellon.

At Carnegie-Mellon University, the Doctor of Arts is currently offered in English, history, mathematics, music, and the visual arts. Of these, only mathematics also offers the Ph.D. In that department, the D.A. differs from the Ph.D. only in the nature of the thesis.

In English, the D.A. program at Carnegie-Mellon requires two academic years beyond the bachelor's degree with the M.A. being granted after the first. There are no language requirements. The doctoral dissertation may grow out of either traditional literary research or applied curricular or pedagogical investigation and should relate literary scholarship to the teaching of literature. The requirements are similar in history where the dissertation is based primarily upon curriculum research and should consist of an original application of existing historical knowledge. In music and fine arts, the D.A. course is planned for students who have come through a professional master's program stressing creativity rather than scholarship and is designed to give them a sufficient overburden of subject-matter courses so that they can teach generally at the college level in the field of history of art or music appreciation. In these fields, the D.A. virtually becomes a four-year program as it involves two years and dissertation on top of what is normally a two-year professional performance program to begin with.

Our impression is that the Doctor of Arts programs at Carnegie-Mellon in mathematics, music, and the fine arts are at the doctor's level. In the humanities the parallel programs are essentially designed, by departments which do not offer the Ph.D., to upgrade secondary school and junior high school teachers in programs stressing curriculum development rather than scholarship.

Interest in the Doctor of Arts degree is widespread. The pros and cons of a teaching doctorate parallel to the Ph.D. are under discussion at many major institutions, among them Illinois, Wisconsin, and University of Washington. After a thorough study, the Coordinating Council for Higher Education of the State of California (1968) recommended not establishing the Doctor of Arts degree.

We take the position that it is preferable to meet the legitimate demands for a doctoral program better suited to the preparation of college teachers through the shortening, better structuring, and broadening of the Ph.D. rather than by creating a new degree. For institutions that cannot or choose not to do this, though, we recommend the Doctor of Arts in parallel to the Ph.D. and warn against its development as an inferior degree, particularly by departments which do not also offer the Ph.D. option.

If the Doctor of Arts is to be established, we suggest the general application of the principles laid out by Douglas S. Allen (1968) for the field of chemistry. He recommends that the program for all doctoral students should be the same for the first two years in that all would complete the same course work and take the same examinations irrespective of a teaching or research objective. All should carry out a research project during this period. After receiving the intermediate degree, the prospective college teacher would spend a third and usually final year of study. In chemistry, Allen suggests that during this period the student would prepare a modest thesis based upon his research, develop a review paper in collaboration with a research scientist, undertake a study in the history and philosophy of science, undertake a teaching internship, become knowledgeable concerning modern instructional media, and broaden his exposure to allied disciplines. If similar requirements could be developed for other fields of study, the Doctor of Arts or comparable teaching degree would not be a second-class degree and should attract numbers of high-quality students committed to a career in college teaching. Allen suggests that the degree given in chemistry be entitled Doctor of Science.

DOCTOR OF SCIENCE Repeated suggestions have been made that the teaching doctorate in science parallel to the Doctor of Arts should be the Doctor of Science (D.Sc.). In view of the existing practice in the United States to offer both the bachelor's and the master's degree in both science and the arts, nothing could be more logical. Established usage for the Doctor of Science degree, however, argues against this proposed practice.

We have already pointed out that in England, the faculties of science and the arts are separate. There, it is clearly desirable to assign the bachelor's and master's degree in arts to one faculty and the same degrees in science to the other. A similar distinction is possible in western European countries where programs taken under different faculties can be identified with differently named degrees.

These were the conditions under which the doctor's degree was introduced to several American universities. Harvard, for example, introduced the Ph.D. through its faculty of arts and the D.Sc. through its faculty of science at the same time in 1872. Princeton and Cornell also offered both degrees, while Chicago provides an example of an institution which has stuck to one earned doctorate (Ph.D.) despite considerable faculty debate on the subject.

Over the years, however, several usages have developed. In the United States, faculties of arts and sciences have been combined and have agreed upon only one earned doctorate in the traditional arts and sciences, that being the Ph.D. As of 1960, Eells and Haswell report only eight institutions offering the D.Sc. These are predominantly engineering schools and only MIT among them gives the degree with any regularity. The merging of the two degrees into the Ph.D. was a natural result of the merging of the separate faculties of arts and sciences into a combined faculty of the liberal arts. At the present time, therefore, the practice of giving only one doctorate, the Ph.D., is more logical than the residual practice of giving separate bachelor's and master's degrees in the arts and in the sciences.

Over the same period, the D.Sc. in the United States has become an honorary degree. More than 200 institutions offer it in this manner.

In England and other Commonwealth countries, the Doctor of Science has become the higher doctorate, earned years after the completion of the Ph.D. through the submission of the body of one's published work to the university with which the scientist is most closely related. Doctoral candidates from these countries studying in the United States, therefore, naturally opt for the D.Sc. rather than the Ph.D. if given a choice. At home, the former is the higher degree and its initials carry very much higher status without any explanations needing to be made. Other countries follow this same practice. The approximate equivalent of the American Ph.D. in the U.S.S.R. is the Candidate in Science, while the Doctor of Science there is granted at the height of the scholar's career on the basis of his published work.

Because the title *Doctor of Science* has been preempted in the United States as an honorary degree and in Europe as a higher doctorate, we do not recommend its adoption as an earned teaching degree. It is not good practice to use the same degree title in two senses. In this case, it would be downright misleading.

PROFESSIONAL DOCTORATES

The original learned professions of the Middle Ages were theology, law, and medicine. Thus the term *profession* became in the scholarly world an antonym for arts or philosophy, and the professional doctorates were those in the learned professions in contradistinction to the doctorate in philosophy. Certainly, the distinction is of limited importance today as the Ph.D. is clearly a professional degree in any sense of the word, and we are becoming increasingly aware of the illogicalness of such dichotomies as between pure and applied science or between professional and philosophical studies. Nonetheless, the professional doctorates provide a useful category to discuss doctoral degrees named otherwise than arts, sciences, or philosophy and granted on the recommendation of faculties other than those in the traditional arts and sciences.

Professional doctorates fall into two general groups: the first are in the newer professional fields that are more or less allied with the arts and sciences (e.g., engineering, business administration); the second are those given in the traditional *learned* professions (medicine, theology, and law) and in professions that have spun off from them.

The graduate school associations have published a joint statement on the doctor's degree in professional fields which briefly summarizes practices and desirable standards (Council of Graduate Schools in the United States, 1966).

In the first group, most institutions give the Ph.D., others give a professional doctorate, and still others give both—the one for a research doctorate and the other for a professional doctorate. Examples would be education, where we have already discussed the differences between the Ph.D. and the Ed.D.; engineering, discussed later; business administration, where 10 schools offer the Doctor of Business Administration and the great majority offer the Ph.D.; public administration, where the Doctor of Public Administration is similarly used at four institutions; and social work, a field in which five schools offer the Doctor of Social Work.

In the learned professions, the professional doctorate has in general much higher status and is the predominant degree. This is particulary true in the health sciences where the Doctor of Medicine degree is so dominant that it has become synonymous with the title *doctor* in the minds of professionals and laymen alike. The Doctor of Dental Surgery degree is also well established. Other professional doctorates in the health sciences of various degrees of difficulty and professional status are Doctor of Public Health, Doctor of Veterinary Medicine, Doctor of Osteopathy, Doctor of Optometry, and Doctor of Pharmacy. In law and theology, the first professional degree has traditionally been the bachelor's. In law in the United States, however, the doctor's degree Juris Doctor (Doctor of Jurisprudence) is currently being substituted for the baccalaureate. A similar movement is under way in theology.

Several of the professional doctor's degrees may be earned in less than seven years by acceptance of the student into the professional school after only two to three years of liberal arts. While the graduate professional program may require four years, the reduction of the preparatory liberal arts program from four to two or three years results in reducing the total time period involved. This occurs commonly in dentistry and to a lesser extent in medicine and law.

Engineering Engineering provides an example of the professions allied to the arts and sciences where the Ph.D. has high prestige. Only a few engineering schools have chosen to offer the Doctor of Engineering degree. Nonetheless, the 1968 report of the Goals Committee of the American Society for Engineering Education concluded that the benefits of the Doctor of Engineering degree could be both practical and symbolic in that its adoption by the engineering faculty would free it from the restraints of university-wide graduate schools. At the University of California, Berkeley, though, where the two alternative doctorates are offered, only about 10 percent have elected the Doctor of Engineering degree. We agree with the implications of the Goals Committee report that a Doctor of Engineering degree offered by the faculty of engineering will continue to have lower status and acceptance than the Ph.D. in an engineering field offered through the graduate school. The same conclusion will apply to most other professional fields.

Medicine In medicine, the conventional four-year postbaccalaureate program leads to the Doctor of Medicine degree. The physician interested in pursuing a career in the basic medical sciences will usually either study initially for the Ph.D. or will take the Ph.D. as a second doctorate after he has completed his M.D. training.

The Association of American Medical Colleges is currently completing a study of curricular development in medical schools in Canada and the United States. Quite obviously, the medical faculties are becoming increasingly concerned with the long period of medical training, the desirability of providing greater flexibility in the medical curriculum, and the need for catering to the increasing social awareness of the medical student.

The recommendations arising from the study were adopted by the AAMC executive council on November 1, 1968. They include the overriding recommendation that medical schools must actively revise the content and methods used in the total span of the education of the physician so that his professional competence will be most relevant to meeting the changing health needs of the people. With regard to curriculum, the recommendations were that medical schools must individualize the education of the physician and that new curricula should be developed by interdepartmental groups rather than by faculty.

A large number of medical schools (about 45) have curricula which permit students to work toward the M.D. and the Ph.D. at the same time with some saving of total effort and total elapsed time. Only seven, however, have as many as 10 students currently enrolled in such a program. These are Chicago, New York University, Northwestern, Minnesota, Indiana, Baylor, and Albert Einstein.

This is not the place for a full discussion of these important issues. We should mention, however, the radical reorganization of the presentation of medical knowledge to students initiated by Case-Western Reserve, the substantial increase in electives at Harvard and other schools, and the trend toward combined B.A.-M.D. curricula permitting ambitious and select students to reduce the conventional eight-year period needed for these two degrees to six or even five. Some four or five schools have adopted these combined curricula. Most, however, simply cram the undergraduate through this bachelor's program with around-the-seasons study before and during the preclinical phases of medical school and have little effected the medical curriculum itself. There seems no question but that an academically defensible combined curriculum is possible if the undergraduate and medical faculties can work together to design a single combined curriculum in which the teaching of such subjects as organic and biological chemistry and of basic and human biology are integrated into single sequences and if training in the liberal arts and in medicine can be carried out contemporaneously throughout most of the five- or six-year combined curriculum.

Dentistry The professional degree in dentistry is Doctor of Dental Surgery. Many dentists, however, continue their studies to the Master of Science degree in a clinical field, and some go on to the Doctor of Philosophy in a related basic science. The general status of graduate education in the sciences related to dentistry is available in the report of a recent workshop on that subject (American Association of Dental Schools, 1969). Consensus was reached that the master's degree in clinical areas should not be considered as a terminal degree, that research and thesis should be emphasized in master's programs to a greater extent, and that the scope of advanced programs in dentistry needs to be broadened and upgraded. The participants in the workshop encouraged the development of combined Ph.D.-D.D.S. programs.

Theology The matter of degree nomenclature in theological education is under active consideration by the American Association of Theological Schools.[4] The trend is toward raising the title of the first professional degree. Nearly one-third of the accredited seminaries award the degree Master of Divinity (M.Div.) for essentially the same three-year program as for the Bachelor of Divinity (B.D.). Meanwhile, some schools have moved toward a four- or five-year professional doctoral program for the Doctor of Religion (D.Rel.), Doctor of Ministry (D.Min.), or Doctor of Divinity degree. The first two names are newly coined while the last is widely granted as an honorary degree.

In religion and theology, the Master of Sacred Theology (S.T.M.), Master of Theology (Th.M.), and Doctor of Theology (Th.D.) are utilized primarily as research degrees, earned subsequent to the completion of the first professional degree.

[4] Personal communication, Richard L. Rising, July 7, 1969.

12. Postdoctoral Recognition

Formal postdoctoral study has grown phenomenally. Beyond that, the expectation that scholars will continue to carry out research and publish the results of their investigations continues to rise. How should postdoctoral scholarly activities be recognized? Traditionally, we have done this in America through the conferring of higher academic rank, higher classes of membership in scholarly societies, election to national honorary bodies, the awarding of medals and prizes, and the bestowing of honorary degrees. Besides considering these briefly, we must address ourselves to the additional possibility of instituting a higher level of doctoral degrees on the well-established European models.

Should the Ph.D. be the highest earned degree in American graduate education? One can raise this question only with the greatest of trepidation for the principle that the Ph.D. should be the highest earned degree is solidly entrenched in the dogma of the graduate school in the United States. When the earned doctorate was introduced by Yale in 1861, that institution chose the Ph.D. over the science faculty recommendations of the D.Sc. Other institutions offered the alternative doctorate but, before long, the Ph.D. had clearly won the distinction of being not only the highest degree but also the only highest degree that would be awarded.

In 1924, the Association of American Universities formally resolved that the Ph.D. should be the highest earned degree in the arts and sciences and that higher doctorates should not be awarded:

The Association of American Universities considers the establishment of higher degrees above or in place of the Ph.D., M.D., J.D., Ed.D., D.P.H. inadvisable and detrimental to the standards and prestige of these degrees and reaffirms its previously pronounced policy that the Ph.D. degree shall be open as a research degree in all fields of learning, pure and applied, and that for the accepted professional higher degrees a standard equivalent to that of the Ph.D. shall be maintained so that these higher professional degrees shall represent the highest type of university professional training.

It took much debate and battle over half a century to eliminate the honorary form of the Ph.D. and to establish this one degree as the hallmark of the research scholar. These gains are not lightly to be given away.

Why, then, should the issue be reopened? The reason is simply that the prevailing concept of the American Ph.D. today presents us with an unsolvable dilemma if only one doctorate is to be awarded. Whether we like it or not, it is the required credential for a university or major college professorship. At the same time, it is the highest honor that a faculty can bestow for research and scholarly productivity. These two characteristics are irreconcilable. Obviously, not everyone can attain the highest honors and yet this is what our present earned degree structure presumes. As W. S. Gilbert put it in the Gondoliers:

When ev'ryone is somebodee
Then no one's anybody.

There are two general solutions to this dilemma. The first is to create a separate doctorate or a lower degree to qualify the rank and file of college teachers. This has been discussed at length in previous chapters. Berelson (1960) aptly sums up the general failure of this approach over the past decades:

A broadened and enriched Master's has never caught on as a degree for college teachers mainly because it was not the doctorate, and the two-track system at the doctoral level has sooner or later come up against the question of which track would get the Ph.D. and what, then, the other would get.

This alternative is completely logical. It has not worked thus far although developments such as the emergence of the respectable intermediate degree in the liberal arts and pressures from two- and four-year colleges for better teacher preparation somewhat enhance its promise in the present day.

The second solution is to recognize that the Ph.D. has become accepted as defining a wide range of training and competence, that it represents high-level competence in both teaching and research in varying mixtures for different fields and different individuals, and that it should be awarded routinely in three or four years to a high percentage of qualified applicants, thus satisfying the job market. The second alternative is simpler, more pragmatic, and perhaps more feasible—although it runs counter to the argument of the academic pursuit that the Ph.D. is a research degree and that it should be conferred only upon the chosen few who have demonstrated real research accomplishment, regardless of how many years it has taken to do it.

If the second alternative is selected, then the possibility of a higher degree should be explored. If we accept the modern Ph.D. for what it has become—a general higher degree required of all prospective university faculty—then we open the doors to the possibility of recognizing a higher doctorate for those who continue on past the Ph.D. to distinguished scholarly accomplishment. In fact, such is the practice throughout most of the rest of the world. In the major British universities, for example, the D.Sc. or similar higher doctorate may be awarded to an individual who submits the body of his published work either to the faculty under which he worked as a student or to that with which he is currently associated. A review committee is appointed. Standards are both high and strictly enforced. Those approved have indeed earned the higher doctorate in the strictest sense. A similar practice exists in the U.S.S.R. and other Eastern bloc countries where the Candidate in Science is the highest degree earned on campus, and the Doctor in Science is awarded on the basis of published scholarly achievement much later, usually about the time a man is promoted to full professorship.

As a basis for exploring the possibility of introducing a higher doctorate in the United States, we should first take a brief look at the current development of postgraduate education, and then examine the various mechanisms by which we currently recognize scholarly accomplishment after the earning of the Ph.D.

POSTDOC-TORAL STUDY In the field of medicine, much of the training of the physician takes place after he earns the M.D., through internship, residency, and postgraduate study. A similar development has taken place for the more amorphous group whose careers are in the universities or in research outside of the universities, only their experiences are less formalized and the pattern of obtaining them less standardized. Through postdoctoral fellowships, term appointments at universities, sabbaticals, and leaves for public service, the university professor spends a good portion of his career in becoming better qualified as a scholar, in full-time research assignments, and in professional self-renewal.

The establishment of the Institute for Advanced Study at Princeton in 1933 symbolized formal acceptance of the concept of postdoctoral study in the United States. Prior to that, however, the National Research Fellowships (1919) and the Guggenheim Fellowships (1925) had provided off-campus study opportunities for many American scholars. Postdoctoral study came of age after World War II. Fellowships became more abundant with the ready availability of Fulbright Fellowships and the establishment of the National Science Foundation and National Institutes of Health postdoctoral fellowships. The supply of scholars available for postdoctoral study was increased by the affluence which permits universities to make sabbatical leaves a matter of course rather than an exception. The increasing use of university faculty in national and world public service added to the diversity of activity of the university scholar. By 1960, postdoctoral study had become an accepted part of our system of higher education, particularly in the physical and biological sciences. Berelson (1960) reports that more than 60 percent of the graduate faculty in the natural sciences felt that postdoctoral training was necessary or highly desirable for proper advancement. The population of American postdoctoral scholars in all fields was approximately 8 thousand in 1960 (Berelson, 1962).

More and more Ph.D.'s are obtaining postdoctoral fellowships to finance their first postdoctoral work activity. Data provided by the National Research Council (1968) indicate that 11 percent of all Ph.D.'s from 1963 to 1966 secured such appointments. The highest percentage was in the biological sciences (34 percent), followed by chemistry (32 percent), physics and astronomy (23 percent), health sciences (20 percent), psychology (12 percent), and earth sciences (11 percent).

The status of postdoctoral study in the United States has recently been surveyed by the National Research Council (1969). It was estimated that in the spring of 1967 there were approximately 16,000 postdoctorals including United States citizens either here or abroad and foreign citizens in the United States. The number had doubled since Berelson's study in 1960. Two-thirds are post-

Ph.D.'s and one-third post-M.D.'s. Over 90 percent are in the natural and health sciences.

Should these postdoctoral scholars have the opportunity of earning a higher doctorate, either while actively engaged in their research on a university campus or by submitting their published papers at a later date? The NRC study unearthed no interest across the country in a higher degree although it did turn up substantial interest throughout the country in better defining, classifying, and understanding the role of the postdoctoral scholar. The conclusion reached[1] was that the relationship between the postdoctoral scholar and his mentor at the host institution is sufficiently fragile that attempts to formalize the interaction would probably be destructive. This conclusion has been verified by most of the educators interviewed in our own study.

The evaluation of postdoctoral experience is conventionally based upon the individual's published work and the recommendations of those who best know him and his scholarly promise. It is difficult for many Americans to see how formal certification by a university would effectively summarize the evaluation process.

This brings us to mention that the vita of the mature scientist or scholar provides the data for the evaluation of his past performance in the same sense that the academic transcript summarizes his career as a student. The very fact of appointment to a postdoctoral fellowship or traineeship is significant, particularly when amplified by the particular award, the institution where the study was undertaken, the colleagues with whom the postdoctoral scholar worked, and the published results. Ultimate recognition is conferred by tenure appointment at a prestige institution, inclusion in *Who's Who in America,* election to fellowship rank in a scientific or scholarly society, senior postdoctoral appointments to such centers as the Institute for Advanced Study or the Center for Advanced Study in the Behavioral Sciences, etc. For the favored few in the right disciplines, recognition may come through election to the National Academy of Science or selection for a Pulitzer or even a Nobel Prize.

HIGHER DOCTORAL DEGREES The earned higher doctorate is well established in Europe (Chapter 13). In the United States, our experience with it has been extremely limited.

[1] Personal communication, Richard B. Curtis, April 14, 1969.

The University of Chicago announced the availability of an earned LL.D. in 1892, but withdrew the offer in 1895. That is the only early trail our desultory investigation has turned up.

More recently (1966) the New England Institute in Ridgefield, Connecticut, established an interdisciplinary postdoctoral program leading to the advanced degree of Doctor of Natural Philosophy (D.Nat.Phil.). The program is small, with three students in residence after two years of operation. Applicants must have the Ph.D., M.D., or equivalent. The candidate's background, interests, needs, and ultimate goals are considered by a general area committee (physical sciences, chemical sciences, or life sciences), after which tutorial assignments are made. After a period of intensive study of approximately 30 months during which periodic reviews of progress are made, the candidate will be examined for his mastery of the basic language, theory, and phenomenology, and some of the techniques of the other disciplines he has studied. If he demonstrates appropriate knowledge and understanding of the subject matter, he then undertakes an interdisciplinary thesis. His progress will be periodically reviewed, his completed thesis examined, and the higher doctoral degree awarded.

Since the program has been initiated, the institute[2] has been exploring how it should add some study requirements in social, behavioral, and communications sciences. Its purpose is to produce widely trained leaders in education and science who obviously require abilities outside the natural sciences to make them most effectual.

One other institution has received legal authority to grant the higher doctorate but has not as yet instituted the practice.[3] The Worcester Foundation for Experimental Biology at Shrewsbury, Massachusetts, has received from the Commonwealth of Massachusetts the right to grant the earned Doctor of Science degree to a selected group of postdoctoral students who come to the foundation with either the M.D. or the Ph.D. and who would like to have recognition for their stay. The desire for such formal recognition is especially strong for foreign postdoctoral scholars. That the Worcester Foundation has not put its program of study into operation is due to restrictions imposed by current fiscal regu-

[2] Personal communication, James H. Green, April 17, 1969.

[3] Personal communication, Hudson Hoagland, March 25, 1969.

lations of the National Institutes of Health rather than to any lack of interest on the part of students or of programs on the part of the foundation.

HONORARY DEGREES The line between an earned higher doctorate and the honorary degree is not a sharp one. As with the earned higher doctorate, the honorary doctorate may be bestowed on an individual in recognition of distinguished scholarship as evaluated by a jury of the faculty. The difference lies in that the spectrum of honorary degrees covers not only the recognition of scholarship but also the recognition of fame, public service, and philanthropy as well.

The imaginative creation of honorary doctoral titles is chronicled by Eells and Haswell (1960) and Eells (1963), and their uses and abuse have been surveyed by Epler (1943). The successful effort to stamp out the practice of giving the Ph.D. as an honorary degree is summarized by Lady (1967).

We repeat our recommendation in Chapter 2 that the choice of names for honorary degrees be greatly restricted and that increased effort be made by governing boards of our colleges and universities to follow national practice in using titles for honorary degrees completely different from those used for earned degrees. Certain honorary degree titles in the United States, however, might well be reserved in the future for earned doctorates. *Doctor of Science* and *Doctor of Arts* are cases in point.

RECOMMEN- DATIONS Quite clearly, there is little support in the United States at the present time for the establishment of higher earned doctoral programs and degrees. Neither the postdoctoral study of the National Research Council nor our own interviews across the country have turned up any ground swell in this matter.

Nonetheless, the higher doctorate is well established and of practical value in Europe. The experiments with it at small interdisciplinary research institutes in this country appear to have merit. More importantly, there is considerable logic in reopening the possibility, not for the purpose of adding to our hierarchal degree structure, but rather as an upper force that will exert pressure to compress the Ph.D. program into more manageable form.

Such are the import of several recent proposals. One is Barzun's (1968) suggestion that the Ph.D. be granted on the passing of the comprehensive examinations and that a second Ph.D. with honors be awarded on the successful submission of a thesis. Carl Kaysen[4] comes up with the same idea but in a lower key, picking up the Russian idea that the candidate's degree completes education and the preparation for a professional career in the university, with the research scientist submitting his published work back to the original faculty at a later date for the appropriate doctor's degree. More generally, the concept of two levels of doctoral recognition is implicit in the hopes of many that students electing a Doctor of Arts program and thus qualifying for a career teaching undergraduates can convert their degree to the Ph.D. at a later date by submitting a successful research dissertation, and thus become certified to move up into a university post. This implication, however, is directly contrary to the explicity provision of these same advocates that the Doctor of Arts should be equal to and have the same status as the Doctor of Philosophy.

In effect, all of the above proposals call for the establishment of two levels of doctorate and differ simply in whether the magic letters Ph.D. are assigned to the first, to the second, or to both levels.

We think it unlikely that the Ph.D. can be reserved for the higher doctorate. Its use as the general doctoral degree qualifying for a wide range of research and teaching positions is too thoroughly established.

We also think it unwise to degrade the Ph.D. below a three- to four-year program incorporating the demonstration of a substantial competence in independent scholarship. Devaluation of our currency seldom solves our problems.

In the belief the Ph.D. should be structured as a high-quality program involving four years of study past the baccalaureate for the average, able student, we have already recommended the establishment of a general liberal arts degree at a level intermediate between the master's and the doctor's. We find similar merit in the possibility of higher doctorates which can be earned through the submission of published works to the faculty from which the Ph.D. was earned. By so bracketing the Ph.D. between a lower degree which recognizes the completion of the general studies phase of graduate education and a higher degree which takes the pressure off the necessity for a long and drawn-out Ph.D. dissertation, we

[4] Interview, September 19, 1968.

may well end up with a stronger and more compact Ph.D. program in the United States.

Since our present climate is not propitious for a major development of post-Ph.D. degree programs, we recommend continued experimentation and probing along the lines of the programs at the New England Institute and the Worcester Foundation for Experimental Biology.

Regarding names, we recommend that the generic *Doctor of Natural Philosophy* might do well for all fields of learning. An acceptable alternative would be the English pattern of *Doctor of Science* (D.Sc.) and *Doctor of Letters* (D.Litt.). Whatever degree titles are chosen, they should be reserved for this purpose and cease to be used as honorary degrees.

13. Degree Structures in Selected European Countries

Academic degree structures in the United States derive historically from those in Europe, particularly from Great Britain and Germany. Although the bachelor's, master's, and doctor's programs in the United States differ substantially from similarly named programs in western Europe, their comparative study is of mutual interest, not only because of the traditional American interest in learning from our European antecedents, but also because of developing European needs for the democratization and modernization of its systems of higher education.

Although we have surveyed the pertinent literature and have spent time visiting European institutions, we make no pretense with regard to expertise or exhaustive study on these matters. The best source of general information on higher education in other countries is Volume IV of the *World Survey of Education* published by UNESCO (1966). The Organization for Economic Cooperation and Development (OECD) in Paris is completing a series of studies on innovation in higher education in selected countries which is particularly relevant to the development of academic degree structures.

The western European universities for the most part are more restricted to the traditional faculties and disciplines than are their American counterparts. Thus, they commonly have faculties of arts, sciences, law, theology, and medicine although the pattern differs from country to country. Engineering is usually taught in separate institutions. The technological universities of England, *grandes écoles* of France, and *Technische Hochschulen* of Germany have generally achieved university status and are awarding degrees or comparable diplomas. Teacher-training institutions are also generally separate from the universities and are beginning to evolve toward comparable status.

In summarizing the very complex problems of making comparisons between different national educational systems with regard to equivalence, we have avoided any subjective judgments as to quality or intellectual equivalence and have contented ourselves with citing the number of years at each level and the theoretical age at entrance or completion as summarized by Cramer and Browne (1965) and King (1967).

ENGLAND AND WALES Higher education in the United Kingdom today is changing rapidly.[1] Since World War II, great enhanced opportunities have been made available to students from a broader range of social classes through the opening of a number of new universities, the movement of the technological institutions to university status, and a whole series of internal changes evolving from the Robbins report of 1963 and a more recent series of studies dealing with national needs and employment patterns of scientists and technologists.[2] The rethinking of the role of higher education has resulted in some changes in the nature and structure of the traditional academic degrees.

Great Britain has traditionally provided a superior system of higher education for a limited percentage of its youths who are admitted to grammar schools at age 11, or to "public schools," and who distinguish themselves in a successive series of examinations through to the gaining of the baccalaureate (in Scotland, the master's degree) without blemish or failure. The problem has been to democratize educational opportunities and to provide second opportunities for those who have had the misfortune to falter at one of the many hurdles on the way.

Secondary school students who perform well on their O-level (ordinary) examinations after 11 years of schooling at age 16 enter the sixth form for two years before taking their A-level (advanced) examinations. University entrance is so competitive that most must specialize throughout their late secondary school years to attain honors in the three A-level subjects that are necessary for admission to the curriculum they wish to pursue.

[1] Recent books dealing with British higher education include Brook (1965), Robbins (1966), Beloff (1968), Lawlor (1968), and Layard, King, and Moser (1969). See also Hare (1966), Anderson (1968), Gallie (1960), Daiches (1964), and Lukes (1967).

[2] Identified by the name of the chairman and by the command numbers of Her Majesty's Stationery Office as Robbins (Cmnd. 2154), Jones (Cmnd. 3417), Dainton (Cmnd. 3541), and Swann (Cmnd. 3760).

The Bachelor's Degree In England and Wales, the university student works three years for the Bachelor of Arts degree. Since success depends solely upon the final examination, the student must devote full time to his studies and progress directly through the university if he is to survive the competition. First-class honors virtually guarantee a distinguished future. Upper-second-class honors normally permit advanced study. Lower-second, third, or pass performance spell the end of university experience. Many variations exist, tradition being particularly strong at the old universities of Oxford and Cambridge.

In England and Wales the traditional course of study is highly specialized. At its conclusion, the student will have been trained well in his main discipline and perhaps in one or two ancillary subjects. The English student may or may not have obtained a general education in the sixth form depending upon the extent to which he concentrated there on his proposed university subjects in order to obtain university entrance.

Of major concern in the British universities today is the question of broadening the base of the baccalaureate program. In Scotland the first degree is Master of Arts, the earning of which normally requires four years and includes a broader spectrum of study than the English B.A. The University of Keele has for a number of years offered a four-year baccalaureate curriculum with one year of general studies, but the guidelines of the University Grants Committee for establishing the newest universities call for three-year undergraduate programs. There is a feeling against a generalized first degree in England, but it is breaking down. The trend today is to at least offer the undergraduate the opportunity to spread his studies over a broader field. Cambridge has in fact a rather broad science degree in contrast to Oxford or London where the student tends to study only chemistry or physics or mathematics. At Cambridge, the student in science takes several subjects during his first two years and does not concentrate upon a single one until his third year.

Although the English baccalaureate has been granted solely on the basis of the student's performance on the final examination, this practice is increasingly being reappraised. The University of London is developing a unit system in the sciences similar to the Harvard course system to permit the student to elect 9 to 12 units, over a three-year undergraduate period, in which they are examined independently in addition to the final general honors examination.

This system is designed to emphasize that a broad curriculum can be just as high quality as a narrow curriculum in a single subject. Traditionally, the broad baccalaureate program has been considered inferior.

At the University of Sussex, students in the arts and social studies are exposed to a broad B.A. program. Of the nine papers required for the final examinations, only five are in the major subject while four are in contextual subjects related to the major. Furthermore, students elect their majors from schools which are interdisciplinary in nature: African and Asian studies, educational studies, English and American studies, European studies, and social studies. While a student in several of these schools may major in economics, his contextual subjects will be different in each case. Efforts to broaden the opportunities for nonspecialist study in the undergraduate curricula of the new universities in England have been summarized by Campbell (1966).

In the field of engineering, students at the colleges of advanced technology (CATs) could not earn degrees until the National Council for Technological Awards was established with the power to grant the Diploma in Technology (Dip.Tech.) after a four-year "sandwich" or work-study, course. The first Dip.Tech. was awarded at what is now the University of Aston in 1958. The higher degree recognized at this time was Membership in the College of Technologists (M.C.T.). Neither degree was particularly successful. Probably not more than 20 of the latter were ever awarded. With the movement of the CATs to university status on the recommendation of the Robbins report they now grant the B.Sc., the M.Sc., and the Ph.D.

Students at teacher-training institutions do not earn degrees. Under a new arrangement, however, these institutions are now colleges of education, and each is affiliated with a nearby university through an Institute of Education. The Institute of Education at the University of London, for instance, is a federation of the university department of education with some 34 small colleges of education in the area. It performs several functions. First, it trains graduates with the regular B.A. degree from the university for careers as secondary school teachers. This one-year course, similar to the American M.A.T. program, leads to a graduate certificate of education. A second function of the institute is to provide a fourth-year program so that the best of the three-year graduates of the colleges of education can continue on for a fourth year at their college but under the supervision of the institute and receive the Bachelor of Education (B.Ed.) degree from the university.

One highly speculative proposal for the reform of degree structures in British universities has been put forward by A. B. Pippard (1968), professor of physics at Cambridge, who proposes changing the present pattern of three years for the bachelor's degree and one year for the master's to two years for each. Pippard suggests that the first two years should be rather light, leaving ample time for extracurricular activities and for the general process of maturation that takes place in the university. It should suffice for most students who aspire to a university education. The next two years leading to the master's degree should be really tough and so difficult that only a small percentage of students will elect to try it. Pippard believes that by compressing the undergraduate program into two years, more students could be handled in the university and less reliance would have to be placed on other institutions (such as the polytechnic colleges and other colleges of further education) to take care of the overload.

Master's Degree

The degree Master of Arts (M.A.) is routinely granted at Oxford and Cambridge without additional university work past the baccalaureate. Elsewhere, however, it and the companion Master of Science (M.Sc.) have been given as a one- to two-year research degree on the completion of a satisfactory thesis. A recent major trend in England has been toward a master's degree in course based upon advanced course work analogous to the American master's degree. Along with the broadening of the baccalaureate, this development has been the major innovation in recent English degree structure.

Nomenclature of the master's degree in England has not become standardized so that one must interpret the particular degree only from a knowledge of the individual institution. In general, the M.A. and M.Sc. are now predominantly degrees based upon the completion of advanced course work, while other master's degrees are increasingly given for research short of that expected for the Ph.D. As in the United States, the master's degree fulfills several functions. For some the master's program provides an opportunity for further specialization; for others a chance to specialize after a broad undergraduate program; and for still others a chance to broaden, as in area studies, after a specialized first degree course of study. For many it is a step upward. For others, particularly at the prestige universities, it may be a consolation prize if they are unable to attain the doctorate. As in America too, there is something of an inverse relationship between the quality of the master's degree and the prestige of the university that gives it.

A few examples will suffice. At the University of London, the M.A. and the M.Sc. are primarily degrees in course, while the Master of Philosophy (M.Phil.) degree is a short research degree requiring only a shorter and less significant thesis than that required for the Ph.D. Postgraduate students may be admitted to the M.Phil. program on the understanding that they may be upgraded to the Ph.D. if their academic performance so justifies. It is also possible, although not loudly admitted, that the M.Phil. may be used as a consolation prize for a failed Ph.D.

At the University of Sussex, all graduate students in the arts and social studies are now admitted initially only into a probationary first year. At the end of two terms (out of a three-term academic year), some may either elect or be directed into the M.A. program which is a one-year program. In this case, they begin work in the third term on a dissertation which they must complete by the end of one calendar year from the beginning of their postgraduate study. The dissertation is normally from 10,000 to 20,000 words in length and must be completed within a 12-month period from the opening of the fall term, thus giving them about 6 months. Other students will be permitted to continue on either for the M.Phil. or the D.Phil. The M.Phil. is a two-year program of residence and involves a thesis of around 40,000 words, while the D.Phil. is a three-year program and involves a thesis of around 80,000 words. The difference between the three postgraduate programs lies in the length of residence and the length of the dissertation.

At the University of Wales, the M.A. and the M.Sc. titles are used to recognize the completion of advanced courses and the passing of an advanced examination and, alternatively, as a postgraduate research degree. The same is true at the University of Aston where the M.Sc. by course and examination is generally considered somewhat a better degree than the M.Sc. for research. At Oxford, the M.A. is vestigial, but the Bachelor of Philosophy (B.Phil.) is the equivalent of the London M.Phil. The Franks Commission in 1966 saw no reason why the B.Phil. should not be renamed the M.Phil., but concluded that the university should retain the present anomalous position of the M.A. because of its historical association with the constitution of the university. At Cambridge, the M.Sc. and M.Litt. are consolation prizes for a dissertation that doesn't meet Ph.D. levels. The Master of Philosophy has been made available as a new two-year degree, but no faculty as yet has submitted a proposal to the board of graduate studies for approval to grant the degree.

To the extent that one can summarize such a complex situation, current thinking in English education seems to favor the development of a one-year postgraduate course program leading to the M.A. or M.Sc., a two-year M.Phil. with a short research thesis, and the conventional three-year Ph.D. or D. Phil. The Master of Education (M.Ed.) degree is the professional second degree for those who teach.

Doctor of Philosophy In contrast to American practice, the Ph.D. in England and Wales (D.Phil. at Oxford and Sussex) has traditionally been based solely upon full-time research activity in residence leading to the doctoral dissertation. Consequently, it is normally earned more quickly (three to four years elapsed time) and at an earlier age than its American counterpart.

Again in contrast to the United States, the British Ph.D. dissertation has historically dealt with "pure" scholarship in the arts and sciences. English Ph.D. students have found employment in the field of higher education to a much greater extent than have ours. Few Oxford or Cambridge doctoral students go into industry and governmental research. Those who do tend to find the people above them are neither very good nor very sympathetic and sooner or later come back to the universities.

Most of the changes in the Ph.D. program in England and Wales today relate to the scientific manpower needs of the nation and to the desire to provide a greater variety of talents in the research scholars produced. The feeling is growing that the straight research doctorate constitutes ridiculous overspecialization. There are growing doubts about the value of many theses and about the training that this exercise provides. The Science Research Councils are deliberately cutting down on support for pure research and are encouraging support for research that has potential applications or is otherwise related to industry. Part-time doctoral research is being permitted on a trial basis. Scientists employed in governmental or industrial laboratories are being increasingly permitted to submit their experimental results to a supervising university to be considered for acceptance in satisfaction of Ph.D. requirements. These innovations are radical in England although the same practices are common in the United States. At the University of London, advanced doctoral students may work on their doctoral dissertation while employed in nonuniversity laboratories. At Aston and two other technological universities, the "sandwich" principle is being applied at the Ph.D. level with postgraduate students alternating study on campus with research in an industrial laboratory. Students are accepted only when the employer provides the opportunity for full-time research on the job and where there is a suitably qualified supervisor of research both on the job and at the university. One objective of this program is to train managers who have an understanding of research rather than straight research scientists.

On a more restrained note, Cambridge has reduced the residence requirement for postgraduate students from six to three terms (two years to one), thus making it possible for a doctoral student to spend as much as two years in a nearby governmental research laboratory working on his dissertation as long as he lives within 10 miles of the university.

At Cambridge, in addition to the common pattern of earning the Ph.D. through research carried out in residence, it may be earned by a Cambridge graduate after a minimum of eight years on submission of his published work to the faculty. This second alternative is in essence a lower level Doctor of Science. Since the practice was introduced in 1946, some 40 Ph.D.'s have been awarded on this basis.

We should note that the Ph.D. is not considered as essential in the humanities in England as it is in the United States. One can still get a major university post in languages and literature on the basis of scholarship alone without the Ph.D.

Higher Doctorates English and Welsh universities grant higher doctorates for distinguished published work submitted a number of years after graduation. The basic degrees are Doctor of Literature or of Letters (D.Litt.)[3] and Doctor of Science (D.Sc.). Similar advanced doctor's degrees based on scholarship are the Doctor of Laws (LL.D.), Doctor of Music (Mus.D.), and Doctor of Divinity (D.D.). The

[3] Doctor of Letters at Oxford (D.Litt.) and Cambridge (Litt.D.); Doctor of Literature (D.Lit.) at London; Doctor in Litteris (D.Litt.) at University of Wales, etc.

number awarded is small. For example, Cambridge (where the order of the letters is reversed) in 1968 granted 23 Sc.D., 4 Litt.D., 1 Mus.D., 1 D.D., and no LL.D. degrees. In contrast to the American honorary degree, the scholar must apply for the higher doctorate and must submit his published works for detailed scrutiny by faculty examiners. Typically, the earned higher doctorate is obtained after the age of 40 by a scholar who originally graduated from the university or who is currently on its faculty. The higher doctorate not only provides for further recognition of a distinguished Ph.D. but also serves as the first recognition at the doctoral level for scholars who did not earn the Ph.D. but went directly from the baccalaureate into a university career. This latter circumstance is most common in the languages and literatures. The degree also serves to recognize scientists who have developed an impressive research publication record in industry.

While the highest recognition in science in England is election to the Royal Society, the recipients of the Doctor of Science tend to constitute the pool from which the Fellows (F.R.S.) are selected. Scholars with the Doctor of Letters degree similarly hope for election to the British Academy. In the humanities, the D.Litt. is considered a desirable high honor everywhere except for a few departments at Oxford and Cambridge where a form of inverse snobbery leads distinguished faculty to disdain the degree because A. E. Houseman and Lord Keynes didn't put in for it.

All in all, the higher doctorates seem to occupy an important place in English degree structure, not only as an incentive for continued scholarly activity past the Ph.D. but also as a means of providing doctoral recognition for those who did not go the Ph.D. route.

The Binary System, Second Entry, and External Degrees

British universities cannot begin to accommodate the flood of incoming students who aspire to higher education. Despite the upgrading of the CATs to university status and the creation of a whole series of new universities within the last decade, there are not enough places to meet the demand. In an effort to meet the numbers crisis, the government has created the "binary system" for England and Wales, sponsoring and encouraging the establishment of a large number of colleges of further education which provide two- and three-year courses without having the authority to grant degrees. In a broad sense, they are similar to the American community college. These include the polytechnic colleges, colleges of teacher training, colleges of commerce, and other nonuniversity institutions of "further" education.

Traditionally, students in such institutions as well as students studying on their own can aspire to university degrees through taking the University of London external examinations. These examinations are designed to recognize performance comparable to that expected of students in residence at that university and they have considerable status. They do, however, create problems for the university faculty who must make parallel changes in external degree requirements for every change made in the university's internal degree structure.

In recent years, national diplomas and degrees have become available through the Council of National Academic Awards (CNAA) established in 1964 on the recommendation of the Robbins committee. Offering a complete range of external degrees, it is the degree-granting authority making it possible for students to qualify for academic degrees on their own or while studying in nondegree-granting institutions of further education. Both the London external examination and the CNAA provide second or third chances for students who fail any of the successive examination hurdles on the conventional degree route. The British university system has long been high in quality but unrelenting in its requirement for consistent high academic performance from adolescence onward. The development of the binary system and of national external degrees provides some flexibility by making available alternate routes to academic success.

The technological universities also provide safety nets in that they accept students with other professional qualifications than prior academic performance. At Aston, for instance, one-third of the graduate students in mechanical engineering come in with qualification other than a university degree.

The democratization of English education has not gone far as yet. It is, however, developing rapidly.

WEST GERMANY University education in Germany is oriented around the doctorate rather than the baccalaureate. At the age of 10, after four years of primary school, about 15 percent of the children in West Germany enter a *Gymnasium* for a nine-year course specifically aimed at university admission. Curricula emphasize classical languages, modern languages, or mathematics and natural science. A small proportion of the 25 percent of the age group who go to the *Mittel-schule* for a six-year course can also shift to a *Gymnasium* and qualify for university admission. All in all, about 50 to 60 thousand students earn their *Abitur* or secondary school leaving certificate each year and therefore have the right of access to higher education. The major problem in West Germany today is that there is not enough room in the universities and *Hochschulen* (technical institutes) for these students.

University students spend at least four years before qualifying as secondary school teachers through the passing of a *Staatsexamen,* and a minimum of eight years from their *Abitur* (average of 10-13 years) before receiving their *Doktor* degree. The doctorate is usually the first earned degree at the university in subjects not taught in secondary school. In psychology, for example, the university student has no stopping point short of the doctorate.

The *Staatsexamen* is, as the name says, a state examination qualifying one for appointment as a secondary school teacher and is not a degree. It must be passed in two separate but related subjects. Most students do not take a degree at this point. A *Diplom,* however, is available in a number of specific fields such as law, economics, psychology, and sociology.

About five years ago, a parallel degree, *Magister artium* (Master of Arts) was introduced but comparatively few students take it. The concept behind it was to increase the value of the doctorate and also to provide recognition for foreign students who were not continuing on to the doctorate and for whom the *Staatsexamen* was of no use.

While theoretically the *Staatsexamen, Diplom,* and *Magister* degree are all equal, there are tremendously complicated status considerations that make them unequal in differing orders in almost every field. For instance, in chemistry the *Staatsexamen* is lower in status than the *Magister* degree, and a person who takes it is considered inferior. In history, however, it is the other way around. These differences are well known within the professions but not among the prospective candidates. Basically, the *Magister* is purely a university degree, the *Staatsexamen* a state civil service examination for teaching in a subject-matter field, and the *Diplom* is a document given out by the university in conjunction with various professional qualifications. At the University of Konstanz, the *Magister* is being awarded in all fields automatically to all who pass the *Staatsexamen* in an effort to eliminate the status difference and to establish the *Magister* as the general university degree.

After obtaining the *Doktor* degree, the prospective student obtains employment as a research or teaching assistant and continues his studies for the *Habilitation* which confers on him the right to teach and eventually to become a university professor. The *Habilitation* is, therefore, analogous to a higher doctorate and fulfills roughly the same general function as the British Doctor of Science or Doctor of Letters, the Soviet Doctor of Science, and the French *doctor d'Etat.* The *Habilitation* is conferred by the university where the *Doktor* works and is required for professorial appointment anywhere in the country. There is much talk in Germany about combining the doctorate and the *Habilitation* in some way or other, but no major change in the present dual structure seems likely.

The basic structure of German education, then, leads to the *Staatsexamen, Diplom,* or *Magister* after four years, the *Doktor* after at least another four years, and the *Habilitation* some years after that. Efforts are currently being made to introduce the bachelor's degree after three years and the licentiate between the master's and the doctor's.

No one has introduced a three-year bachelor's program yet, but the concept is being pushed in the state of Baden-Württemberg to recognize the successful completion of an academic program that qualifies the student for teaching through the first six years of the secondary schools and for a variety of positions that already exist in a number of technical and professional fields (Dahrendorf, 1967). The course of study and the precedent already exist. At the University of Konstanz, the founding committee suggested that the degree *Baccalaureus* be granted upon the passing of the traditional *Vordiplom* examination after three years, but no action has been taken on this proposal.

Konstanz, however, has introduced the *Lizentiat*[4] degree to recognize completion of all phases of the doctoral program up to the dissertation. This degree is thus similar to the American Candidate in Philosophy and Master of Philosophy degrees. The *Lizentiat* is given at Konstanz with two general goals in mind. First, it is given to students who continue their postgraduate studies in

[4] The degrees offered are *Lizentiat* in natural science (Lic.Rer.Nat.), social science (Lic.Rer.Soc.), law (Lic.Jur.), and philosophy (Lic.Phil.).

the same field as their undergraduate studies but wish to qualify as advanced professionals rather than as research scholars. Second, however, it is available to students who wish to change subjects during their university sojourn and thus broaden themselves by qualifying in two related areas. Thus far, two *Lizentiat* degrees have been awarded, one in law and one in political science. The degree also recognizes the partial completion of the doctorate. The successful candidate may continue to work for the higher award.

Although the *Lizentiat* is an innovation at Konstanz in its form as a general intermediate graduate degree, the degree itself has a long history in Germany. Its main usage has been in theology where it was generally given as the highest earned degree rather than the doctorate. This is still the case at the University of Halle.

FRANCE The "revolution" of May, 1968, has put French higher education into such a state of flux that it is difficult to characterize its academic degree structures with any certainty. Substantial changes have already been made, other changes have been announced but not yet put into effect, and others are still in the offing. As with the U.S.S.R. and Italy, France's system of higher education is an arm of the government. Its degree structures are determined by the Chamber of Deputies and the Minister of Education. University reform, therefore, is a highly political issue, particularly since student revolts have been perhaps the major factor in recent French politics.

The traditional first degree in France has been the *license,* granted after three years of study at the university to students who entered at the age of 18 with the *baccalauréat* from secondary school. The rate of failure is very high. Although a student may repeat his examinations, it is estimated that perhaps only one in every three or four ever earn the degree.

The *maitrise* degree was introduced in 1964 to recognize the completion of a four-year program. It was designed to replace the *license* but it is currently taken one year after it in many instances. In a sense, the new degree is in limbo: some authorities think that it will be the basic university degree, and indeed it is currently required for admission to the doctorate; others feel that the concept will not be fully activated. At the present time, the student completes his first cycle of studies at the university in two years receiving a *diplôme universitaire d'études litteraires* or *d'études scientifiques.* He then enters his second cycle with the choice of either taking an additional year of study for the *license* or following a separate two-year track involving the preparation of a thesis and leading to the *maîtrise.*

As the *maîtrise* becomes more important, the *license* retains a meaning for the training of secondary school teachers. The prospective teacher, however, must go on for a fourth year at a teacher-training institution before final qualification. A four-year program thus already exists for teachers under the new system.

The *license libre* and *maîtrise libre* are available in the faculty of letters and humanities for students who follow their own choice of studies. The social problem is to determine the types of employment for which such graduates may be qualified.

The *agrégation* is not a degree but an examination held by the state which students must pass to qualify for secondary school teaching positions. It is usually taken after the earning of the *maîtrise* or the similar-level *diplôme d'études supérieures.* The *agrégation* has been widely criticized as being inappropriate and may be supplanted by a *concours superior.* How different the new program will be remains to be seen.

An earned doctorate more or less similar to the American Ph.D. was introduced in 1964. The *doctorat du troisième cycle* requires from 2½ to 4 years of study past the *maîtrise* and involves the preparation and defense of a thesis. The *doctorat du troisième cycle* is designed to replace the *agrégation* as the qualification for lower ranks of university appointment. It was established for the science faculties in 1954 and has spread rapidly, but is only now taking form in the faculty of letters and humanities.

French universities also award the *doctorat d'université,* primarily to foreigners. It is given after one or two years of university study and the defense of a thesis. It is a weak degree and does not qualify its holder for teaching positions in France.

The ultimate French degree is the *doctorat d'État;* it is awarded after not less than two years of additional study past the *doctorat du troisième cycle* on the basis of a new and major thesis. In the past, the alternative track has been through the *agrégation* to the *doctorat d'Etat,* and this is still the common pattern in letters and humanities. In actual practice, the *doctorat d'État* requires from 3 to 4½ years of advanced study in the sciences and up to 12 to 20 years in letters. It is a requirement for appointment to the rank of professor.

ITALY   Italian universities admit students who attended school for 13 years. Study at the *liceo classico* leads to the *diploma di maturità classica,* which gives admission to all university courses except those provided by the faculty of education. The *liceo scientifico* prepares for the *diploma di maturità scientifica,* which gives admission to all university courses except those provided by the faculty of letters and philosophy (Nonis, 1968).

Upon the completion of a four-year program consisting of required courses and the discussion of a thesis, the student receives the *laurea* degree and has the right to use the title *dottore.* The Italian title of doctor thus recognizes a degree level substantially lower than the doctorate in other western European countries. Only a small proportion of the age group have the opportunity of attending the secondary schools which prepare for university entrance, and only a portion of these receive the diploma which grants university entrance.

Italy, thus, has only one degree level, and that is represented by the *laurea.* University reform is a matter of great political concern in the country at the present time, and universities there are in a current state of flux and disruption. A major element of the proposed reforms involves the establishment of two additional degree levels[5]—a technical diploma after two years of study and therefore preceding the *laurea* by two years and a research doctorate after two or three years of study past the *laurea.* The whole question of legal privileges attached to degrees is being discussed as well as the question of degrees granted by private universities. No action has been taken by the Italian Parliament on the proposed reform in degree structure as of the time of writing,[6] nor has the effort been successful to establish a research doctorate at the International Studium of Molecular Biology in Naples along the lines of the American Ph.D. program despite a grant from our National Science Foundation to the University of California at Berkeley to provide staff support to the institution.[7]

U.S.S.R.   The Soviet Union is similar to the United States in that a large percentage of its youth have the opportunity to attend an institution of higher education. The entering age at the university is 18,

[5] Personal communication, Russell L. Harris, December 6, 1968.

[6] *Science,* 161:451-452, August 2, 1968.

[7] *Science,* 163:1306-1308, March 21, 1969.

and the basic diploma course averages five years in length. Competition for admission is high and subsequent attrition low.

At the postgraduate level there is a three-year course involving special examinations and the preparation of a thesis leading to the candidate's degree *Kandidat Nauk* (Candidate in Science), a recognition roughly equivalent to the American Ph.D. Again, competition for postdoctoral appointments is stiff but subsequent attrition is slight.

The highest degree, *Doktor Nauk* (Doctor of Science) is awarded on the basis of published scholarship over a long period of years at about the time a scholar is appointed to a full professorship. In effect, it is formal certification by the university that the scholar is qualified for the highest level of university rank.

The term *science* in the Soviet Union covers all knowledge and is therefore much broader than in its English-language usage. Information on Soviet education was obtained from Grant (1964) and Terman (1965).

GENERAL
COMMENTS

Whereas a large percentage of the youth in the United States and the U.S.S.R. are exposed to some sort of higher education, this is not true for western European countries. As recently as 1955, the enrollment in higher education in western Europe ranged from five to seven percent of the population of the 20 to 24 year age group (Table 9). Although the institutions of higher education in western Europe have expanded greatly over the past decade, the proportion of the age class in these institutions is still only about one-quarter of that in the United States. Since universities in western Europe are more limited in scope than those in the United States, the proportional university population is substantially less. We should not forget that engineering and teacher training are commonly taught in America in the universities but in separate institutions of higher education in western Europe. This fact must be kept in mind when comparing enrollment statistics.

Most American educators are generally impressed with the more rigid and intensive instruction given in European secondary schools and with the relatively loose pattern of higher education. There is a tendency to generalize the conclusion that European secondary education is better and that, in some countries at least, the first university degree is more equivalent to our master's than to our bachelor's despite the fact that the student receives his first degree at the same age after the same number of years of study as

TABLE 9
Enrollment in all higher education as a percentage of population of 20-24 year age group

Country	1955	1960	1965
United States	25	32	41
Canada	9	14	24
France	7	10	17
United Kingdom	7	8	12
Italy	5	6	11
Germany	5	6	9
Switzerland	6	7	8

SOURCE: OECD, Paris.

are taken by an American student of similar intelligence in earning the bachelor's degree.

We cannot avoid making comparisons of degree levels if for no other reason than to classify students who move from country to country in the course of their education. Indeed, we have evolved workable guidelines for so doing. In a more basic sense, however, such comparisons are inevitably superficial and cannot adequately take into account differences in the total cultural and educational experience of different populations. Our own impression is that European and American education are quite comparable for students of similar intelligence, similar age, and similar number of years of formal education. As a general rule, most western European countries extend their primary and secondary school education through 13 years in contrast to the 12-year period in the United States. It follows that, other factors being equal, three years of university training in these countries should bring the students to the same point that four years accomplish in the United States. At the present time, the trend in western Europe is to learn from and borrow from American higher education, rather than the other way around. American graduate education has long been admired and emulated in Europe. American undergraduate education is similarly serving as a model for the democratization of education while providing superior opportunities for promising youth.

The widening scientific gap between the United States and western Europe is of increasing concern. It is at the core of the British worry about the "brain drain" and about ways and means of increasing the utilization of scientists by industry. It has also concerned more broadly the Organization for Economic Cooperation and Development. In a recent analysis of the relationship between fundamental research and the universities, Ben-David (1968) argues for the development of "ecological centers" such as the Oxford-Cambridge-London triangle and the University of Paris which possess advanced facilities, great resources for research, and the capacity of bringing together large groups of trainees in most fields of science. Such multipurpose university centers of research should deal with both pure and applied science and should have the authority to confer at least graduate degrees. As Ben-David sees it, the need for western Europe is to internationalize its system of advanced higher education.

14. A Proposed Generalized System of Degree Structures

In terms of academic degree structures, the system of higher education in the United States should be so designed to create a fluid and interconnecting pattern that will facilitate the movement of the student within the system and develop his academic potential. By keeping our degree structures few and broadly defined, we can consciously plan to keep our system adaptable and evolutionary. If, on the other hand, we allow degree programs at any given level to become more discrete, mutually exclusive, and inevitably more numerous, we are apt to limit opportunities of students to maximize their educational opportunities and to change their degree goals as they themselves mature and develop.

Each level of graduate study should be characterized by a broadly accepted generic name. At each there should be as few specific degree names as possible. The student must pass through each level as his higher education progresses. All students should be admitted as applicants only for the particular phase for which they are qualified. Each level should mark successful attainment to date, and its completion should carry no implications as to what a student elects to do in the following stage of his education or career. Care should be taken to avoid categorizing any level as being either terminal or intermediate. Inevitably each will be terminal for some and intermediate for others. A selection of noninvidious progressive choices should be available to the student at each recognition gate.

DEGREE LEVELS There are six general levels of academic recognition that have become established in the United States and that should be considered in the evolution of any general set of degree structures. These levels are (1) associate, (2) bachelor, (3) master, (4) intermediate graduate, (5) doctor, and (6) postdoctoral or higher doctoral. Each has been discussed separately in earlier chapters. In each case the degree or certificate should be further named by an appropriate modifier such as arts, science, or philosophy. The fewest possible degree titles should be given general usage within each level while allowing for substantial variation within each with regard to subject matter, emphasis, quantity, and even quality of effort. When more than one name is used within a given level, each should carry a clear connotation of distinctive meaning.

Associate The first level is that of associate. It signifies the qualification for undergraduate specialization and is recognized by the granting of the Associate of Arts or Associate of Science certificate or degree. The associate's degree clearly has an important place in American higher education, particularly in view of the burgeoning role being played by community colleges throughout the United States.

It would seem desirable to require the recognition of the associate's level en route to the baccalaureate in order to endow that step on the academic ladder with greater status and prestige than it carries when it is associated primarily with the junior and community college movement. Then the associate's degree could no longer be interpreted as a mark of a second-track academic career, but would rather represent the successful completion of the first phase of higher education. By bracketing together all who reach the two-year level with the associate's degree, whether on the completion of an academic or in a technical-vocational program, all successful students at this point will share the prestige and recognition and the sense of satisfaction and completion that comes from the possession of a college degree.

Were the associate's degree to be universally required en route to the baccalaureate, it would be desirable to so categorize the requirements for the degree that it could be earned in transit and that no additional effort or work would be required by the student planning to continue on to the baccalaureate over what would be required for the baccalaureate alone.

In addition, however, the possibility exists of using the associate's degree to stimulate the qualified student to move more rapidly through his undergraduate program into graduate education. Whereas the two-year requirement can serve as a useful maximum, provision should be made for early completion of this stage through advanced placement and other qualifying examinations demonstrating that the student has met his general education requirements and is qualified to begin undergraduate specialization. The normal range of full-time study, therefore, would be from $\frac{1}{2}$ to 2 years.

It is presumed that recognition at the associate's level will continue to be in the form of a degree at the community and junior colleges, but that it may also be in the form of a certificate at four-year institutions.

Bachelor   The second level is normally marked by the granting of the Bachelor of Arts or Bachelor of Science degree in recognition of the completion of undergraduate general education and specialization requirements. Four academic years of full-time study are commonly required from college matriculation to the baccalaureate. Two years of study thus separate the associate's from the bachelor's level.

There is no reason why the student should not be recommended for the bachelor's degree with fewer formal credits as soon as he has met the levels of academic attainment set for the general education (distribution), specialization (concentration), and other curriculum standards. Such a relaxation in the duration of the baccalaureate program would seem to have general merit. Furthermore, advanced credit toward the master's degree should be available to advanced students wishing to enjoy the four-year undergraduate experience while pursuing graduate-level studies in the last year of this period.

Master   The third level of academic degrees is normally recognized by the granting of the Master of Arts or Master of Science degree after a minimum of one year of full-time academic study at the graduate level. Many professional master's degrees and the Master of Philosophy degree require two years of graduate work.

We recommend that all students graduating with the baccalaureate pass through the master's stage and not be admitted to study for more advanced degrees until they do. As a result the master's degree would become a required and necessary stepping stone en route to the doctorate. The fact that all students would be admitted only as candidates for the master's and must earn this degree means that the master's degree would always mark successful forward progress. It would therefore, be a more appropriate stopping place than it now is for those who choose not to go further. It is only the fact that many graduate schools admit students fresh out of the baccalaureate into doctoral programs that gives the connotation of consolation prize to the master's degree. Efforts to strengthen the master's degree by requiring an extra period of study or a more carefully planned academic program may be desirable in themselves but may not create a really respectable degree if the students who are accepted into the program are separately chosen and segregated from those who are chosen at the baccalaureate level to continue on directly to the doctorate.

The master's program should have a finite maximum time duration, tempered by incentives for early completion of an accelerated program. Probably the maximum duration for the student passing through an M.A. or M.S. program en route to a doctorate should be one academic year. At the other extreme, students might well earn the master's degree at the same time that they complete the requirements for the baccalaureate. The successful passing of doctoral qualifying exams, commonly given by many departments in the first year of graduate study, could also qualify the student for the master's degree, permitting him to move after one semester or one or two quarters into the doctoral program. The master's program would thus be equated with the qualifying stage of doctoral studies and become an integral part of the continuum of liberal arts study. The requirement for a master's thesis should not be universal. Students could be encouraged, though, to elect courses in which major effort is placed on the preparation of a substantial term paper, a paper which could well be called a thesis under appropriate conditions.

Intermediate Graduate

The fourth level marks the completion of graduate learning and the qualification of the student as a scholar possessing a general knowledge and competence in his chosen field of specialization. No single degree name has achieved wide acceptance. Candidate in Philosophy, Master of Philosophy, and Specialist in Education are the most widely used titles at the present time. Licentiate in Philosophy or Diplomate in Philosophy, however, would seem to be more specific and less misleading in their connotations.

The intermediate graduate degree or certificate requires one academic year's work past the master's and may take as much time as two calendar years. The student receiving this recognition, therefore, will have had at least two years of graduate study but hopefully not more than three.

The time required could well be shortened by granting the degree or certificate upon the passing of comprehensive examinations and the completion of other requirements for the doctorate up to the dissertation. In short, the intermediate graduate recognition should occupy the same general position as the "A.B.D." but should represent an affirmation of accomplishment to date rather than an implication of failure to complete the dissertation.

Doctor Upon successful completion of the intermediate graduate stage, the student, in addition to having the opportunity of deciding to terminate his graduate studies at this phase, could well be given the opportunity of electing alternative programs demonstrating his ability to carry out individual, independent scholarly activity. He who elects to carry out independent scholarly research and investigation and to prepare the conventional doctoral dissertation would receive the Doctor of Philosophy degree. Others who are more professionally oriented could well demonstrate their capacity for individual work and reporting by appropriate activity as defined by that profession. For instance, the Doctor of Education could well be granted to the student who elects an essentially pedagogical or professional education individual project as opposed to individual research or scholarly investigation. Others could write an expository thesis for the Doctor of Arts degree. Still others could submit creative literary projects for the Doctor of Literary Arts degree.

The great value in the Doctor of Arts programs would be to offer parallel and respectable alternatives to the Doctor of Philosophy in the liberal arts. Just as the Doctor of Musical Arts offers a parallel in the field of music, the proposed Doctor of Literary Arts could offer a parallel in creative writing, and the Doctor of Education, if properly restricted, could offer a parallel and respectable alternative to the Ph.D. in that professional area. Only if elected by the student after successful completion of the next previous academic level will the degree Doctor of Arts truly become a respectable and acceptable academic degree. If it is so handled, however, there appears to be no reason why it cannot meet the career goals of many who are qualified and interested in becoming college teachers in subject-matter specialties covered by the liberal arts departments but who do not have the interest and perhaps not even the ability to carry out independent research in their chosen field.

The doctor's program should be structured similarly to the lower degrees in that it could be earned by the steady and competent scholar in a specified time span. At the same time, the exceptionally motivated student should be offered incentives to complete the program in a shorter period of time. Standardized maxima in terms of full-time academic study from the master's should perhaps be two years for the completion of general studies and for the passing of the comprehensive examinations (the intermediate level) and one to two years for the preparation of a thesis. The one-year minimum is probably attainable in the Doctor of Arts program, but two years will often be required in Ph.D. programs. Within these suggested time limits, however, it would seem desirable on many counts to so structure the doctor's program that the exceptionally qualified and able student should be able to take his comprehensive examinations a year after the completion of his master's and that he should be given a thesis topic capable of being completed in an additional 12-month period.

Postdoctoral Recognition

It is to be expected that postdoctoral studies will attract increasing numbers of scholars either in the formal sense of full-time postdoctoral study at a university or in the informal sense of continuing postdoctoral education throughout a scholarly career. The possibility exists, therefore, of recognizing accomplishment at this level with a higher doctorate, awarded by the faculty that had previously granted the Ph.D. and given in recognition of distinguished published creative activity over a period of years. If distinguished scholarly achievement following the doctorate should be recognized by a higher doctoral degree, the pressure for making every Ph.D. dissertation into a *magnum opus* could well be reduced. We opt for the generic title *Doctor of Natural Philosophy* for this highest earned degree.

REDUCTION OF NUMBER OF LEVELS

The fact that we recognize six generic degree levels should not be taken to imply that we advocate that all should necessarily be included in any overall degree pattern. On the contrary, there is much merit in reducing the number if the surviving degree levels can be so handled as to meet the multiple needs of our student population. A number of alternatives suggest themselves.

To begin with, the bachelor's and doctor's levels are so well entrenched as to warrant their inclusion in any set of structures. Greater flexibility should be introduced into the bachelor's degree, both in terms of providing greater opportunities for earlier completion of the degree and for advanced study applicable to graduate credit. For the Ph.D., major efforts must be made to encourage more students to finish in less time. Both degree levels, however, will remain a part of any future structure.

Our present system involves three levels: the bachelor's, the master's, and the doctor's. If the master's level can be strengthened and made a requirement, and if the doctor's level can be tightened up, the same total structure would serve us very well.

By so patterning the master's and doctor's programs, the completion of the bachelor's program would require 3 to 4 years, the master's program ½ to 1 year, and the doctor's program from 2 to 3 years. The total range of study from college matriculation to the Ph.D. would therefore occupy a time span of approximately 6 to 8 years. The maxima placed on the different components of the system, however, might result in a substantial reduction of total time elapsed under present practice. The modal enrollment time from matriculation to the Ph.D. today is nine years—four years for the baccalaureate and five years for the doctorate. This period could well be reduced by two years to approximately seven years under the system described.

While there is a great deal of merit in the simplicity of the three-stage system of higher education described above, this system is probably not sufficient to deal with the complexities of present-day American higher education. To accomplish this end, therefore, we must introduce into our pattern one or more of the additional three stages that have actually evolved. These are the associate's stage marking an intermediate point in undergraduate education, the comparable intermediate level in the doctoral program marking the completion of the general studies phase of graduate education, and finally the postdoctoral or higher doctoral stage of scholarly recognition.

The introduction of the associate's stage results in a two-stage pattern of undergraduate education, and this is the pattern we recommend. While the four-year colleges can continue to do without the associate's level, its omission by them will make it more difficult to integrate the two-year colleges into a single system of higher education.

For graduate education, the master's and the intermediate graduate level could well be combined into a single two-year program for all students at this level. The difference between a strong two-year master's program (such as the Toronto M.Phil.) and a two-year program for doctoral students culminating in comprehensive examinations and admission to candidacy (such as the Yale M.Phil.) is so little that the two could well be amalgamated by a graduate faculty ready to eliminate both the one-year master's and the drawn-out doctor's programs.

The resultant program should constitute a regular stage through which all doctoral students pass. It should require two full years of graduate study for the well-prepared student pursuing at the graduate level the same field he studied at the bachelor's. The program should not take more than three years for the student coming into graduate study from a related discipline or otherwise needing a preparatory year after the baccalaureate.

Whether or not a formal higher doctorate should be established in the United States hinges upon the effect such a doctorate would have in streamlining the Ph.D. Our thought is that the establishment of such a higher doctorate would not hurt, and that it might help. The concept seems worthy of further experimentation.

A number of possible patterns thus emerge for graduate degree structures. Put in overly simple terms, the most obvious are as follows:

1 A one-year master's program followed by a three-year Ph.D. program. This is essentially our present structure except that the master's level would be compulsory.

2 A one-year master's program followed by a one- to two-year graduate intermediate program followed by a one- to two-year doctoral program. In this variant, we introduce the intermediate level and alternative doctorates to the Ph.D.

3 A one-year master's program followed by either a two-year Doctor of Arts or a three-year Ph.D. program. While the two doctoral programs would be equal in concept, we would here hope to hold the Doctor of Arts to the same three years of total graduate work that is the rule honored in the breach for the Ph.D.

4 A two-year graduate intermediate program followed by a two-year Ph.D. program. We like this formulation but are not sanguine about its acceptableness.

In closing, we reiterate that the formalities of our academic degree structures are important only to the extent that the form can influence the educational process itself. Nomenclature and regulations are important only in the effect they have on the faculties, the students, and prospective employers. The revisions in our academic degree structure suggested above may well result in the improvement of our system of higher education. The projected reforms will cost but little and may accomplish much.

References

Allen, Don Cameron: *The Ph.D. in English and American Literature,* Holt, Rinehart and Winston, Inc., New York, 1968, 248pp.

Allen, Donald S.: *New Degree Programs of Potential Interest to the Two-Year College Chemistry Faculty Member and Administrator,* State University of New York at Albany, Albany, 1968, 22pp. (mimeographed).

Altman, Robert A.: *A Study of the Establishment of Upper Division Colleges in the United States,* U.S. Office of Education Project 8B073, 1969, 64pp.

American Association of Dental Schools: "Workshop of Graduate Education in Sciences Related to Dentistry," *Journal of Dental Education,* **33** (1):1-67 (1969).

American Association of Junior Colleges: *Preparing Two-year College Teachers for the '70's,* Washington, D.C., 1968, 24pp.

American Association of State Colleges and Universities and National Conference on the Intermediate Degree: "The Specialist Degree: A Statement [1969] by A.A.S.C.U. and N.C.I.D.," 8pp.

American Association of University Professors: "Requirements for Master's Degree," *AAUP Bulletin,* **18**: 169-185 (1932).

American Institute of Biological Sciences: "The Candidate's Degree: Is the Ph.D. Inadequate?," symposium, presentations by Kenneth V. Thimann, Gustave Arlt, E. J. Boell, and Stephen H. Spurr, *Bio-Science* **18** (3):179-189 (1968).

American Society for Engineering Education: *Goals of Engineering Education: Final Report of the Goals Committee,* E. A. Walker, chairman, Washington, D.C. 1968, 74pp.

Anderson, G. Lester: "Higher Education in England," *Journal of Higher Education,* **39** (8):442–452 (1968).

Arlt, Gustave: "The First Ph.D.'s under Title IV," *Journal of Higher Education,* **34** (5):241-249 (1963).

Association of American Universities: *Report of the Committee on Problems Relating to the Master's Degree,* Thirty-seventh Annual Conference, 1935, pp. 32-37

Association of American Universities: *Report of the Committee on Graduate Work Beyond the Master's Degree for Teachers in Secondary Schools,* Thirty-eighth Annual Conference, 1936, pp. 41-57.

Association of American Universities: *Report of the Committee on Graduate Work,* Forty-sixth Annual Conference, 1945, pp. 108-137.

Association of Graduate Schools in the Association of American Universities: *Report of Committee on Policies in Graduate Education, Journal of Proceedings and Addresses,* Ninth Annual Conference, New York, 1957, pp. 35-48.

Association of Graduate Schools in the Association of American Universities: *Report of Committee on Policies in Graduate Education, Journal of Proceedings and Addresses,* Tenth Annual Conference, New York, 1958, pp. 35-48.

Association of Graduate Schools in the Association of American Universities: "Proposed New Degrees," panel discussion, presentations by John Perry Miller, Robert H. Baker, Horace W. Magoun, and Stephen H. Spurr. *Journal of Proceedings and Addresses,* Eighteenth Annual Conference, New York, 1966, 137pp.

Atkinson, Carrol: *Pro and Con of the Ph.D.,* Meador Publishing Company, Boston, 1945, 172pp.

Barzun, Jacques: *The American University,* Harper & Row, Publishers, Incorporated, New York, 1968, 319pp.

Barzun, Jacques: *Teacher in America,* Little, Brown and Company, Boston, 1945. Paperback edition, Doubleday Anchor Books, 1959, 280pp.

Bean, Mary V.: "Development of the Ph.D. Program in the United States in the Nineteenth Century," Ph.D. dissertation, Ohio State University, Columbus, Ohio, 1953. Abstract in *Dissertation Abstracts* 18 (4):1,325-1,328 (1958).

Beloff, Michael: *The Plateglass Universities,* Secker & Warburg, London, 1968, 208pp.

Ben-David, Joseph: *Fundamental Research and the Universities: Some Comments on International Differences,* OECD, Paris, 1968, 111pp.

Berelson, Bernard: *Graduate Education in the United States,* McGraw-Hill Book Company, New York, 1960, 346pp.

Berelson, Bernard: "Postdoctoral Work in American Universities," *Journal of Higher Education,* 33 (3):119-130 (1962).

Blegen, Theodore C.: "How Can Graduate Schools Increase the Supply of College Teachers?" *Journal of Higher Education,* **30**: 127-133 (1959).

Bowdoin College: "The Development of Doctoral Programs by the Small Liberal Arts College," symposium, Brunswick, Maine, 1967, 181pp.

Bowers, Fredson: "Doctor of Arts: A New Graduate Degree," *College English* **27** (2):123-128 (1965).

Bowles, Frank: *Access to Higher Education,* UNESCO and the International Association of Universities, New York, 1963, vol. 1, 212pp., vol. 2, 648pp.

Bowles, Frank: *The Refounding of the College Board, 1948-1963,* College Entrance Examination Board, New York, 1967, 336pp.

Boylan, Laurence C.: "The Present Status of Sixth-Year Graduate Programs," *Proceedings Fourth Annual Meeting of Graduate Schools in the United States,* Washington, D.C., 1964, pp. 48-68.

Bretsch, Howard: *A Study of Doctoral Recipients, 1938-58,* University of Michigan Graduate Study No. 6, Ann Arbor, 1965, 104pp. (mimeographed).

Brickman, William W., and Stanley Lehrer, (eds.): *A Century of Higher Education,* Society for the Advancement of Education, New York, 1962, 285pp.

Brinkman, J. Jean: *Associate Degrees and Other Formal Awards Below the Baccalaureate, 1965-66 and 1966-67,* U.S. Office of Education OE-54045, 1969, 135pp.

Brinton, Crane (ed.): *The Society of Fellows,* Harvard University Press, Cambridge, Mass., 1959, 268pp.

Brook, G. L.: *The Modern University,* Andre Deutsch, London, 1965, 192pp.

Brubacher, John S., and Willis Rudy: *Higher Education in Transition: A History of American Colleges and Universities, 1636-1956,* Harper & Row, Publishers, Incorporated, New York, 1958, 494pp.

Burkett, J. E., and Paul G. Ruggiers (eds.): *Bachelor of Liberal Studies: Development of a Curriculum at the University of Oklahoma,* Center for the Study of Liberal Education for Adults at Boston University, Boston, 1965, 107pp.

Campbell, Malcolm B.: *Nonspecialists Study in the Undergraduate Curricula of the New Universities and Colleges of Advanced Technology in England,* The University of Michigan Comparative Education Discussion Series No. 10, Ann Arbor, 1966, 516pp.

Carmichael, Oliver C.: *Graduate Education: A Critique and a Program,* Harper & Brothers, New York, 1961, 213pp.

Cartter, Allan: "The Supply and Demand of College Teachers," *Journal of Human Resources,* 1 (1): 22-38 (1966).

Cartter, Allan, and Robert Farrell: "Higher Education in the Last Third of the Century," *Educational Record,* 4 (2): 119-128 (1965).

Chase, John L., and Deborah B. Breznay: *The Number and Kinds of Second Level Degrees Conferred by United States Institutions of Higher Education in 1963–64,* U.S. Office of Education, 1965, 14pp.

Commission on the Training and Utilization of Advanced Students of Mathematics: "Report on the Training of Teachers in Mathematics," *American Mathematical Monthly,* **42**: 265 (1965).

Committee on Higher Education: *Higher Education: Report of the Commission Appointed by the Prime Minister under the Chairmanship of Lord Robbins 1961-63,* Her Majesty's Stationery Office, London, 1963, 335pp.

Coordinating Council for Higher Education: *Approaches to Preparing Prospective College Teachers,* A staff report for presentation to the council, prepared by Willard Spolding and Leslie Wilbur, Sacramento, 1968, 53pp.

Cordasco, Francesco: *Daniel Coit and the Protean Ph.D.,* E. J. Brill, Leiden, 1960, 160pp.

Council of Graduate Schools in the United States: *The Doctor's Degree in Professional Fields: Joint Statement by the Association of Graduate Schools and the C.G.S.,* Washington, D.C., 1966, 9pp.

Council of Graduate Schools in the United States: "The Functions and Future of the Master's Degree," panel discussions, *Proceedings Third Annual Meeting,* Washington, D.C., 1963, pp. 111-127.

Council of Graduate Schools in the United States: "An Intermediate Graduate Degree," panel discussion, Stephen H. Spurr, chairman, presentations by Robert H. Baker, Sanford S. Elberg, Charles T. Lester, John Perry Miller, and F. Kenneth Hare, *Proceedings Sixth Annual Meeting,* Denver, Colorado, 1966, pp. 103-122.

Council of Graduate Schools in the United States: *The Master's Degree,* Washington, D.C., 1966, 20pp.

Council of Graduate Schools in the United States: "A Model Time Schedule for Completing the Ph.D.," *Proceedings Second Annual Meeting,* Washington, D.C., 1962, pp. 38-54.

Council of Graduate Schools in the United States: *New Doctor of Philosophy Programs,* Washington, D.C., 1965, 8pp.

Council of Graduate Schools in the United States: "The Preparation of Junior College Teachers," panel discussion, Joseph L. McCarthy, chairman, papers by Alvin H. Proctor, Robert H. Koenker, Jack E. Reese, and Roger Garrison, *Proceedings Seventh Annual Meeting,* Washington, D.C., 1967, pp. 77-99.

Council of Graduate Schools in the United States: "Preparation of Secondary and Junior College Teachers," panel discussion, Archie N. Solberg, chairman, papers by Laurence C. Boylan, George C. Feliz, Alan M. Hollingworth, Robert H. Koenker, and Raymond O. Rockwood, *Proceedings Fourth Annual Meeting,* Washington, D.C., 1964, pp. 47-93.

Council of Graduate Schools in the United States: "Teachers for Junior Colleges," panel discussion, papers by Edmund J. Gleazer, Jr., William H. Macmillan, Creatus Williams, and Lloyd A. Helms, *Proceedings Sixth Annual Meeting,* 1966, pp. 123-144.

Council of Graduate Schools in the United States: "The Ph.D. in Transition," third plenary session, presentations by John K. Folger, Don Cameron Allen, Stephen H. Spurr, D.C. Spriestersbach, and Sterling M. McMurrin, *Proceedings Seventh Annual Meeting,* Washington, D.C., 1967, pp. 45-76.

Council of Graduate Schools and Association of Graduate Schools in the United States: *The Doctor of Philosophy Degree,* Washington, D.C., 1964, 14pp.

Cramer, John F., and George S. Browne: *Contemporary Education—A Comparative Study of National Systems,* Harcourt, Brace and World, Inc., New York, 1965, 598pp.

Dahrendorf, Ralf: *Bildung in neuer Sicht, Hochschulgesamtplan Baden-Wurttemberg. Empfehlungen zur Reform von Struktur und Organisation,* Schriftenreihe des Kultusministeriums Baden-Wurttemberg zur Bildungsforschung, Bildungsplanung, Bildungspolitik, Reihe A Nr. 5., 1967. 203pp.

Daiches, David: *The Idea of the New University: An Experiement in Sussex,* Andre Deutsch, London, 1964, 269pp.

Doermann, Humphrey: *Baccalaureate Origins and Performance of Students in the Harvard Graduate School of Arts and Sciences,* preliminary draft, 1968 (typewritten).

Dressel, Paul L., and Frances H. DeLisle: *Undergraduate Curriculum Trends,* American Council on Education, Washington, D.C., 1969, 83pp.

Eells, Walter Crosby: *Degrees in Higher Education,* The Center for Applied Research in Education, Inc., New York, 1963, 118pp.

Eells, Walter Crosby: *The Junior College,* Houghton Mifflin Company, Boston, 1931, 833pp.

Eells, Walter Crosby, and Harold A. Haswell: *Academic Degrees,* U.S. Office of Education Bulletin 28, 1960, 324pp.

Elder, J. P.: "Reviving the Master's Degree for the Prospective College Teacher," *Journal of Higher Education,* **30**(3):133-136 (1959).

Epler, Stephen Edward: *Honorary Degrees: A Survey of Their Use and Abuse,* American Council on Public Affairs, Washington, D.C., 1943, 224pp.

Fuess, Claude M.: *The College Board: Its First Fifty Years,* Columbia University Press, New York, 1950, 222pp.

Gallie, W.: *A New University: A. D. Lindsay and the Keele Experiment,* Chatto & Windus, London, 1960, 152pp.

Garrison, Roger H.: *Junior College Faculty: Issues and Problems,* American Association of Junior Colleges, Washington, D.C., 1967, 90pp.

Gleazer, Edmund J.: *American Junior Colleges,* 7th ed., American Council on Education, Washington, D.C., 1967, 957pp.

Gleazer, Edmund J.: "Preparation of the Junior College Instructor," *Junior College Journal,* **35**: 3-4 (1964).

Goodman, Paul: "Compulsory Mis-education, and 1963," *The Community of Scholars,* Reprinted in one volume paperback edition, Vintage Books, Random House, Inc., New York, 1962, 339pp.

Grant, Nigel: *Soviet Education,* 2nd ed. Penguin Books, Harmondsworth and Baltimore, 1968, 192pp.

Haggerty, Melvin E.: "The Professional Training of College Teachers," *The North Central Association Quarterly,* **2**(1):108-123 (1927).

Hare, F. Kenneth: "The Intermediate Graduate Degree in the United States," *Proceedings of the Sixth Annual Meeting of the Council of Graduate Schools in the United States,* 1966, pp. 116-122.

Harvard University: *Report of the Committee on the Future of the Graduate School,* Cambridge, Mass., 1969.

Haskins, Charles Homer: *The Rise of Universities,* Henry Holt and Company, Inc., New York, 1923. Paperback edition, Great Seal Books, Cornell University Press, Ithaca, New York, 1957, 107pp.

Hawkins, Hugh: *Pioneer: A History of the Johns Hopkins University, 1874-1889,* Cornell University Press, Ithaca, N.Y., 1960, 368pp.

Heard, Alexander: *The Lost Years in Graduate Education,* Southern Regional Education Board, Atlanta, Ga., 1963, 39pp.

Heiss, Ann M.: *The Preparation of College and University Teachers,* Center for Research and Development in Higher Education, University of California, Berkeley, 1968, (mimeographed).

Hofstadter, Richard, and Wilson Smith: *American Higher Education: A Documentary History,* 2 vols., University of Chicago Press, Chicago, 1961, 1,016pp.

Hollis, Ernest V.: *Toward Improving Ph.D. Programs,* American Council of Education, Washington, D.C., 1945, 204pp.

James, William: *Ph.D. Octopus—in Memories and Studies,* Longmans, Green & Co., New York, 1917, pp. 329-347.

Jencks, Christopher, and David Riesman: *The Academic Revolution,* Doubleday & Company, Inc., Garden City, N.Y., 1968, 580pp.

Jernegan, Marcus W.: "Productivity of Doctors of Philosophy in History." *American Historical Review,* **33**(1):1-22 (1927).

John, Walton C.: *Graduate Study in Universities and Colleges in the United States,* U.S. Office of Education Bulletin 1934, No. 20, 1935, 234pp.

King, Edmund J.: *Other Schools and Ours,* 3rd ed., Holt, Rinehart and Winston, Inc., New York, 1967, 360pp.

Koenker, Robert H.: "Sixth-Year Graduate Programs—Ten Years Later," *Proceedings National Conference on the Intermediate Graduate Degree,* Kansas City, Mo., 1967, pp. 9-24.

Lady, R. Andrew: "Honoris Causa, An Examination of the Doctor of Philosophy Degree," *Journal of Higher Education,* **38** (4): 197-205 (1967).

Lawlor, John (ed.), *The New University,* Columbia University Press, New York, 1968, 200pp.

Layard, Richard, John King, and Claus Moser: *The Impact of Robbins,* Penguin Education Special, London, 1969, 153pp.

Lukes, J. R.: "Binary Policy: A Critical Study," *University Quarterly,* **22:** 6-46 (1967).

Malden, Henry: *On the Origin of Universities and Academical Degrees,* John Taylor, London, 1835, 173pp.

Mathematical Association of America: *Qualifications for a College Faculty in Mathematics,* Committee on the Undergraduate Program in Mathematics, Berkeley, Calif. 1967, 16pp.

Mathematical Association of America: "Report on the Training of Teachers of Mathematics," *American Mathematical Monthly,* **42**: 263-277 (1935).

Mayer, Martin: *Diploma: International Schools and University Entrance,* The Twentieth Century Fund, New York, 1968, 250pp.

McGrath, Earl J.: *The Graduate School and the Decline of Liberal Education,* Institute of Higher Education, Teachers College, Columbia University, New York, 1959, 65pp.

Mezes, Sidney E.: "Professional Training for College Teachers," in Paul Klapper (ed.), *College Teaching,* World Book Company, New York, 1920, 583pp.

Midwest College Art Conference: "The Present Status of the M.F.A. Degree," *Art Journal,* 24(3):244–249 (1965).

Midwest Modern Language Association: "M.A.?, M.Phil?, D.A.? C.D.? Ph.D.: Intermediate Graduate Degrees," Robert Scholes, moderator, presentations by Don Cameron Allen, F. Andre Paquette, Stepehen H. Spurr, and James R. Squire. *Bulletin Midwest Modern Language Association,* 1(1):1-39 (1967).

Modern Language Association: "Recommendations Concerning the Ph.D. in English," *Proceedings,* New York, 1967, 81pp.

Moise, Edwin: "The Proposed Doctor of Arts Degree," *Notices.* 8 (2): 112-115, American Mathematical Society, 1961.

Miller, John Perry: "The Master of Philosophy: A New Degree Is Born," *Ventures,* 6(1):1-4 (1966). Also *Journal of Higher Education* 37(7):377-381 (1966).

Mooney, Joseph D.: *Attrition Among Ph.D. Candidates: An Analysis of a Cohort of Recent Woodrow Wilson Fellows,* Princeton University, Princeton, N.J., Manuscript: 1967, 27pp. (mimeographed).

National Academy of Sciences: *Doctorate Recipients from United States Universities, 1958-1966,* Washington, D.C., 1967, 262pp.

National Conference on the Intermediate Graduate Degree: *Sixth-year and Other Intermediate Programs,* Kansas City, Mo., 1967, 1968.

National Faculty Association of Community and Junior Colleges: *Guidelines for the Preparation of Community/Junior College Teachers,* Washington, D.C., 1968, 11pp.

National Research Council: *The Invisible University: Postdoctoral Education in the United States,* National Academy of Sciences, Washington, 1969, 310pp.

New England Institute: *A New Interdisciplinary Postdoctorate Program*

Leading to the Advanced Degree of Doctor of Natural Philosophy, Ridgefield, Conn., 1966, 24pp.

Nonis, Flavia: *Notes on Education in Italy,* American Commission for Cultural Exchange with Italy, Rome, 1968, 53pp.

Pippard, A. B.: "Science as a Constituent of University Education," *Nature,* **219** (5,161):1,307–1,308 (1968).

Physics Survey Committee: *Physics: Survey and Outlook,* National Academy of Sciences, National Research Council, Washington, D.C., 1966, 119pp.

Putnam, H.: "Suggested Intermediate Graduate Degree," *School and Sociology,* **95**: 182-183 (1967).

Radcliffe, Shirley A.: *Advanced Standing: New Dimensions in Higher Education,* U.S. Office of Education, No. 8, QE-54014, 1961, 24pp.

Rashdall, Hastings: *The Universities of Europe in the Middle Ages,* 2d ed., F. M. Powicke and A. B. Emden (eds.), Oxford University Press, Oxford, 1936, vol. 1, 593pp., vol. 2, 342pp., vol. 3, 558pp.

Reese, J. E.: "New Titles and New Directions in Graduate Education; Masters of Arts in College Teaching," *Journal of Higher Education,* **38**: 250-256 (1967).

Robbins, Lord: *The University in the Modern World,* Macmillan, London, 1966, 157pp.

Rosenberg, Ralph P.: "Eugene Schuyler's Degree," *Journal of Higher Education,* **33**: 381-386 (1962).

Rosenberg, Ralph P.: "The First American Doctor of Philosophy Degree," *Ventures,* **6** (1): 31-37 (1966).

Rosenberg, Ralph P.: "The First American Doctor of Philosophy Degree: A Centennial Salute to Yale, 1861-1961," *Journal of Higher Education,* **32**: 387-394 (1961).

Rosenhaupt, Hans: *Graduate Students' Experience at Columbia University, 1940-1956,* Columbia University Press, New York, 1958, 129pp.

Rudolph, Frederick: *The American College and University: A History,* Alfred A. Knopf, Inc., New York, 1962. Paperback edition, Vintage Books, 1962, 516pp.

Rudy, Willis: *The Evolving Liberal Arts Curriculum: A Historical Review of Basic Themes,* Institute for Higher Education, Teachers College, Columbia University, New York, 1960, 135pp.

Ryan, W. Carson: *Studies in Early Graduate Education,* The Carnegie Foundation for the Advancement of Teaching, Bulletin 30, New York, 1939, 167pp.

Schachner, Nathan: *The Medieval Universities,* Paperback edition, Perpetua 4075, A. S. Barnes and Co., New York, 1962 (first published in 1938), 388pp.

Schmitt, Hans A.: "Teaching and Research: Companions or Adversaries?" *Journal of Higher Education,* **36**: 419-427 (1965).

Sinnott, Edmund Ware: "Three Dimensions in Graduate Education," *Graduate Journal,* **2**: 54-60 (1959).

Snell, John L.: "The Master's Degree," in Everett Walters (ed.), *Graduate Education Today,* American Council on Education, Washington, D.C., 1965, pp. 74-102.

Spivey, H. E.: "The Role of the Graduate School in the Promotion of Scholarship," *Graduate Journal,* **1**: 144-154 (1958).

Spurr, Stephen H.: "The Candidate's Degree," *Educational Record,* **48** (2): 126-131 (1967).

Stansbury, Paul William: *The Master's Degree for Secondary School Teachers,* Ohio State University Studies, Contributions in Education No. 3, Columbus, 1939, 75pp.

Storr, Richard J.: *The Beginnings of Graduate Education in America,* The University of Chicago Press, Chicago, 1953, 195pp.

Storr, Richard J.: *Harper's University: The Beginnings,* The University of Chicago Press, Chicago, 1966, 411pp.

Strothmann, F.W.: *On behalf of the Committee of Fifteen: The Graduate School Today and Tomorrow,* Fund for the Advancement of Education, New York, 1955. 42pp.

Summerskill, John: "Dropouts from College," in Nevitt Sanford (ed.), *The American College: A Psychological and Social Interpretation of the Higher Learning,* John Wiley & Sons, Inc., New York, 1962, pp. 627–657.

Tappan, Henry Philip: *University Education,* George P. Putnam, New York, 1851, 120pp.

Terman, Frederick E.: *Education in Engineering and Science in the U.S.S.R.,* Stanford University, Stanford, Calif., 1965, 131pp. (mimeographed).

Thomas, Flavel S.: *A Dictionary of University Degrees,* C. W. Bardeen, Publisher, Syracuse, New York, 1898, 109pp.

Thwing, Charles Franklin: *The American and the German University,* The Macmillan Company, New York, 1928, 238pp.

Thwing, Charles Franklin: *A History of Higher Education in America,* D. Appleton and Company, New York, 1906, 501pp.

Tronsgard, David T.: "A Common-sense Approach to the Dissertation," *Journal of Higher Education,* 34(9):491-495 (1963).

Tucker, Allan, David Gottlieb, and John Pease: *Attrition of Graduate Students: At the Ph.D. Level in the Traditional Arts and Sciences,* Michigan State University Office of Research Development Publications 8, East Lansing, 1964, 296pp.

UNESCO: *World Survey of Education: IV Higher Education,* New York, 1966, 1,433pp.

Veysey, Laurence R.: *The Emergence of the American University,* University of Chicago Press, Chicago, 1965, 505pp.

Walters, Everett (ed.): *Graduate Education Today,* American Council on Education, Washington, D.C., 1965, 246pp.

Ward, F. Champion: "Returning Coals to Newcastle," in Wayne C. Booth (ed.), *The Knowledge Most Worth Having,* University of Chicago Press, Chicago, 1967, pp. 29-57.

West, Andrew Fleming: "The American College," in Nicholas Murry Butler (ed.), *Education in the United States,* J. B. Lyon Co., Albany, New York, 1900, pp. 207-249.

Whaley, W. Gordon: "American Academic Degrees," *The Educational Record,* **47**: 525-537 (1966).

Wilson, Kenneth M.: *Of Time and the Doctorate,* Southern Regional Education Board Research Monograph 9, Atlanta, Ga., 1965, 212pp.

Woodring, Paul: *The Higher Learning in America: A Reassessment,* McGraw-Hill Book Company, New York, 1968, 236pp.

Wooton, Edwin: *A Guide to Degrees,* L. Upcott Gill, London, 1883, 724pp.

Wortham, Mary: "The Case for a Doctor of Arts Degree—A View from Junior College Faculty," *AAUP Bulletin,* **53**(4):372-377 (1967).

Yale University: "New Graduate Programs in the Humanities," *Ventures,* **9**(1): 10-19 (1969).

Appendix: Alphabetical List of Persons Interviewed

Aigrain, Pierre, Délégation Générale de la Recherche Scientifique, Paris, May 22, 1969.

Algate, F. M., Secretary of the Board of Graduate Studies, Cambridge University, May 14, 1969.

Altman, Robert A., City University of New York, December 17, 1968.

Annon, Baron, Provost, University College, University of London, May 8, 1969.

Aron, Raymond, Ecole Pratique des Hautes Etudes, Paris, May 20, 1969.

Ashby, Sir Eric, Vice-chancellor, Cambridge University, May 13, 1969.

Balbir, J., Programme Specialist, Division of Higher Education, UNESCO, May 21, 1969.

Barzun, Jacques, The University Professor, Columbia University, December 17, 1968.

Bender, Ignaz, Assessor, Universität Konstanz, May 27, 1969.

Besse, Ralph M., President, Cleveland Electric Illuminating Company, April 7, 1969.

Betz, Margaret J., Assistant Planning Director, Vassar College Institute for the Advancement of College and University Teaching, December 16, 1968.

Bowen, William G., Provost, Princeton University, September 19, 1968.

Brewster, Kingman, Jr., President, Yale University, February 25, 1969.

Brooks, Harvey, Dean, Division of Engineering and Applied Science, Harvard University, March 31, 1969.

Butler, C. C., Professor of Physics, Imperial College, University of London, May 5, 1969.

Cerych, Ladislav, Directorate for Scientific Affairs, OECD, Paris, May 19, 1969.

Cowan, C. D., Professor and Chairman, Centre for South East Asian Studies, University of London, May 8, 1969.

Cunliffe, Marcus, Professor of American Studies and Director of Graduate Studies in Arts and Social Sciences, The University of Sussex, May 16, 1969.

Dährendorf, Ralf, Professor of Sociology, Universität Konstanz, May 27, 1969.

Dunham, E. Alden, Executive Associate, Carnegie Foundation, December 16,1968.

Duroselle, Jean-Baptiste, Professeur, Institut d'Etudes Politiques, Paris, May 22, 1969.

Elvin, Herbert Lionel, Director, Institute of Education, University of London, May 8, 1969.

Evans, D. Anderson, Assistant Director of Continuing Education, The University of Sussex, May 16, 1969.

Ferguson, Marjorie, U.S. Embassy, Paris, May 19, 1969.

Ford, Boris, Professor and Dean of the School of Education and Educational Studies. The University of Sussex, May 16, 1969.

Ford, Franklin, Dean, Faculty of Arts and Sciences, Harvard University, October 18, 1968.

Frankel, Charles, Professor of Philosophy, Columbia University, December 16, 1968.

Gay, B., Professor and Chairman of Higher Degrees Committee, University of Aston in Birmingham, May 12, 1969.

Goheen, Robert F., President, Princeton University, September 20, 1968.

Henderson, Algo, Research Educator, Center for Research and Development in Higher Education, UC Berkeley, October 24, 1968.

Hughes, Everett, Visiting Professor of Sociology, Boston College, October 17, 1968.

Jambrun, Lucien, Franco-American Commission for Educational Exchange, Paris, May 20, 1969.

Jeffreys, G. V., Professor of Chemical Engineering, University of Aston in Birmingham, May 12, 1969.

Johnston, Robert L., Harkness House, London, May 6, 1969.

Joselin, A. G., Professor and Dean of Faculty of Social Science, University of Aston in Birmingham, May 12, 1969.

Kaysen, Carl, Director, Institute for Advanced Study, Princeton, September 19, 1968.

Kelly, William, Director, Office of Scientific Personnel, National Research Council, April 10, 1969. Also Robert Wetherall, Massachusetts Institute of Technology.

Kerr, C. William, Associate Provost, Wesleyan University, February 25, 1969. Also Earl D. Hanson (Biology), José Gomez-Ibáñez (Chemistry), Walter H. Gottschalk (Mathematics), Richard K. Winslow (Music), Jules D. Holzberg (Psychology), C. Steward Gillmor (History and Philosophy of Science), and Olin C. Robinson (Student Affairs).

King, Alexander, Director of Scientific Affairs, OECD, Paris, May 19, 1969.

Logan, Sir Douglas, Principal, University of London, May 8, 1969.

Low, D. A., Professor and Dean of the School of African and Asian Studies, The University of Sussex, May 16, 1969.

Lyon, Richard C., Dean of the College, Hampshire College, February 26, 1969.

Mautz, Robert, Chancellor, State of Florida University System, October 12, 1968.

Meadow, Henry, Associate Dean, Harvard Medical School, March 31, 1969.

Morse, Robert W., President, Case Western Reserve University, April 7, 1969.

Moser, C. A., Professor and Director of the Unit for Economic and Statistical Studies on Higher Education, London School of Economics, May 15, 1969.

Müller-Schwefe, Gerhard, Dean, Faculty of Philosophy, Universität Tübingen, May 29, 1969.

Nind, R. A., Secretary of Science, The University of Sussex, May 16, 1969.

O'Connell, Stephen C., President, University of Florida, October 11, 1968.

Olsen, Leonard K., Assistant to the Vice-president and Dean of Faculties. University of Chicago, March 25, 1969. Also Robert E. Streeter (Humanities) and David G. Johnson (Social Sciences).

Onushkin, Victor, Vice-rector, University of Leningrad, May 21, 1969.

Ostar, Allan W., Executive Director, American Association of State Colleges and Universities, April 10, 1969.

Page, Denys Lionel, Master of Jesus College, Cambridge, May 13, 1969.

Pallotino, Massimo, Professor of Etruscology and Italic Antiquity, University of Rome, November 11, 1968.

Papadopoulos, George, Head, Education Division, OECD, Paris, May 19, 1969.

Pifer, Alan, President, Carnegie Foundation, December 16, 1968.

Pippard, A. B., Professor of Physics, Cambridge University, May 14, 1969.

Piret, Edgar, Scientific Attaché, U.S. Embassy, Paris, May 23, 1969.

Poignant, Raymond, Director, International Institute for Educational Planning, Paris, May 21, 1969.

Poli, Bernard, Directeur du College Franco-Britannique, Paris, May 23, 1969.

Price, Don K., Dean, Kennedy School of Government, Harvard University, October 19, 1968.

Pusey, Nathan M., President, Harvard University, October 18, 1968.

Richards, Martin, Research Fellow, Trinity College, Cambridge, May 12, 1969.

Richardson, S. Dennis, Professor of Forestry, University College of North Wales, May 10-11, 1969. Also Paul Richards (Botany), Eric Hughes (Assistant Registrar), and David Kinloch (Forestry).

Ricoeur, Paul, Doyen, Faculté des Lettres, University of Paris—Nanterre, May 22, 1969.

Riesman, David L., Professor, Harvard University, October 24, 1968.

Robbins, Baron, Chairman of the Board, Financial Times, London, May 6, 1969.

Rudolph, Lloyd I. and Susanne, Associate Professors of Political Science, University of Chicago, March 25, 1969.

Saunders, Sir Owen, Vice-chancellor, University of London, May 8, 1969.

Schadewaldt, Wolfgang, Professor of Classics, Universität Tübingen, May 29, 1969.

Schein, Edgar H., Professor, Sloan School of Management, Massachusetts Institute of Technology, April 1, 1969.

Shannon, William G., American Association of Junior Colleges, April 10, 1969. Also Derek S. Singer.

Snyder, Benson R., M.D., Psychiatrist-in-chief and Professor of Psychiatry, Massachusetts Institute of Technology, October 17, 1968.

Steinberg, Erwin R., Dean, Carnegie-Mellon University, December 12, 1968. Also Edwin Fenton (History), Orville Windsand (Fine Arts), Richard A. Moore (Mathematics), Robert Slack (English), and Allen F. Strehler (Graduate School).

Sutherland, Sir Gordon, Master of Emmanuel College, Cambridge, May 14, 1969.

Todd, Baron, Master of Christ's College, Cambridge, May 14, 1969.

Toepfer, Kenneth H., Associate Dean, Teachers College, Columbia University, December 17, 1968. Also Alan B. Knox (Education) and Jonas F. Soltis (Philosophy and Education).

Trow, Martin, Associate Professor of Sociology, UC Berkeley, October 24, 1968.

Tyler, Elizabeth, Assistant to the Dean, College of Liberal Arts, Boston University, October 17, 1968.

Venables, Sir Peter, Vice-chancellor, University of Aston in Birmingham, May 12, 1969.

Vickers, Sir Geoffrey, April 1, 1969.

Walters, Everett, Academic Vice-president, Boston University, October 17, 1968.

Ward, F. Champion, Vice-president, Division of Education and Research, Ford Foundation, December 16, 1968. Also Frank Bowles and Robert Schmid.

Wolfenden, Sir John, Director, The British Museum, May 8, 1969.

Wright, Gordon, Cultural Attaché, U.S. Embassy, Paris, May 23, 1969.

Zuckerman, Sir Solly, Hon. secretary, The Zoological Society of London, May 7, 1969.

Index